FOR HARMONY AND STRENGTH

Published under the auspices of
THE CENTER FOR JAPANESE AND KOREAN STUDIES,
University of California, Berkeley

THOMAS P. ROHLEN

For Harmony and Strength

JAPANESE WHITE-COLLAR ORGANIZATION
IN ANTHROPOLOGICAL PERSPECTIVE

UNIVERSITY OF CALIFORNIA PRESS

BERKELEY · LOS ANGELES · LONDON

University of California Press
Berkeley and Los Angeles, California
University of California Press, Ltd.
London, England
Copyright © 1974, by
The Regents of the University of California
First Paperback Printing 1979
ISBN: 0-520-03849-5
Library of Congress Catalog Card Number: 73-91668
Printed in the United States of America
1 2 3 4 5 6 7 8 9 0

FOR MY THREE FAMILIES

CONTENTS

ACKNOWLEDGMENTS

My interest in investigating a Japanese company predates my interest in anthropology by some years, and the number of people who have guided my studies, introduced me to Japan, and encouraged me in this undertaking is commensurately large. I wish to thank Marius Jansen, Eleanor Jorden, Francis L. K. Hsu, Anthony F. C. Wallace, Ward Goodenough, Igor Kopytoff, and Teigo Yoshida, under whom I have studied. To Ezra Vogel, Robert Cole, Keith Brown, James Donohue, and my colleagues at the University of California, Santa Cruz, I am most grateful for much helpful encouragement and advice.

I also gratefully acknowledge the support provided me by an NIMH Predoctoral Fellowship (No. 5–FO1–MH–36190–04 CUAN) and by two faculty research grants from the University of California at Santa Cruz.

The Uedas, with whom I lived for a year during my earlier studies, I count as my own family. For their gracious hospitality and warm friendship I am grateful beyond words. If my opinions of Japan are oversympathetic, the Uedas are most responsible. Hitoshi Ueda, a fellow anthropologist and a close friend, shared his own fieldwork and his perceptive grasp of Japanese society with me throughout our years together. Jun Katada, Koichi Maruyama, and others too numerous to name also contributed greatly to the pleasantness of my stay and to the excitement of my work.

A good friend from another bank, Takashi Kondo, has been a most cooperative teacher on the subject of Japanese business.

My greatest debt of gratitude is owed to the people of the Ueda bank. Without their cooperation, tolerance, and good will this study would have been impossible. They took the time to answer my naive questions and to share an evening or two with me during their very busy lives.

During the preparation of the several drafts of this book, Patti Rahm, Phyllis Halpin, Charlotte Cassidy, Pam Fusari, and Wanda Jett have cheerfully assisted with the typing. Patiently supporting me during the trying process of writing and rewriting have been my parents, my brother and sister, my wife, and my children. I hope this book in some measure redeems all the sacrifice and trouble they have so willingly endured.

INTRODUCTION

"Harmony and strength" (*wa to chikara*) is the official motto of Ueda-gin, a Japanese bank I studied for eleven months in 1968–69 using the participant-observer approach.[1]

A study of a large, modern bank is not the kind of research normally undertaken by cultural anthropologists, yet our discipline's central concern with culture and cultural variation must be extended to the study of modern organizations particularly as they assume more significance in the non-Western world. Japan is one obvious place for this kind of study, since it is the non-Western nation most characterized by industrial development, urban concentration, and modern organization. It is safe to estimate, for example, that more than half of the working population of the country is employed in a company of one kind or another. Uedagin is one such company. It is considerably larger than average, employing three thousand people, and its commercial rather than industrial nature places it in the category of a white-collar organization having more in common with government bureaus than with factory situations.

There are many reasons why one would decide to study such a company. The extraordinary vigor of Japan's economic growth has generated a good deal of general interest in Japanese companies, and scholars from a variety of disciplines (primarily business management, sociology, and industrial relations) have in the last decade been studying the subject with growing intensity.[2] The major social science focus, however, has been blue-collar workers in industrial firms, and there is an obvious need for more information on the kind of company Uedagin represents. White-collar workers, white-collar work, and companies in which these predominate deserve greater attention, and this case study of a bank will hopefully reveal many new avenues of inquiry and comparison.

My intention here is primarily to demonstrate the general applicability of the anthropological perspective to the study of modern or-

1 An account of my fieldwork methods appears in the last chapter of this book.
2 The list of significant studies is too long to include here, but in the course of this book most will be mentioned in footnotes at the relevant juncture.

ganizations. I began my research with the conviction that what scholars in other fields have labeled, and often dismissed, as "traditional" Japanese patterns of thought, organization, and interrelationship would be readily found to be integral and lively aspects of contemporary organizations, if, that is, a fieldwork approach was coupled with a concern with grasping the inherent meaning of organizational structures, official explanations, daily events, and all the other material that constitute the social life of a company.[3] This is a most common intention of anthropological fieldwork, and I can make no claim to theoretical innovation except in the application of old techniques and insight to the questions of modern organization.

Although some scholars (especially Abegglen, 1958; Ballon, 1969; Brown, 1969; Nakane, 1970; and to a degree Whitehall and Takezawa, 1968) have used cultural continuity as an explanatory device in discussing Japanese company organization, none has offered detailed documentation of what is being specified as particularly Japanese. What they point to seems vague, and often it is interpreted by them and their critics as "values" that can be readily measured by attitude surveys and the like, a point of view unacceptable to contemporary cultural anthropology. The meaning of cultural patterns cannot be reduced to discrete opinions or beliefs that are easily measured, and when such an approach is taken the results have been a gross oversimplification of the problem. The development of a polarity within social science between those emphasizing "cultural factors" (under rubrics such as values, religion, traditional world view, etc.) and those emphasizing "functional" ones has grown in this context, and in Japanese social studies this has resulted in something of a split between those advocating and those eschewing the use of cultural factors in explanation. The former group, of course, emphasizes continuity, while the latter focuses on change, and the twain seem to meet less and less.

In this account I seek to circumvent this impass by the strategy of examining my empirical data without the intent of proving one particular explanation. The reader will find in this regard that I purposefully adopt no single vocabulary of description. In large measure my goal is to explore, illustrate, and interpret the vocabularies of daily, particular reality as found in the company's organization and as given

---

[3] The term *meaning* has enjoyed great currency in anthropology lately, and it is one focal concern of numerous theoretical proposals and debates in the field. I assume that other anthropologists will intuitively understand my use of the term, but for others who have doubts, Geertz (1966) is suggested reading. Berger and Luckman (1967), in sociology, attempt to clarify the relationship of cultural meaning and institutional form and their work would also serve as a good introduction.

in the explanations and actions of Uedagin people. Functionalist perspectives are not forsaken, for they are common among Uedagin people, but the universal dominion of the functionalist vocabulary and world view is denied. Instead I chose to view the life of organizations as informed by a multiplicity of points of view, interpretations, and contextual-specific realities, some of which are indeed universal in nature. The bank is a business and a large administrative structure, and as such it shares certain realities with all such organizations. Uedagin people, like mathematicians who can converse internationally without each other's language, are fluent with the more or less universal languages of finance, economics, and administration. They find concepts like efficiency, the maximization of returns in business, or the workings of a market to be perfectly logical, yet in details of practice and, more importantly, in many spheres of company life dominated more by human relations than by the flux of economics, there is clearly a world of difference between Japanese and foreign understanding. It is here that foreign management in Japan has either failed miserably or feared to tread, and it is here that an anthropological approach is most revealing.

The Mayo or human relations school of industrial studies had one great virtue. It illustrated decisively that within any organization, the "rational" interpretations derived from abstract organizational logic are laid down over the same situations for which rather different common-sense interpretations already exist. The two (or three or four) may make strange bedfellows, but coexist they do. People can view any event in a variety of lights, and complex organization preserves and even sponsors variety while it seeks to control the consequences. I will follow this basic insight in the following account and extend the field of inquiry beyond the work group alone to a wide variety of levels, subsystems, and separate contexts within the organization.

My primary effort is to comprehend and express the particular, local aspects of human relations and organization, and to do so I have assumed a familiarity on the reader's part with many universal aspects of business and administration. Each reader is encouraged to establish his own dialogue with the material in these terms. Furthermore, since I have directed my attention to basic and taken-for-granted matters, it may seem that I have been overly eclectic in my approach to data collecting and interpretation. Everything from company ceremonies to briefly observed interactions find a place in this account. While strict social scientists may object to a lack of proper methodology, it is my understanding that the meaning of any observed phenomenon derives from its place in one or more larger configurations, and this traditional idea in anthropology is my justification for casting a wide net. Rather than a lexicon I hope to provide photographs, and even these are far inferior in texture and dimension to the enveloping experience of Uedagin life gained in fieldwork.

BACKGROUND INFORMATION

In order that the bank remain anonymous, not only its true name, but its location, and a few other features cannot be included. The statistical information presented has also been disguised by making small but consistent changes in magnitude. None of the changes is great enough to alter the nature of the data. Large figures have also been rounded off, but again without any significant distortion. Throughout this description the present tense will be used, although the actual date of the fieldwork was 1968–69.

On an average day approximately three thousand persons work for the bank. The actual total varies according to a regular annual pattern. In April, when some three hundred new recruits enter, the total increases above this figure, and during the rest of the year it gradually decreases to below three thousand due to retirements and other departures. Of the total, two thousand are men and one thousand are women. The profile of age and sex distribution within the bank is presented in Figure 1.

It is estimated that an additional six to seven thousand people are related to Uedagin as members of the families of men working in the bank.

The number of stockholders in 1969 was around 7,700. This figure includes institutions as well as individual persons. The ten largest stockholders are all institutions, other banks and insurance companies. They hold about one-third of the total stock. Many men in Uedagin have bought stock in their own bank, invariably in small amounts. Uedagin's stock is neither concentrated in the hands of a family nor controlled by a few individuals. Nor is it held by a set of interlocking companies. The largest single interest (10 percent) is held by another, much larger, bank. The other major institutional stockholders have 2 to 3 percent each. Only one individual, a person not part of the bank's administration, has a considerable amount (2 percent). The stock owned by the president and directors does not alltogether equal 1 percent of the total.

The role of stockholders today is of little direct significance. The law presently requires banks of the Uedagin type to pay 10 percent of each year's profit as dividends, and it is the common practice of Ueda-

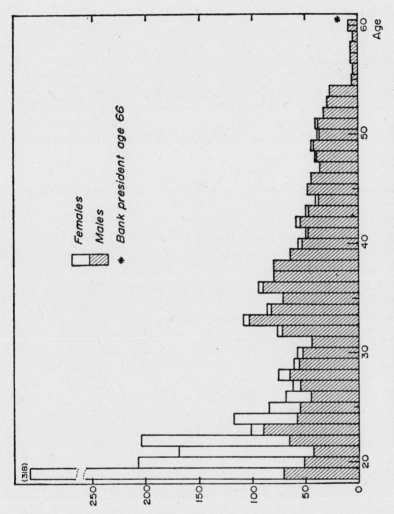

FIG. 1. Age and sex profile of the bank population (members only).

gin and other banks to arrange their accounting to maintain a constant annual rate of profit year after year regardless of the ups and
downs of business.

Profits are seldom mentioned in official pronouncements, and since
the bank has avoided serious trouble, paid dividends, and continued
to grow, it has been free of overriding concern from its stockholders.
Never did I hear any comment to the effect that the company was run
primarily for stockholders. Most often the benefits of greater welfare
facilities, increased job security, higher wages, and more prestige for
Uedagin workers were presented as the bank's goals and the rewards
of its business success.

Given the rule stabilizing dividends, the interests of stockholders
and the interests of the people working in the bank cannot be directly
compared as long as the company remains successful, but it is worth
noting that the market value of the stock has not increased at anywhere near the rate of increase in salaries and benefits. The profit
motive typically played down in official pronouncements in Japanese
companies, is said to be of increasing significance in many firms, but
within Uedagin the primary goal remains growth, for it brings greater
security, power, and status to the organization, and better promotion
opportunities, security, and material benefits to Uedagin people.

UEDAGIN'S POSITION

According to statistics for 1967 there are 1,224 private financial institutions in Japan divided by law into two general categories: banks
with national scope and those of less than national scope.[4] The latter
specialize in financing small and medium businesses and must by law
give a percentage of their loans to such companies. Uedagin is one of
the largest banks in the second category, and it is about the thirtieth
largest bank in Japan. The country's four greatest banks are each
approximately eight times Uedagin's size.

The home office is located in the city of Aoyama,[5] a regional urban
center of eight hundred thousand people that lies outside the industrial megalopolis that stretches between Tokyo and Osaka. Uedagin is
one of the city's two largest banks. Its rivalry with an older national
bank extends throughout the region and is a much-discussed factor
motivating both companies.

[4] This and the rest of the statistics in this paragraph are from The Fuji Bank,
Ltd. (1967).
[5] This is a fictitious place name.

A distribution map of the bank's operations indicates that 25 percent of its 120 branches are in and around the city of Aoyama where its base is strongest; 60 percent are in the other cities and towns of its home region, and finally 15 percent are located in major cities outside the region. The last group includes some of the largest and many of the most recent branches. The bank is thus a bridge between a regional economy (even to the extent of having offices in rural areas) and the national economy (through its offices in most of Japan's largest cities).

HISTORICAL BACKGROUND

Compared to most other medium and large Japanese banks, Uedagin has a short history. In 1944, five mutual loan associations, or *mujin*,[6] were merged into a new company, Ueda Mujin. It is this date that has been chosen to mark the bank's establishment. All five constituents were themselves products of amalgamations of even smaller mujin during the years just prior to 1944. All of this combinational activity was effected by the Tokyo government as part of a program for the rationalization of the wartime financial system. The war ended before the program could be completed, but amalgamations continued for several years thereafter. In total, twenty-four mutual loan associations were merged into what ultimately became the Ueda Bank.

It is doubtful that these mergers would have occurred without government intervention, for the tremendous problems of reorganization and integration that were created would not, in all probability, have been voluntarily chosen by the various mujin companies themselves. Creating a uniform system of operations was only part of the problem. Most difficult and painful of all was the task of merging the separate personnel hierarchies into a single viable framework in which previous loyalties and fresh antagonisms were subordinated to the new organization. Japanese business custom ruled out the possibility of extensive lay-offs and new hiring as a solution. These difficulties were further compounded by the economic collapse and general social chaos that followed the war. According to the older men in the bank, this

---

6 Embree in Suye Mura (1939) has a lengthy description of one such association in the Japanese village he studied. It is fitting that thirty some years after his study of a savings and loan association of the most rudimentary kind located in an admittedly "backward" part of Japan, we now consider the modern, urban counterpart of such an arrangement. Embree's type *ko* is ancestor of the mujin companies of prewar Japan from which Uedagin arose. There is also an even more detailed account of such associations in China in Gamble (1954), pp. 260–268.

early period was a time when simply feeding the bankers and their
families was an overriding concern. Perhaps such stark necessities
served to draw people together. In any event, the hardships of the
early years from 1944 to 1950 are remembered today with great nostalgia by the remaining old-timers. The leaders of that period, almost
all of them dead or retired now, have come to occupy the position of
founding fathers of the bank, and their heroic efforts in the face of
air raids and postwar economic collapse are a major component of
the bank's tradition.

Mujin were not prestigious institutions like the regular banks of
the prewar era. Japan's first modern banks were established in the
late nineteenth century primarily by men of the samurai class seeking
a new form of employment consistent with their status and training.[7]
The Meiji government encouraged them to open banks and equated
banking with national service, thus making it a suitable occupation
for a class whose traditional ethic despised business and finance. Consequently, the original staff of regular banks were men who enjoyed
prestige as members of the upper class. By contrast, mujin, particularly
the commercial variety, had no prestige, for their organizers and participants were commoners and small merchants who, in reputation at
least, were motivated by a "vulgar" interest in financial speculation
and gain. Even now, many people in Uedagin are sensitive about the
mujin origins of their company, an illustration both of the close relationship between institutional and individual identity and of one kind
of social classification to which companies are liable. A social ambition on the part of the bank to shed its "merchant" image can be
detected in a number of its programs, particularly those emphasizing
public service. The president of the bank, incidentally, is of samurai
origin; and most personnel trace their ancestors to farm backgrounds.

Coincidental with the series of initial mergers, Uedagin was placed
under the patronage of one of Japan's largest banks (the largest stock-
holder today). Several young executives were sent to help with the
new organization, and they remained as part of the early leadership.
Some twenty-five years later this special relationship still exists, and
some observers are inclined to label Uedagin as a dependent (*kogaisha,*

---

[7] Hirschmeier (1964) writes in his study of entrepreneurship in the Meiji period,
"Along with the publication of the revised banking act of 1876 went a drive to
stimulate participation of the samurai in founding new banks. The investment of
bonds and cash in the establishment of banks were propagandized as a service to
the country. Bankers were declared patriots who contributed to the building of
strong national economy. Thus they were not associated with the much hated and
despised money exchangers of Tokugawa days."

literally "child company") of the larger bank even though by most measures Uedagin is now thoroughly independent and considerably more vigorous than its original patron.

From 1951 to 1969 the bank expanded its capital assets and operations remarkably. In 1969 deposits were thirty times the 1951 amount. The number of branch offices doubled. The geographical spread of branches increased proportionally, and the number of people working in the bank increased to the present three thousand. Obviously, much of this growth is directly attributable to the general economic growth of the country, but even so Uedagin is regarded as a dynamic company.

BUSINESS ACTIVITIES OF THE BANK

Like any bank, Uedagin maintains itself financially by earning interest on the loans it makes to customers. The money it has to loan comes in great measure from deposits for which it must pay interest. It earns additional income by clearing and guaranteeing financial transactions between other parties. The efficiency with which these operations are performed is certainly one factor affecting the ability of the bank to maximize its income. As a rule, the larger the volume of transactions the more efficiently they may be conducted. Computerization of record keeping and other functions has been strongly pursued since 1966.

A second factor influencing the bank's income is the security of its loans. If loans fail to be repaid, the bank suffers a loss. Therefore, reducing the risk without reducing the interest is another way to increase income. In Japan, the amount of risk tends to be in inverse relationship to the size of the company. It is highly predictable, for example, that in economic downturns small companies will suffer most. The larger the organization, the greater the security and the better the growth rate, is a principle understood to operate throughout Japanese life.[8]

When loans are made, something more than a one-way financial transaction occurs. A relationship between the bank and its customer is established. The customer is expected to become a depositor, and often this is part of the initial understanding. If a relationship exists, more transactions are likely to be made in the future, and the two companies may cooperate in developing new kinds of business beneficial to both. Good relationships are the lifeblood of successful bank-

---

8 In Broadbridge (1966) the differences in performance, security, wages, and other factors related to company size are examined and documented statistically.

ing, and the larger the bank becomes, the more large customers it will be able to attract.

Since relative size is a key, perhaps the single most important key, to success, Uedagin works hard to boost its standing in the banking world. The pressure to increase deposits is relentless, and the competition is extreme. The bank's branches are best understood as collection agencies with assigned territories and monthly goals. To obtain the receipts of companies and to attract the savings of housewives, Uedagin salesmen, some five hundred or so, go out daily from their branch offices calling on depositors and potential depositors requesting business for their bank. These salesmen, young men in their late twenties and thirties, travel by foot, by motor scooter, and by public transport throughout their territory, ringing doorbells, doing small favors, developing friendships, and, in general, doing anything that might lead to greater deposits. Their approach is amicable, polite, and persistent. Competition comes from other banks, savings institutions, farm cooperatives, and even the post office savings plan. In all, about thirty different institutions in the city of Aoyama use essentially the same methods to collect deposits. Rival salesmen often pass each other in the streets of their mutual territories.

In addition to salesmen, the bank has a bus converted into a small mobile bank that visits the newer housing projects to make depositing easier for housewives in those locations. Wives hold the family purse strings in Japan.

Calls on larger customers are generally made by members of top management, and their chauffeur-driven cars can be seen coming and going from the main office on such missions. Attendance at the weddings and funerals of important people, participation in public events, and expense-account entertainment are also part of their effort to strengthen Uedagin's ties in higher business and political circles.

No one in the bank escapes the duty of gathering deposits, and everyone is expected to seek funds from friends, relatives, neighbors, and acquaintances. The patronage of a restaurant, for example, might be accompanied by a request that the restaurant owner deposit with Uedagin. Deposits given as "favors" result, in turn, in further obligations on the bankers. Many Uedagin people find themselves uncomfortably involved in the tangle of such affairs. The distinction between business and personal relations is impossible to maintain under the pressure of the organization's drive for greater deposits.

Loans, deposits, efficiency, competition, security, and income constitute the framework of the business perspective, one that is present throughout the bank, but especially in the offices and conference rooms of top management.

THE JAPANESE ECONOMY IN 1968–69

A study of any institution as deeply involved in a national economy as Uedagin requires an introductory statement as to the condition of the economy at the time of fieldwork, for the organization, morale, and other aspects of a company are likely to be affected by this factor. During the period 1968–69 the Japanese economy experienced a remarkable 14 percent real growth rate of gross national product. This came at the end of two decades of almost continuous rapid expansion at rates averaging 10 percent annually. It was estimated by a number of serious scholars using these statistics that Japan would overtake the U.S.S.R. and then the United States in GNP by the end of the twentieth century. One problem that would have to be solved for growth to continue at a high rate was the growing labor shortage. The work force was not expanding rapidly. Seventy percent of all companies surveyed by the Bank of Japan in 1969 indicated a shortage of labor to be their principal problem. In spite of this, predictions for the future were optimistic on the assumption that greater capital investment and the rationalization of labor use would raise productivity enough to compensate for the constriction of labor supply. As might be expected, unemployment was at a low 1 percent, and failures of medium and large enterprises were minimal. In short, this study was made during a period of economic boom, and this condition was reflected in the state of the bank's business.

Per capita income had also risen during the sixties at a rate only slightly less than the rate of increase of GNP. The average salaried worker in the nation's largest 155 companies reportedly enjoyed a doubling of his income from 1966 to 1969. During the latter year, for example, 85 percent of all families owned refrigerators compared with 35 percent in 1964. By all measures except urban congestion and pollution, the standard of living of the Japanese was improving the fastest in the world. When this study was done, the people of Uedagin were satisfied with the direction of their lives in terms of material gain, and they perceived a direct relationship between improvements in their living and the success of the national economy as a whole. They were, in fact, becoming increasingly conscious of the possibility that Japanese accomplishments, rather than something to be embar-

rassed about, were things to take pride in. This was a significant departure from the postwar tendency to worship anything that was not
Japanese. Among the things that began to come in for praise was the
Japanese company system, one example of which we now turn to consider in detail.[9]

[9] See Itō (1969) for one outspoken example of this.

1

THE BASIC FORM OF THE COMPANY

Many approaches to a description of this bank might be taken, particularly if we realize that Uedagin people experience life in their company in a complex manner that is often quite removed from the conceptual frameworks of social science and certainly different from the linear mode of explication required in writing. I have opted to begin by setting forth the major outlines of the social organization because a grasp of the basic social divisions and their labels is prerequisite to an understanding of the more detailed material to be discussed in subsequent chapters, and because we can perceive in the basic form of the company many characteristics that will remain central to our generalizations about Uedagin life throughout this account.

THE COMPANY AS A SOCIAL BOUNDARY

Like any modern society, Japan today contains a wide variety of institutions including, of course, families, villages, cities, government agencies, religious entities, and the like. Among them the company is undoubtedly the most significant, if sheer numbers of participants and centrality to national livelihood is considered. In the past, the country's villages were preeminent by these standards, but the last hundred years has witnessed a tremendous increase of commercial and industrial organizations, and they now far surpass villages as Japan's major type of social institution.

The boundaries between a company and other institutions turn out to be clear and invested with considerable importance. A strong sense of "we" and "they" is developed in each, and the result is a degree of company isolation and parochialism, and an intensity of internal activity, that would be surprising in the modern West.[1] The company

[1] A large number of authors have made this point, including Cole (1971a), Nakane (1970), and Yoshino (1968), to mention three of the most recent. The important points to note about this generalization are (1) that it hinges on a comparative

label is generally the most important classifier of people, activities, and loyalties in urban Japan today. It defines the realm of primary social involvement. The company boundary, as we shall see, shapes many things beside the organization of work.

Uedagin, for example, is not regarded in everyday thought as primarily a legal entity or a complex money-making machine, but more as a community of people organized to secure their common livelihood. This conceptualization is doubted and repudiated at times, but it occupies a powerful central position in the world of implicit understandings. The extension of terms of reference from village and household to modern company life reveals this perspective. One often hears companies referred to as "our house" (*uchi*) and "your house" (*otaku*), the same expressions as are used for actual households and household enterprises. People working in the bank are known to others as "Uedagin people," while their occupational labels (for example, banker or teller) are of secondary importance. The "company-as-household" image is not taken literally by any means, but its constant reiteration preserves a strong sense of analogy. A major "we-they" distinction in Japan today follows the lines that circumscribe individual companies.

The importance of the company boundary is also reflected in the fact that most of a man's social relations and activities take place in the company framework. Company membership, for example, is a highly significant prediction of companionship patterns. Ambitions for advancement are virtually limited to upward mobility in the bank, to take another illustration. One is tempted to say that Uedagin, by American company standards, is an island unto itself.

A company's status and reputation are related to its size and power, and also to the quality of its personnel. Illegal or improper acts by Uedagin people reflect badly on their company and there is an implicit sense that the company should take responsibility, at least in part, for such misconduct.[2] Related is the fact that a high level of employee education, neatness, courtesy, and the like contributes greatly to any company's image, and individuals are, in turn, judged by the prestige of their company. In such personal matters as marriage, the extension of credit, the rental of housing, and precedence in public places, one's company affiliation can speak as loudly as per-

---

framework of cross-cultural scale and is thus dependent on a vague (but real) sense of what is typical of an entire country, (2) that a comparison among Japanese companies would reveal considerable variation, and (3) that the evidence to support this generalization as it applies to Uedagin is contained throughout this description.

[2] Companies are, for example, often expected to assume responsibility for damages caused by an employee in the case of traffic accidents going to, and during work.

sonal income, education, or family background. It is valuable to belong to a powerful company, and it follows that working to increase the power and prestige of one's firm is regarded as natural and proper.[3]

Another crucial aspect of company boundaries is their influence over interpersonal relations. The "we-they" distinction is confirmed by the fact that trust, trustworthiness, and the other ingredients of long-term mutual involvement are notably greater within the company realm than in those areas of social interaction that lie outside. For white-collar workers, in particular, only family, kinship, and early friendship are more important sources of security and intimacy. To belong to the same company is to have an expectation of reliable, continuous, and, in many cases, close involvement. As in most in-looking social situations, this creates a cautious propriety, a willingness to enter into fellowship, and a sensitivity to the nuance of interaction. People in one's own company are by definition important, whereas other people (including those in the same neighborhood, or those with the same political perspective) are strangers by comparison.

Nakane Chie refers to this concentration effect using the concept of social frame (ba or waku). She writes,

> Even in terms of physical arrangements, a company with its employees and their families forms a distinct social group. In an extreme case, a company may have a common grave for its employees, similar to the household grave. With group consciousness so highly developed there is almost no social life outside the particular group on which an individual's major economic life depends. The individual's every problem must be solved within this frame. Thus group participation is simple and unitary. It follows then that each group or institution develops a high degree of independence and closeness, with its own internal law which is totally binding on members [1970:10].

This same general phenomenon is referred to as "a semi-closed social grouping" by Cole (1971) who studied the more fluid life of blue-collar workers in two relatively small industrial companies. Whatever the label selected, the implication is that the relationship of the individual with his company and the nature of social life and organization

---

3 Vogel in his study of white-collar families noted this quality. He writes, "Yet the rationalizing process in large Japanese enterprises has not resulted in the same patterns of social organization that one finds, for example, in the United States. The basic mode of integration of the man into the economic order is not through his occupational specialty, but through his firm. His commitment to the firm is ordinarily more basic and longer lasting than to any occupational specialty. The individual's security and his sense of identity derive from membership in a particular firm or government bureau [1963:264]."

within the company are different from what Western experience has decreed to be characteristic of modern company organization. Whitehall and Takezawa conclude from their comparative questionnaire survey of American and Japanese blue-collar workers that,

> Japanese workers more readily accepted their company as something more than a place to earn money for their living. One out of every ten workers selected the extreme end of the continuum, which posed company life as being even more important than personal life. It is, indeed, a deep sense of involvement that characterizes those who chose this item.
>
> An additional six of every ten workers selected the second item, which attaches "at least equal" importance to company life as to personal life. This position reflects an affirmative, positive attitude toward both personal life and work, and seems characteristic of most contemporary Japanese workers. Identity with the company seems definitely greater among Japanese than U.S. workers [1968:112].

There are many other similar observations to the effect that the relationship of a Japanese to his company is more intense and more complicated than similar relationships in the West. This subject is a central concern of this entire description, and at the start we can only alert ourselves to the fact that throughout Japanese society the prominence of company boundaries sets the stage for the extensive elaboration of each company's internal life.

FORMAL ORGANIZATION

Our description of the bank's social organization will begin with outlines of its most elementary forms. The purpose here is not to deal exhaustively with any single facet of the bank, but rather to lay the groundwork for subsequent more thorough description. We are therefore interested in definition and structure, the former being in fact dependent on the latter. The first of the three elementary forms is constructed of a set of *categories* each of which defines a different relationship between individual workers and the bank. The second is comprised of a set of *ranks*. This form establishes hierarchy and its associated qualities. The organization of work into *group functions* and *individual roles* is the third form to be considered. All three forms have been created, promulgated, and enforced by the management of the bank and are therefore the official foundations for Uedagin organization. There are other criteria (such as sex, age, affect, personal indebtedness, and the like) that are relevant, but they exist outside the official scheme, and we will take them up separately.

Categories

Variations in the relationship between the bank and individuals working for it result in a number of different categories within the general Uedagin population. These categories express fundamental distinctions within the bank that do not correspond to the usual divisions found in the organization of Western business enterprises.[4]

The differences involved between categories center on what I will term the concept of membership. The major category of persons in Uedagin is that of *kōin*, a compound composed of two characters, one abbreviating "bank" (*kō*), and the other "member" (*in*). Thus *kōin* means "member(s) of the bank."[5] A second possible translation is "bank personnel," but this is too inclusive a term to be appropriate, for kōin is actually a category within and not the entire retinue of bank personnel. *Ginkōin* means banker in other contexts, but "banker" is not an appropriate translation here. About 90 percent of all people in Uedagin are kōin or "members." The remainder occupy four other categories: *junkōin* or "quasi member(s)," *rinji jūgyōin* or "temporary employee(s)," *shokutaku* or "commissionee(s)" and *untenshū to sono ta* or "drivers and others." Quasi members constitute 5 percent of the bank and the others 1 to 2 percent each. People are in one and only one of the above five categories. For convenience, temporary employees, commissionees, and drivers and others will be lumped together at times under the heading "nonmembers."

[4] They are not by any means unknown to Western modern organization, however, since there is implicit in the fundamentals of school, religious, and other kinds of organizations (that are not in our terms exclusively "economic") much that parallels the distinctions reflected in Uedagin categories. Company organization in the West is also much less purely "contractual" in practice than in theory and in explicit definition. Only fieldwork in Western firms directed at the study of meaning in all its complexity will provide the necessary data for detailed cross-cultural comparison of the kind discussed here.

[5] The translation of *kōin* as "bank member" is of special interest. Normally authors of accounts of Japanese industrial organization stay close to Western usage and apply the term employee to all but the "owners" and "managers" of a company. I have chosen to eliminate the logic implied in this vocabulary, since I feel it is misleading in the Uedagin case, and a barrier to the perception of the underlying character of the relationship between an individual and his company. No doubt there are individuals in Uedagin who feel they have a simple employee-employer relationship with the bank, but this is beside the point since it is not mentioned except in the context of union activities. I have chosen to translate the term *jūgyoin*, which appears occasionally in union documents, as "employee" since this word is closer in spirit to the English term. In any event, at the end of this description the reader may make his own judgment of this issue.

The distinctions between categories are not simply those of role, salary, or status, even though such things are influenced by category lines. There are cases, for example, of people of different categories performing the same role and of persons being transferred from one category to another without any change of actual role performance. To distinguish correctly between categories the relationship between the individual and the bank is crucial. In each instance it is an exchange relationship, yet categories represent more than variations in the details of what is exchanged (such as time, skill, and reward). More significantly, categories represent different "philosophies" of relationship. In particular, there is a profound difference in the spirit of the member-bank relationship compared to the others.

Members.—The basic distinguishing characteristic of this relationship is an implied mutual commitment (on the part of individual and bank alike) to the general interests of the other party. The member agrees to work wholeheartedly for the organization, and the bank agrees to serve the needs of the member. Money and labor are central, but they must be understood as resulting from a more general commitment. To understand this we must appreciate that Uedagin is envisioned in official pronouncements as an enterprise created to combine the efforts of individual members for the achievement of their common goals.

Membership, therefore, means sharing in the community of interest and endeavor. When a person enters the bank as a member he discards his independence (something less of a preoccupation in Japan to begin with) and accepts the burdens of responsibility as a participant. It is also understood that in return Uedagin assumes the position of provider for the individual's security and welfare in the face of whatever problems may arise. This general agreement, lacking details and specifications, is implicit. It is the actions of both parties that illustrate it, and it is their actions that over time confirm or deny it, preserve or destroy it. This is obviously different from the usual contractual relationship found in most Western employment situations.

New members sign a statement, called a "contract" (*keiyaku*), that documents only two things: recognition of the person as a member of the bank, and his pledge to follow the rules of the organization.[6] No

---

[6] In two articles the legal scholar Kawashima Takeyoshi (1963 and 1967) has discussed the traditional pattern of relationship in Japan and used it to explain the relative absence of contracts and litigation in modern Japanese society. He explains that traditionally most forms of relationship have been characterized by (1) indeterminateness of obligation, (2) reciprocity of good will, (3) personal acquaintanceship and involvement, and (4) a reliance on the spirit of harmony (*wa*) rather than on legal sanction. He adds that the interests of the collectivity are assumed to

other details are included. Neither rights nor duties are specified and no procedures for redress, renegotiation, or termination are listed. Nor are sanctions of any sort mentioned.

Rather than limiting the relationship, the unspecific nature of the commitment extends its possibilities far beyond the confines of a normal contract and creates a situation in which the actual give and take may vary considerably. The independence of each party from the other, which the specified limits of a normal contract express, is thus disregarded in the case of Uedagin membership. The result is an elasticity of relationship that would be impossible if a detailed contract were in force.[7]

With detailed contracts, terminations are built into the relationship as sanctions against the breaking of terms by either party, as outlets for the election of more attractive possibilities, and so on. In contrast, the member-bank relationship we are discussing emphasizes and seeks to realize an expectation of continuity and mutual good will. Definitions separating interests, motives, and forms of redress are avoided, and the ideal model of relationship is one closer to that of a family than to that of an impersonal employment situation.

The deemphasis on termination as a sanction creates a situation in which either party may misuse or otherwise alter details of the relationship without it being quickly terminated. The company is reluctant to fire people, and members do not quit without considerable thought and preparation. Mutual trust, then, is crucial—both as the basic principle of the relationship and as a most necessary ingredient of those daily actions and choices that would substantiate the principle. The elasticity of the relationship is expressed by the fact that in the event the exchange becomes "unbalanced" (that is, unsatisfactory to one party), it may continue for a considerable length of time utilizing the reserve of forbearance, good will, and trust implied in the original commitment. Ideally neither party should be inclined to misuse this inherent flexibility, for according to the basic concept of membership

supersede those of the individual which are "not made distinct and fixed." Yoshino has characterized this aspect of the Japanese "permanent employee system" in the following terms: "It is not a contractual relationship in which each party agrees to an employer-employee relationship, bearing certain conditions and terms, which can be terminated at the option of the parties involved. The Japanese employment relationship is an unconditional one, requiring total commitment on the part of employer and employee [1968:229]."

7 A glimpse of the assumption of community and the elasticity of relationship in times of company crises is provided by one of Robert Cole's blue-collar informants, who remarked, "My idea of a good company is one that when it gets into economic difficulty doesn't fire but asks the workers to go all out, and everyone works together to solve the problem [1971a:118]."

the interests of both parties are viewed as united. Imbalances do occur, however, and a diffuse sense of dissatisfaction is a commonplace. The important point is that this dissatisfaction remains vague in large measure because the limits of the relationship are vague. Patient forbearance is and has been seen as highly virtuous in Japan.

About one third of all Uedagin members are women, and officially their membership provides them with the same relationship to the bank as their male counterparts. In actuality, however, they have neither as deep nor as lasting a relationship with the bank. Women must leave upon marriage. They are never found in positions of responsibility, and it is assumed that their involvement cannot become as strong as in the case of men. Thus women are partial exceptions to the foregoing generalizations about the nature of membership. Their case highlights the fact that the standard for Uedagin conceptualization is the relationship of men to the bank.

Because the commitment is general and its limits vague, everything having to do with the relationship between the company and its male members is, in the final analysis, part of a proper definition of membership. Consequently, the entirety of this description should be taken as serving to clarify what membership is about. Definitional outlines, on the other hand, are logically created through the establishment of contrasts, and in this case the significant contrasts are those between member, quasi member, and nonmember. Here the story is rather less complicated.

Quasi Members.—As the term implies, quasi members are like members, but not exactly. The major difference lies in the fact that quasi members do not do banking work, but occupy support positions such as custodians, cooks, and the like. They belong to a system of roles that is separate from the office organization, and they cannot be transferred or promoted to positions in the office organization. Their status is consistently lower than that of members. Except for these limitations, however, quasi members have essentially the same kind of relationship to the bank as members. They are also expected to be motivated out of loyalty to the relationship, rather than out of contractual necessity. Their interests are thought to merge with the bank's. They automatically join the company union along with members. While the distribution of fringe benefits to quasi members is often made separately, they are eligible, the same as members, to participate in the bank's welfare and security programs.[8]

8 See Abegglen (1958), Whitehall and Takezawa (1968), Cole (1971a), and Dore (1973) for discussions of categories in contemporary industrial firms.

Nonmembers.—Unity of interest and extensive reciprocal commitment are not assumed in the case of nonmembers. Terminations are anticipated, and nonmembers are conceptually part of the organization only in terms of the actual work situation. Nonmembers are excluded from the company union, from the bonus and welfare programs, and, as a rule, from social activities.

It is not always possible to make sharp distinctions among the three nonmember categories. Stated as simply as possible, the basic differences are that temporary employees are hired for the shortest periods and usually do office work, that commissionees may be above retirement age, have an annual contract, and do office work, and that "drivers and others" do not do office work.

Temporary employees are hired separately from members, and the criteria upon which they are selected relate to the specific function they will perform. People who work part time and those who supply a skill needed for only a brief period are hired in this category. They often do clerical or other skilled work. The wages they receive are determined by agreement, and the term of employment is usually less than a year.[9]

Commissionees may do banking or support work, but the terms of their employment involve a contract that must be renewed annually, thus it can be easily terminated for economic reasons. Many commissionees are persons who have been retired automatically from the bank at age fifty-five and are simultaneously reemployed, often in the same job.

Telephone operators, card punchers, and other women with a special skill not taught in the bank's training institute also work for Uedagin as commissionees. Their salaries are determined at the going market rate for their occupation. They are not allowed to join the union or to participate in the bonus program, and the bank may terminate the relationship at the end of each year. In short, they work on a contractual basis.

Those who stay with the bank for a few years tend to develop a desire to be one with the members. Working alongside members in an office, they often come to wish they, too, were members, for this would

9 Abegglen (1958) mentions temporary employees in the manufacturing companies he surveyed and notes they serve as "buffers" against the consequences of economic and technological change. He contrasts temporary workers with permanent workers and observes that temporary workers constitute about 10 percent of an average company's total work force. This figure is considerably higher than for Uedagin. Dore's (1973) more recent study indicates that in manufacturing the labor shortage makes hiring temporary people difficult and that part-time women are now increasingly important.

"settle" their place in the group. Furthermore, as they befriend people in the bank, many come to feel close to the organization, and the greater involvement of membership more closely approximates their actual feelings about the relationship. Conversion to member status has occurred.

Many men had been hired as commissionees during the period of postwar dislocation. They had lost their wartime jobs and were in great need of employment. Uedagin was willing to hire them, but only as commissionees. The problem of securing the welfare of the existing membership was tenuous enough in those days, and the bank, in effect, retained the option of treating these men as second-class citizens. They could be laid off if economic necessity required. These commissionees were not asked to undergo transfer to other offices, but neither could they reach supervisory levels. In time, with the rapid growth of the bank, the shift from a labor surplus situation to one of increasing labor shortage, and the long association of this group of commissionees, their categorical place came to be less and less satisfactory. In the early sixties a wholesale transfer of commissionees to member status took place, much to everyone's satisfaction.

An analogous extension of full membership status to more and more blue-collar workers has been a prominent trend in the history of modern Japanese industrial relations, especially as companies sought to retain skilled workers, and today this inclusive quality is pronounced for both white- and blue-collar workers, especially in large and medium-sized companies.

People following unskilled occupations in which there is high labor mobility, such as chauffeurs, are usually employed on a contractual basis for a limited period. They are not included in the society of the bank and are simply paid at the going rate for work performed. There is no wider commitment by either party involved, and the turnover is often high, yet even among drivers one can find examples of intense loyalty to Uedagin or to a particular executive. Drivers may become quasi members if they wish to deepen and make permanent their relationship with the bank.

It would be useful to summarize some of the most apparent practical differences between membership, quasi membership, and nonmembership. Persons accepted as members are all tested, interviewed, and selected in a standard manner. They invariably come to the bank directly out of school. By contrast, quasi members and nonmembers are hired individually any time during the year, and the procedures used in their selection may vary from case to case. Often they have been out of school for some time and have worked previously for some other organization. People coming into the bank as members may be characterized as "pristine," because they are young and have no history of commitment to and subsequent divorce from another enterprise. They also have a higher education than most quasi members and nonmembers, giving them higher status.

A Typical Quasi Member

In order to visualize some of the behavioral patterns that follow category lines, let us consider briefly one of the hundred or so quasi members who serve as custodian-guards for branch offices. These men constitute the most numerous group outside the membership category. They generally live with their families in quarters set aside for them in branch office buildings. Time and again I was struck by the resemblance between their position in an office group and the position of trusted family servants.

The junkōin moves quietly about the branch office during business hours, always with a degree of caution not to interfere with the more important business of the members. He is on friendly terms with them, and if they are not busy he will converse amicably with them. He maintains a strict attitude of subordination to the older and higher-ranking men, using respectful language and gestures. With the younger people his behavior is more varied. Ultimately he knows he must show subordination if they should demand it, but he would prefer to deal intimately with them, as an "uncle from the country" might. To those younger members who grant him their respect because he is an older man, he will be grateful and ready to offer assistance. If any younger member assumes superior airs toward him, on the other hand, he will grow resentful, and if the situation is not remedied it may sour his attitude toward his work and the entire group. It is widely understood that quasi members and their families are susceptible to feelings of inferiority and are acutely aware of status differences between themselves and members. A good branch chief will watch for subtle signs of discontent and psychic injury from his quasi member custodian-guard and attempt to relieve the situation through delicate manipulation. He may warn the younger men and women of the office to be more polite and respectful "even though he is a quasi member."

If there is an office party, the junkōin may be invited, but he is not automatically included. If he attends he will studiously stay in the background. If called before the attention of the group, he will be notably hesitant and embarrassed.

He and often his wife are responsible for cleaning the office at the end of each day. He prefers to wait to do this until the members have left. Besides not wishing to disturb their work, he wishes to avoid being observed doing this, the most menial of his tasks. During the day, he may wear a suit and do errands or other business for the office, but when he washes the floor his inferior status has no disguise.

There is a revealing case in which the daughter of a quasi member expressed strong resentment against the bank because of her father's low position. This occurred even though, because of her father, she herself had been accepted into the bank as a member and given a job in the main office after graduation. Her resentment took the form of resistance to the norms of dress and makeup expected of Uedagin girls. She dressed and spoke in a loose, offensive manner at work, yet outside the office her behavior was above criticism. After this kind of resistance to the bank had ended, she admitted to having harbored a terrible sense of anger and shame about her father's position. She said she often recalled his helplessness in the face of careless insults from others. This is an extreme case, yet it illustrates the problems to which all quasi and nonmembers are vulnerable.

Our discussion of Uedagin subsequent to this chapter will deal almost exclusively with members. This too is a reflection, however regrettable, of the inferior status and the relative obscurity of quasi members and nonmembers alike.

Ranks

Figure 2 illustrates the manner in which the membership is organized into a system of ranks not unlike the ranks of a military organization. These ranks are hierarchically arranged. From the top down they are: (1) department head (*buchō*); (2) branch or section chief (*shitenchō* or *kachō*); (3) assistant chief, inspector, or researcher (*jichō, kensa yaku,* or *chōsa yaku*); (4) deputy (*dairi*); (5) regular (*shūnin*); and (6) ordinary (*ippan kōin*).[10]

Some heads of departments are simultaneously on the board of directors (Figure 3), a body that includes no outsiders to the bank organization. Collectively these men are known as *jūyaku,* or "directors."

The title "researcher" is most interesting. It is handed to men who have been demoted from the rank of chief, and placed on the inactive list. Only people inside the bank, however, appreciate this fact, since the title in many firms is one of considerable responsibility. It is, there-

---

10 Ranks characterize almost all Japanese companies. Those in commercial firms appear to have historical antecedents in both the rank system of the early government bureaucracy and the rank orders of merchant-run business houses during the Tokugawa period (Hazama, 1963).

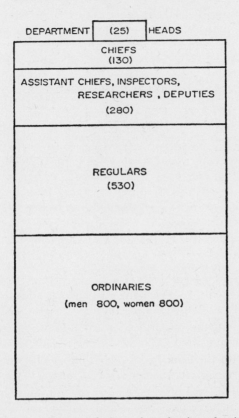

FIG. 2. The population of ranks (members).

fore, a face-saving title for those who, after failing in relatively high office, have been shelved. The bank keeps them on out of obligation and protects their status, but gives them no significant responsibility.[11] Rank is the key factor in the determination of roles, authority, and rewards, but other factors such as age, years of service, and the peculiarities of each office situation also must be considered to understand these somewhat distinct matters. The hierarchy of ranks serves as a common denominator within the total organization, but it does not specify the details of work or interrelationship.

Alone, rank primarily expresses status. Others recognize a person's importance and achievement from his rank. Although they may not

11 A number of special ranks have also been established to solve problems within the organization centering on situations where the position and authority normally belonging to a chief is temporarily or conditionally given to a man of lower rank.

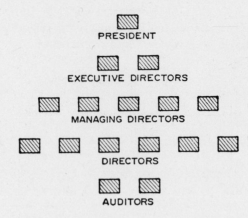

FIG. 3. The Board of Directors.

know what his actual authority, role, or amount of reward is, people respect a person's rank. The bank's titles have universal currency in Japanese society and this is important, for the greater status that promotion brings is a most important reward in itself.[12]

The rank of chief is the crucial watershed. Little social distinction is connected with the ranks below chief, but in the white-collar world, a man's achievements become worthy of general notice and respect when he is appointed to head a section or branch. The rank connotes a leader, a man of responsibility, and, particularly, a person with a group of subordinates. Deputies may share the managerial duties with their chief, but their rank carries little status. Certainly the young men who have made deputy before the crowd will be noted by others for the distinguished career ahead of them, but older deputies can expect only sympathy for the unfortunate fact that their careers will termi-

12 In the West, banks are also notable for their use of titles and their emphasis on general rather than special skills. American banks, for example, often have an extraordinary proliferation of titles (such as second vice-president) within the managerial level. As in Japan these titles are viewed as important rewards in themselves. It would not be correct, however, to conclude from this that Uedagin's organization is a product solely of its nature as a bank, for there are as many similarities between Uedagin and other forms of Japanese commercial organization as there are similarities with non-Japanese banks. In Japan, the bureaucracy, and before that the military, occupied the highest status as organizational models, and ranks were prominent in both. According to Hazama (1963) and Sugaya (1963) business organizations have imitated these two organizational styles. Banks in the West can be said to show similar affinities with the bureaucratic styles of their own countries.

nate short of chief. In most respects, chief is the lowest rung on the ladder of status in the world of intercompany relations and its satellite, the world of nightclubs, restaurants, and bars.

No insignia or uniforms provide clues to a person's rank. All men dutifully wear their Uedagin lapel pin and dress in dark suits with white shirts and conservative neckties. The women wear uniforms resembling stewardess outfits of the forties. For all this rather drab uniformity, there is little confusion about rank, however, for close attention to the implications of behavior and the arrangement of groups allows those with a practiced eye to perceive differences in rank readily. For example, when people of differing rank sit down together, a definite seating order placing the highest ranking either at the head or the center of the table is followed. On a stroll the highest ranking person will walk slightly in front of his associates, and also he will be the first through a door and the first to sit down. Because age and rank are correlated, one judges the person's years and then looks for signs of distinction in those cases where group arrangements are of no help. Finally the presence of a Rotary Club pin, the tailoring of the man's suit, and even his bearing are more subtle, but still highly dependable, kinds of information.

Characteristically, forms of address in Japanese companies have involved the extensive use of rank designations (such as "Deputy Tanaka") as in a military system. Uedagin has a policy to discontinue this practice, and now the officially proper form of address is to append *san* ("Mr." or "Ms.") to the person's last name regardless of sex, age, or rank. This second form, preferred because it provides everyone with equal respect, is now much more common than the older style of address.

On the other hand, the use of titles of rank appended to last names is the dominant mode of reference. Conversations in and out of the bank are constantly punctuated with designations of rank. To an outsider the Japanese seem preoccupied with differences of hierarchic level, such as those represented by rank, and the constant use of titles in reference is one source of this impression. It is almost impossible for Uedagin people to be ignorant of the rank of anyone with whom they have contact, and the common practice of exchanging name cards (with titles) when meeting a new person facilitates early classification. In fact, not to know a man's rank can place one in the confusing and uncomfortable situation of not knowing precisely how to act and speak with him.

In subsequent chapters dealing with promotions, rewards, and the organization of work groups, we shall have the opportunity to observe in detail the relationship between ranks and other major elements of the Uedagin system.

The Organization of Work

The third major underlying framework to be considered is the system that orders the actual work of the bank. There are two separate aspects to this. The first involves the division of responsibility and authority throughout a superstructure of command: this results in task assignments to office groups of the section (*ka*) and branch (*shiten*) level. The second involves the organization of work among individuals within these groups. The superstructure is neither heavily populated nor functionally developed, and great emphasis is placed on activities that center in the work groups.

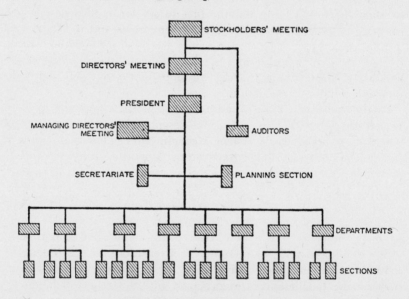

FIG. 4. Organizational chart of the main office.

The ubiquitous organization chart (Figure 4) serves to inform us of the general outline. At the top we find the stockholders' meeting, one we have already noted to be of no serious influence on Uedagin policies. We may also dismiss from serious consideration the two auditors, for although they appear on paper to have independent authority, they are in fact subject to the wishes of Uedagin's other leaders.[13] The

[13] Teraoka (1967) makes this observation about auditors in Japanese companies in general.

real loci of decision making and authority are the directors' meeting, the offices of the president and his two executive directors, and the managing directors' meeting. Since all directors are Uedagin men and since the president is the leader of the directors' meeting, the situation at the top is not so fragmented as it would appear from the figure. The president and his directors have executive authority on an informal basis through the agency of frequent meetings. Major decisions must be worked out within this group of fourteen or so men, but exactly how this is to be done is not predetermined. There are no strict rules of procedure or designations of priority, yet despite this lack of formal definition, decisions appear to be made with expedition and certainty. The exact process by which the inner circle works is a subject beyond the scope of this investigation, but to those in the bank who interest themselves in the politics of management, it is presently axiomatic that the president runs the show. Uedagin is a "one-man company," they say. The directors, who are all his juniors, have been chosen by him and are therefore not disposed to question his leadership. The rule of consensus so commonly mentioned in discussions of Japanese decision making appears to be hardly more than a formality in this case.[14]

Only the president, his two executive directors, and the auditors are exempted from line duty, that is, from direct, daily involvement with task-oriented offices. These few men are the most removed from the daily activities of the organization. The other directors, all department heads or chiefs of large branches, spend most of their time working directly with the offices under their jurisdiction, much like field commanders in the military. For example, the head of the general affairs department has two offices, one on the sixth floor at the center of executive affairs, and another on a lower floor adjacent to the offices of his department. He spends the majority of his time in the latter working closely with his staff. Since this is the practice of most directors, the sixth floor, the hub of executive decision making and the center of the twelve-story main office, is occupied on most days by only

---

[14] When the president retires, however, it is unlikely that any one of the directors will be in a natural position to assume "one-man rule" in his place. It takes some time and maneuvering to build a solid basis of support within the directors' group. Barring the appointment of a finance ministry official as the successor, an oligarchic form of administration at the top is likely to prevail during the interregnum. The rule of consensus would assume great significance at this time, a situation radically different from "one-man rule." It is best that we understand the general nature of Uedagin executive leadership as inherently containing a range of possibilities from total control by the president to an oligarchy of directors including a president. A retired president has also had considerable influence at times as the power behind the throne.

the president, the executive directors, and the small secretarial section that serves them. It is quiet and plush there, leaving one with the feeling that the hum of daily operations never penetrates to disturb the clublike atmosphere.

The essential character of the bank's work organization is indicated by the fact that even staff functions follow the basic pattern of group, rather than individual, work assignment. The planning section is the most appropriate example, for, in addition to planning, it has diverse responsibilities in other areas, such as the operation of the library and the publication of the bank's monthly magazine. The reason these diverse functions have been brought together is important.

Work is conceived as essentially a matter of group effort, and individuals are viewed as essentially members of work groups. Rather than assigning one man to manage the library on an individual basis, for example, the Uedagin approach is first to assign the task of library management to the planning section and then to assign a member of that section to the specific task. In some cases, personnel may pick a person as appropriate for a specific job, but the person will still be assigned formally to an office group rather than the target job. There are no formal job descriptions existing separate from work groups.

This general emphasis on the group context of work is not entirely explained by an interest in supervision or some other technical consideration. It arises from something much more elemental—the inclination, found throughout Japanese society, to organize activities into small face-to-face groups, to enjoy this kind of environment, and to work most efficiently in it. The librarian, informants told me, would be "lonely" if he was not part of some section.

With the two exceptions of the secretariate and planning sections, a three-step hierarchy links work groups with the executive realm. Directors-departments-sections is the top-down sequence in the main office, and for branches the sequence is directors-regional groupings-branches.

The pivotal position in the whole arrangement is the chief. On the one hand, he has a heavy responsibility for the productivity and good morale of his section or branch, and on the other, he acts as the middleman between the executive level and the rest of the organization. He thus faces in two directions and has two sets of loyalties. The position is generally recognized as the most ambiguous and the most demanding within the entire system, and the contradictions built into it have caused numerous reversals of previously successful careers.

Organization charts typically fail to express the various lateral lines of relationship. Periodically, formal conferences of all branch and section chiefs are held, and on a smaller scale there are numerous scheduled meetings between chiefs within the same department or region. Each chief, as the representative of his office, meets with others of his own rank at least once a week. Section chiefs in the home office often meet two or three times a week. These meetings are not to decide policy, but they may serve as the point of initiation for joint recommendations to the directors, the place to achieve better coordination, and a forum for the discussion of common problems. More often, however, these meetings, particularly the larger ones, are treated by the directors as convenient means for the promulgation of new general orders. Even informally there is relatively little interaction along horizontal lines. Chiefs who are close acquaintances meet to discuss business and to enjoy each other's company, but close acquaintanceships of this sort are not numerous.

Change often reveals the essential nature of an organizational structure. In the case of Uedagin, reorganizations have occurred almost every year, and yet none of the numerous changes have altered the basic principles already outlined. New branches and sections have been formed, sections have been shifted from one department to another, and new departments have been created without any disruption of the integrity of the work group or alteration of the basic levels within the hierarchy. While expansion of business and the advent of computerized record keeping have been the major sources of recent structural change, a third factor serving to explain some of the reorganization has been considerations of rank among the top personnel. In order, for example, to promote several men to department head, it was necessary to elevate their sections to departments. Alterations, for any reason, have been accomplished with ease because they have been consonant with the established procedures of hiring, promotion, and transfer. There is nothing static about the organizational chart itself, but the basic principles involved appear to be quite resistant to change.

DISCUSSION

What is there about the Uedagin arrangement of interest to the Western observer? First, there is the elasticity of membership; that is, its noncontractual character and its implicit assumption of mutual involvement and good will. Companies and public bureaucracies in many countries have categories of employment. We find them in banks, universities, the military, and other types of organizations. Highly "elastic" arrangements are found in at least three major places: the military; managerial levels of government, corporations, and other institutions; and organizations with idealistic goals such as religions, political movements, and, to a lesser degree, schools and hospitals. Uedagin is notable, because, although a business organization, its membership category includes 90 per cent of its personnel. This is remarkably inclusive, even acknowledging the place of women in the scheme to be a partial exception to the long-term implications of membership. This inclusiveness reiterates the general conception of the bank as a single community. It encourages, for example, the drawing of the insider-outsider line at the company-outer society boundary rather than, say, between management and employees.[15] It is also one fundamental starting point for the elaboration of ideas, organizational practices and personal sentiments that make this bank (and Japanese white-collar organizations like it) different from their western counterparts.

Because the membership category is so extensive, the rank system is also remarkably inclusive. With the exception of quasi members and nonmembers, it orders the entire personnel into a single hierarchy, like a military system without the barrier between officers and enlisted men. This uniformity is possible because the membership contains only high school and university graduates, and because the work of the bank is broadly homogeneous in nature. Both of these qualities are common to white-collar organizations in Japan.[16]

The bank's rank system does not formally take cognizance of individual skills other than leadership. Specialists among the men are recognized in such areas as computer programming, accounting, law, and training, but they only become specialists after being in the bank for

[15] Argyris (1954) in an interview study of a small American bank, for example, notes that the crucial hierarchical distinction is that between "officers" and "employees" or subordinates. He says that officers are seen by some as a "caste" (p. 94) and that the pejorative term "boss" encapsulates the sense of distance and reserve felt between the two (pp. 59, 96–97). In American banks, officers constitute a very small percentage of the total number of employees, in marked distinction to the Uedagin arrangement. It is also characteristic of large American banks to recruit and otherwise treat future officers in a special way.

[16] Japanese manufacturing firms, with greater educational disparity and distinct types of work, are divided into categories (and separate rank systems) that recognize distinctions along white-collar–blue-collar lines. Uedagin can be said to represent modern Japanese organizations of the white-collar type, yet even within this more narrow field the largest firms usually have separate categories (based on education) for those headed into management and those who are not. The official Uedagin inclusiveness does not discriminate against high school graduates in terms of upward mobility, but informally there is a difference (see chapter 6), and in larger white-collar organizations this ambivalence appears to be resolved by drawing a line between the two.

some time. Their promotions follow the regular rank steps, but in terms of assignments their mid-career patterns involve a minimum of shifting around to different kinds of work. That is, except for a small number of specially trained women, the bank does not hire skilled workers on the open market, but educates its own members to fill its needs. Again, the insider-outsider boundary is strengthened.

The emphasis on the office group as the work unit contrasts with the possibility of organizing work on the principle of individual job distinctiveness. Just as to a large degree membership draws a line around the organization rather than through it, so the arrangement of work circumscribes small face-to-face groups and invests them with great importance. We shall learn in chapter 4 how this group orientation establishes a particular framework for such matters as motivation and authority.

We have, then, a set of basic organizational principles that emphasize the community of work and the uniformity of hierarchical distinctions. These two themes will recur throughout this account. We will find them to be the ingredients of a series of paradoxes generated by the fact that the first principle tends to draw people together while the second strings them out. The first treats them as the same, the second differentiates. Both are obvious necessities, and they can be successfully joined, yet the sense of incompleteness and tension remains. It seems likely that large organizations are inevitably faced with the necessity of attempting to resolve the reality of hierarchy with other powerful principles of social life. In America, hierarchy tends to clash with equality and individual independence. In Uedagin, the differentiation and distance established by rank often appear in marked contrast to the ambitions for a community of common interest and endeavor.

The next chapter, in which we examine the official explanation of the total enterprise, will carry these concerns much farther.

2

SONGS, CEREMONIES, AND
THE UEDAGIN IDEOLOGY

Japanese companies of all sizes and activities pay considerable attention to the philosophy that serves as the official explanation of their
enterprise.[1] No one in Japanese business would be so naïve as to deny
the centrality of economic goals and motives, but this does not detract
from the significance of official ideals and interpretations within each
organization. In Uedagin, not only is there a general requirement for
common direction and meaning, many informants indicate that the
bank's philosophy is useful because it enhances the satisfaction of work
by establishing a sense of joint effort and shared value. To these ends
company leaders expend considerable effort to enunciate a world view
that is acceptable, inspiring, and a bit unique.

By the term ideology is meant the public, official expression of the
ideas and ideals that define Uedagin as a social enterprise, provide
its goals, explain the relationship of its personnel to the bank, and
define the relationship of the bank to the rest of society.[2] The major

[1] For details and discussion of the subject of the history of company ideologies,
the leading sources are Bellah (1957), Hirschmeier (1964), Hazama (1963), Marshall
(1967), Whitehall and Takezawa (1968), Yoshino (1968), and Dore (1969). Two
compendiums of company mottos, principles, and philosophies (Seisansei Chubuchihō
Honbu, 1964, and Sakamoto, 1967) provide some idea of the character of company
ideology for a cross-section of Japanese business and industry during the 1960s. The
extensive writings of Matsushita Konnosuke are indicative of the personal philosophies of many company leaders. The Uedagin ideology has its own flavor and differs
in details of expression from the ideologies mentioned in the above sources, but it
is not at odds with them or different from them on any essential points.

[2] Other designations for this subject matter, including world view, social covenant,
and institutional charter, might possibly be used in place of the term ideology, for
all share its primary focus on the social and doctrinal aspects of ideas and ideals,
but ideology is the least limiting of these possibilities and therefore the most suitable for descriptive purposes. Geertz (1964) has written a fine critique of the mis-
applications of this concept from a cultural anthropologist's point of view, and the
reader is urged to consult this article for an elaboration of the sense of the term
as used here.

responsibility for the maintenance of this ideology rests with the top leaders, the staff of the training institute, those in charge of the company magazine, and the people who arrange company ceremonial meetings. There is no paucity of material of an ideological nature available, but most of it is scattered, fragmentary, and coded in both verbal and nonverbal form. Our task, therefore, is to seek the composite, underlying structure of its message.

THE CEREMONY OF JOINING THE COMPANY

Let us begin by considering in detail one of the richest ceremonial events, the *nyūkōshiki* (literally "entering-bank-ceremony") in which new recruits are officially recognized as members. There are two of these each year, one for women and one for men. It is the latter which we will follow point by point. Without exception all new men who are accepted as members have just graduated from high school or university, and at the time of the ceremony they are in the process of undergoing a rigorous three-month introductory training.

Three groups of participants are involved: the top officers of the bank, the new recruits together with their instructors, and as many parents of the recruits as can attend. The first group, some fifteen or twenty senior men, sit on the stage of the company's large auditorium. The new men, 120 of them in 1969, sit in the front rows of the audience. The parents, well over one hundred in number, sit behind their sons toward the rear of the auditorium. All the men wear dark business suits, and the mothers are dressed quite formally in either kimono or Western attire. Most of the new recruits have fresh haircuts.

As the time for the ceremony approaches everyone has taken his assigned seat except the president, whose conspicuously more comfortable chair at the front of the stage remains empty. Hanging above the stage are the company and Japanese flags and a large banner of congratulations. The president's arrival is the signal that the event may begin. Over to one side, the chief of the personnel section states the name of the ceremony and the year and then announces the company song.[3] Everyone stands and new and old members sing:

[3] Morning ceremonies, company songs, sets of principles, mottos, and the like are common in Japanese companies, as are company flags, badges, and other institutional symbols. The singing of songs and recitation of creeds, while still found in most cases, is today publically regarded as old-fashioned, and among intellectuals as laughable. See Dore (1973:50–53) for a brief account of efforts in a giant manufacturing firm to express company spirit.

A falcon pierces the clouds
A bright dawn is now breaking.
The precious flower of our unity
Blossoms here.
Uedagin Uedagin
Our pride in her name ever grows.

Smiling in our hearts with glory,
For we carry the responsibility for tomorrow's
Independent Japan.
Our towns and villages prosper
Under our banner of idealism raised on high.
Uedagin Uedagin
Our hopes inspired by her name.

Marching forward to the new day
With strength unbounded,
We continue forward step by step.
Oh, the happiness of productive people.
Uedagin Uedagin
Brilliantly radiates her name.

They remain standing to recite in unison the "Uedagin Principles" (*Uedagin kōryō*):

> Constantly abiding by the ideas of cooperative banking, we will, together with the general populace, advance in our mission to serve as an instrument of small and medium business enterprises.
> Intent in the spirit of service, we will contribute to public welfare and social prosperity. Emphasizing trust and possessing an enterprising spirit we will advance scientific administration.
> With mutual respect and affection, we will work with diligence, employed in maintaining systematic order.
> Possessing a spirit of love for Uedagin, we pledge to plan for the prosperity of the bank and for the public welfare and to make the bank the greatest in Japan.

And finally, before sitting down, a second catechism is recited, this one known as the "President's Teachings" (*shachōkun*).

Harmony (*wa*). The bank is our lifelong place of work, let us make it a pleasant place, starting with our greetings to each other each morning.

Sincerity (*seijitsu*). Sincerity is the foundation of trust, let us deal with our customers with a serious and earnest attitude.

Kindness (*shinsetsu*). Have a warm heart. Be scrupulously kind.

Spirit (*tamashii*). Putting our heart and soul into it, let us work with all our strength.

Unity (*danketsu*). Strong unity is the source of energy for our business.

Responsibility (*sekinin*). Responsibility makes rights possible; first let us develop responsibility.

Originality (*sōi*). In addition, let us think creatively and advance making each day a new day.

Purity (*seiketsu*). Have a noble character and proper behavior.

Health (*kenkō*). With ever growing pride let us fulfill the Uedagin dream.

Everyone sits down. The master of ceremonies welcomes the parents and makes some announcements to the effect that following the ceremony there will be a tour of the main office and a luncheon to which all are invited. He then calls on the chief of the training institute to introduce the new men.

Facing the executives on the platform, he describes the group about to enter the bank. There are 120, he says, and all have just finished school. They are fine young men who have worked very hard. In addition they are presently learning to be effective and enthusiastic members of Uedagin. He concludes that the bank should be very proud to receive them.

The president is the next to speak. Representing the rest of the bank, he expresses gratitude that such a fine group of young people are joining the organization. He thanks the parents in the audience for raising such excellent young people. (Many of the parents bow silently in their seats as he says this.) Then in a rambling manner, since he has no prepared speech, the president discusses the history of the bank, the difficulties of contemporary competition, and the problems facing the nation. The stage is set for his direct admonition to the new members.

They are now *shakaijin*, "adult members of society," he says. This means they have heavy responsibilities to serve the society and thus to repay it and their parents for the nurture and sacrifice of raising them from infancy. His tone grows more impassioned as he proceeds to outline the seriousness of working for the bank.[4]

---

[4] All quotations are paraphrases of what was said or written in Japanese and not word-for-word translations. In the case of unprinted speeches and the testimony of informants, it was usually impossible to make verbatim accounts. Original material has also been paraphrased to avoid awkward and confusing sentences.

In contrast to life as a student, working in society brings us face to face with reality each day. That reality is, first, the necessity to work, and, second, the fact that no one is going to care for us. We must care for ourselves. Therefore our decision must be to make the steady progress of our work one of our great lifelong values.

As a shakaijin working in this organization you are expected to fulfill your individual responsibilities as well as you can, for the prosperity of each of us depends on the prosperity of the bank.

I hope you will be conscious and proud that you are members of this bank. Never ignore the fact that our present situation is the result of the blood and sweat of many senior people (*senpai*) who have raised the bank to this high position. I sincerely ask you to get involved with your work in a serious and devoted manner.

The bank is a public institution based on mutual trust. Our lifeblood is trust. Each of you in your heart must become worthy of the trust of others. Your character and skill must deserve their trust and for this reason you must learn every day. This will show that you have the correct spirit.

Finally, addressing the parents, he promises to take responsibility for their children, to educate and care for them, that they may continue to grow as shakaijin.

The president makes speeches of this sort frequently and the themes become repetitious after the third or fourth hearing, yet the man's involvement in what he is saying and his deep personal commitment to the success of the bank remain fresh and at times truly inspiring. He is a large man of impressive posture and energy, yet delivering this speech he has grown so emotional that his voice has broken off and tears have streamed down his face.

The master of ceremonies next calls on the representative of the parents, who walks to the platform and stands before the president. He first expresses the parents' pleasure with the company their children are joining and offers their good wishes for its success. The parents from now on will support the bank's business whenever possible. He requests that the bank discipline and guide their offspring, who are "yet immature and naïve." The parents have brought them this far, he says, it is now the bank which must continue their upbringing. During this brief address the president is also standing, a sign of respect.

When the parents' representative has returned to his seat, the master of ceremonies calls the roll of new members, reading their names and the school from which they have just graduated. As his name is called, each stands and bows with great formality. The president and other leaders nod in response. The list is ordered not alphabetically nor by region, but rather by the status of the schools—national university graduates are first and distant high schools last.

The president again stands to listen to the address by the representative of the new men.

> All 120 of us, the new members of Uedagin, are extremely grateful for our three months of training. Hearing our president's speech today has moved us deeply and made us feel even more grateful.
>
> Looking back, it seems long ago that we left school and our outgrown school uniforms. We entered the gate of the training institute full of high ambitions.
>
> At first, we were primitive and unaware of our responsibilities, but in a correctly ordered environment, we became aware of what Uedagin means, and a sense of devotion grew in our hearts.
>
> We know that Uedagin, for all its rigor and strictness, is, at heart, understanding and sympathetic, yet we are committed to a course of independent self-development within the bank.
>
> Facing a brighter tomorrow, we shall grow. I think the sun will emerge as we advance toward it.
>
> We regard the bank as our life and our career. We are committed to battle with all our strength under the banner and spirit of "harmony and strength." We will trust and aid each other as we face the difficulties before us. We will take our responsibilities seriously, and feel joy in the bank's good name. We are young and as yet spiritually and technically underdeveloped. We ask our seniors to lead and educate us, for we know it is imperative that we become hardy and brave Uedagin men, possessing a spirit of devotion and a capacity for sharp, effective action.
>
> Of late the national long-term debt has increased, the consolidation of the bond market has now speeded up, and the financial world is undergoing a revolution. There is much discussion of the reorganization of the financial system to achieve greater efficiency. Management faces the impending problems of trade

liberalization, the revaluation of the yen, the liberalization of dividends, and many other problems.

It is now time for us to help by enthusiastically working at our first assignments, and, with vision, gaining a better understanding of the financial situation, so that we may report accurately to management.

Furthermore, we must correctly understand what we have been taught about office procedures and seek ways of further rationalizing them.

The words of advice from our president and other executives will be valued advice for the conduct of our lives.

We are deeply grateful for this magnificent ceremony today.

Though still immature, we will energetically go to work like seasoned soldiers.

We humbly request your guidance and discipline from now forward.

The representative and president bow to each other, and then when all have been seated it is announced that the nyūkōshiki is concluded and that the luncheon will begin about an hour later.

Because it is also part of the proceedings, the banquet also requires some description. The luncheon hall is filled with long tables attractively decorated with tablecloths and flowers. At each place has been placed a box lunch, neatly wrapped to indicate a celebration. These have been catered, and inside among the various delicacies is a red sea bream (*tai*), also symbolic of celebration. At the head of the room a microphone has been set up next to the table where the president will sit. The other leaders will sit among the parents and their sons. Several large banners congratulating the new members are hung on the walls.

The president's arrival again is the signal for everyone to sit down and begin eating. Polite conversation ensues. As people are finishing up, the president moves to the microphone to offer his congratulations. He then concludes the program by leading everyone (now standing) in three hearty banzai cheers for the long life and success of Uedagin.

COMMENT ON UEDAGIN CEREMONIES

The bank has numerous such ceremonies throughout the year, and most of them take place in its plush auditorium—perhaps the finest in the city—which holds about four hundred people. The following is a list of the major regularly scheduled ceremonies:

(1) New Year's Ceremony (January)
(2) Entrance Ceremony for New Women (April)
(3) Branch Chiefs' Conference (April)
(4) Award Ceremonies (April and November)
(5) Entrance Ceremony for New Men (May)
(6) Memorial Service for Deceased Members (June)
(7) Graduation Ceremony for Class of Entering Men (July)
(8) Summer Camp Out (August)
(9) Boost Deposits Conference (August)
(10) Retired Members' Association Meeting (October)
(11) Brief End of Year Ceremony (December)
(12) Uedagin Beauty Circle General Meetings (quarterly)
(13) Uedagin Junior General Meetings (quarterly)[5]

In addition to these, the openings of new branch offices (which have lately occurred three or four times a year) are causes for celebration and solemn ritual at the scene. Of all ceremonies, however, the most elaborate and grand are the anniversary celebrations, which occur every five years. Formalities are also associated with some of the bank's charitable activities, but they follow a different pattern.

A few qualities of these ceremonies deserve mention before we interpret their content. First, major ceremonies are among the largest gatherings of Uedagin people during the year, and despite the fact that less than a sixth of the total personnel attend even the largest, they do have the effect of physically representing the Uedagin community, not only to those directly involved, but also to those people who read about them in the bank's magazine. Without such congregations of people from different and often distant offices of the bank, the sense of parochial interests centering on each work group would certainly increase beyond its already significant proportions.

---

[5] The Uedagin Beauty Circle (UBC) and Uedagin Junior (UJ) are youth organizations for unmarried Uedagin members. They were created recently (1969) with the original inspiration coming from the personnel section. This section has fostered their development as a means of raising morale among young people. The idea came from another much larger manufacturing company which has had great success with this kind of association. Besides serving to organize youth-oriented activities and encourage enthusiasm for bank work, it is hoped that the UBC and UJ will become channels of expression from the young people to the older leaders of the bank. The quarterly meetings so far, however, have been characterized by an interest in gaining wide support among the young people in various offices, and as yet little independent activity has been generated.

Ceremonies interrupt the monotony of regular work routines and give them a fresh definition, one that is elevated in significance, dramatic, and impressive. The pageantry and scope of these meetings inspire the audience in a manner far more effective than any printed word.

The general form and symbolic content of Uedagin ceremonies are rather uniform. At least, there is a core of activities that commonly occur. The most important is an exchange of speeches between designated parties. Often one party conducts the meeting and acts as "host," and the other assumes the role of "guest," as represented by the platform-audience division. When the women's association meets, for example, the president sits in the audience.

Such distinctions serve to organize the speeches, but the beginning and end of each formal occasion is the note of Uedagin unity. The singing of the bank song and recitation of the principles and the "President's Teachings" are ubiquitous openers. Since virtually everyone can recite these from memory, an effect of spontaneous unity of purpose is created and the ceremonial proceedings begin on a strong note. The banzai cheer, in which everyone bellows "banzai" thrusting their arms high in the air, is the common finale.

In the ceremony just described the purpose is to solemnize the acceptance of new people into the community of the bank. That so much time is devoted to its preparation, that the top executives give up a morning for it, and that the bank spends a considerable sum on the banquet all give the event weight. The formality, decorations, and shared meal further underline its importance.

The significance given to entering Uedagin is also emphasized by the manifold transitions it involves. Three turning points are marked in the process: a shift in the responsibility for succor and education from parents to the company; the coming of age of the young men as adult social beings (shakaijin); and the beginning of their long career as contributing members of the company. The new recruits are expected to be less dependent and more responsible from this point in their lives, and a new central focus—Uedagin—takes the place of family and school.

Each speaker who reiterates these themes also states the nature of the relationship between the group he represents and the other groups present. The president expresses the bank's gratitude to the parents for providing fine young men, the parents thank the bank for accepting and training their sons, and the new recruits thank parents and bank alike for the care and upbringing they have and will receive.

Gratitude and interdependence, as we shall see, are basic foundations of the structure of meaning erected by the company's ideology.

Pledges of future aid and commitment are also made by the various parties. The representative of the new recruits not only commits his group to the service of the bank, but also to the service of society in general—a long-standing means of showing gratitude to one's parents. In his address the president offers the young men security and education so that they may develop further as adults. The parents, too, acknowledge an obligation to aid the bank in whatever way possible. Gratitude and commitment are closely related, the first serving as inspiration for the latter.

Finally, in the speech of the representative of the young men we are treated to a glimpse of the relationship between themselves and the rest of the Uedagin organization. Senior men (senpai) are acknowledged to be more experienced, wiser, and more perfected. The young men submit to their leadership and discipline, asking for guidance and assistance. This sense of hierarchy is also underlined by the president, who, in speaking of the history of the bank, conveys the idea that Uedagin was built with great sacrifice and devotion by the men who now are retired or in senior positions. The vertical order is thus based on both personal development (experience) and a history of service to the organization (sacrifice).

Ceremonial occasions are but a part of the total effort by which the ideology is broadcast, and it is highly unlikely that the complete story is ever packaged and presented at one time. For people acquainted with Japanese thought (varied as it is), and particularly for people having spent any time in the bank, the fragments of the ideology presented on each occasion are sufficient to suggest the entire arrangement. It is doubtful that Uedagin people consciously examine the coherence and consistency of their bank's official "world view," but it is certain that they understand it.

THE IDEOLOGY SUMMARIZED

It is necessary for us as outsiders to Japan and to Uedagin to make the structure underlying all of this explicit. The interpretation that follows is mine, based on the numerous fragments collected, such as the above entrance ceremony.

The way work is organized is the same as the organization of the body. A variety of people with different functions are put together as an interdependent whole. If everyone does his job well the organization begins to operate successfully and this allows each person to improve his ability even more. In school, where grades were an individual matter, you could get out of doing your work without causing trouble for others, but in banking, if one person is slow or lazy it causes everyone else inconvenience and their work declines as a result. Work is a living thing. Behind the superficial appearances of simplicity lies the living reality of society.

Taking a cue from this explanation offered to new members by a director of the bank, we may summarize the various themes of the Uedagin ideology as forming a conception of the bank and of Japanese society as integrated and hierarchical organisms with all constituent parts (individuals and institutions) interrelated and interdependent. The story of the kingdom lost for want of a nail expresses the same view, for it too presents a picture of a functionally unified system containing levels of ascending integration. Instead of the nails in the shoe of the horse of the knight, the Uedagin view of society begins with individuals, who are workers, related directly to institutions such as Uedagin, which are, in turn, part of the larger society. If the workers are married men, their families are also included. Starting from the bottom we find families dependent on workers who themselves are dependent for jobs on some company. These relationships are hierarchical, but they are also reciprocal, for the worker depends on his family, and the company depends on the worker. Relationships at the higher level of institutional integration are also matters of interdependence. The company succeeds only if the national system succeeds, and the nation depends on the contribution of companies. As long as each constituent element fulfills its tasks, the entire scheme can be expected to operate smoothly. Production is efficiently organized upwards, and this provides sustenance that flows downward to the worker and family levels.

Competition is between companies, rather than individuals, and international competition is clearly recognized as threatening the total Japanese system.

This simple and not unusual conception of society lies at the heart of the entire Uedagin world view. It is in the Confucian tradition (a point we will take up shortly), except in its lack of emphasis on the family. Instead, it elevates the company's importance as the key organizational focus between individuals and the national polity. Let us note a number of logical extensions based on this assumption of organic unity. First, there is no conflict of interest between levels of the system. Individual interests are inextricably interrelated with institutional and national interests, and only institutions are in direct competition. Second, because the hierarchy is reciprocal and levels are interdependent, there is no reason to assume that it is inherently tyrannical or exploitative. Third, institutions have an implied responsibility for the welfare of their workers, just as the government has a responsibility for the welfare of constituent institutions. Finally role fulfillment is a moral duty of individuals and institutions alike.

The difficulties inherent in the problem of creating or maintaining unity without sacrificing the necessary hierarchy is resolved through the concept of organic unity. Hierarchy is natural and proper. It serves to order the organism and therefore preserve its viability. Unity is also natural and proper. It summarizes the interdependence and cooperative character of the arrangement. The two are inseparable and equally necessary, and to the degree people understand and accept this fact, problems between the two principles will not arise. But if equality is a precondition of unity, which it is in the democratic national ideology of Japan today, then problems will arise.

Statements of the ideology are never so explicit or logical as the foregoing account. To be effective, that is, to be reasonably acceptable and hopefully even inspirational, the presentation of the ideology must depend on a set of images more tangible and closer to the important moral sentiments of daily Japanese life. Thus, most messages of an ideological nature revolve around analogies and metaphors that derive not from bank work, but from the daily life of families, schools, and the like.

Uedagin is at times referred to as "one great family" (daikazoku). The implications of this image are extensive. First, the bank, like the ideal Japanese family, is an entity in which the interests of members are secondary to the interests of the family as a whole.[6] It is everyone's duty to work for the well-being and reputation of the family, and in return the family exists for the benefit of all its members. The same relationship holds, by implication, between workers and the bank.

[6] Pelzel (1970) offers the best summary in English of the ideals of the Japanese household (ie) as a social organization. Readers of Japanese should also consult Kawashima (1948, 1950, and 1956) for an exploration of such ideals and their extension beyond the household. As noted by many writers, independence and social distance from parents is not a cultural ideal or psychological ambition in Japan to the degree it is in American culture. Parental authority, dependency, and mutuality within the family, despite all of the postwar changes, continue to be notable from a cross-cultural perspective. This is most true of families operating as an economic unit in agriculture and business. Although generalizations about "the family" may be risky, people in Uedagin do not regard the analogy with the family as a stagnant or authoritarian concept, but rather as one that conveys the traditional and, for them, Japanese value of human involvement and sympathy into the social relations of the company.

The analogy also describes an ideal pattern of interpersonal relations, which should be warm, understanding, and cooperative. As in the regular family, leaders and followers, old and young, men and women, all occupy different roles and have different degrees of authority. It is proper to respect these differences and to be loyal to one's given place in the system. Leaders, like fathers, have a responsibility to watch over the welfare and best interests of their followers, and relations between different generations in the bank should follow the ideals of the family pattern. Older members should advise and educate younger members, and younger members should, out of gratitude and affection, show obedience and respect for their seniors. In time, each generation advances from apprenticeship to responsibility, at which point, like grown children, it assumes the duty of caring for those that went before. The family ideal is clearly a rich source of inspiration, and the high esteem and respect for the institution of the family, combined with its emotionally appealing image, invest this metaphor with considerable persuasive power.

Closely related is the highly valued quality of social concord, most often expressed by the term *wa*.[7] The bank's motto is *wa to chikara*

---

[7] The concept *wa* is a central theme in several articles by Kawashima (1963 and 1967). This important concept has received little attention from Western scholars, and no succinct expression of its meaning exists in English. Kawashima (1967) quotes a prewar nationalist publication: "In individualism there can exist cooperation, compromise, self-sacrifice and so on, in order to adjust and reduce contradictions and oppositions, but in the final analysis there exists no real harmony (wa). . . . The wa of our country is not mechanical cooperation, starting from reason, of equal individuals independent of each other, but the grand harmony (*taiwa*) which maintains its integrity by proper statuses of individuals within the collectivity and by acts in accordance with these statuses. . . . After all, oppositions of opinions, as well as differences of interest deriving from (various) standpoints, are integrated into a unity of grand harmony proper to Japan and originating from a common source. Not conflicts, but harmony is final. [Quoted from a 1937 publication of the ministry of education, *Kokutai no Hongi* (Principles of the National Polity) pp. 50, 51, 57.]" He then adds his own comment: "In a concept of social obligation which does not have the counterbalancing notion of 'right,' the interest of the individual is not made distinct and fixed. Here, an individual is not considered to be an independent entity. Rather, his interest is absorbed in the interest of the collectivity to which he belongs, and the interest of the collectivity is recognized as having primary importance, while the interest of the individual has merely a secondary importance [pp. 262–263]." Nakamura (1969) also discusses the importance of this concept to the early history of Japanese thought. The seventh century Seventeen-Article Constitution, regarded by Nakamura and others as a major keystone of Japanese polity, begins: "Concord (*wa*) is to be esteemed above all else; make it your first duty to avoid discord. People are prone to partisanship, for few persons are really enlightened. Hence, there are those who do not obey their lords and parents, and they come into conflict with their neighbors. But when those above and those below are harmonious and friendly, there is concord in the discussion of affairs, and things become harmonious with the truth. Then what is there that cannot be accomplished? [Translated by Nakamura, p. 5]"

("harmony and strength"), and the assignment of wa to the "President's Teachings" illustrates its preeminent position in a list of values. The term is also to be found in descriptions of the pleasures of company recreational outings, and the New Year's greetings from some offices (which the company magazine publishes) show individual pictures of the staff grouped around the character *wa* written large in the center of the design. Nor is Uedagin at all unusual in this emphasis. Wa is undoubtedly the single most popular component in the mottos and names of companies across Japan.

The precise sense of this notion is not, however, easily defined. The usual translations of "harmony" or "concord" are inadequate to convey the full sense of the term. Wa is not a metaphor. Nor is it some abstract or logical part of a system of distinctions. Rather, it is a quality of relationship, particularly within working groups, and it refers to the cooperation, trust, sharing, warmth, morale, and hard work of efficient, pleasant, and purposeful fellowship. Teamwork comes to mind as a suitable approximation. It is the complex of qualities that makes working relationships successful and enjoyable. Thus, wa is far from a concept of static harmony. It is a directly tangible thing that easily accommodates human frailties and differences as long as participants share a devotion to the success of the common effort and a respect for one another as partners in the enterprise.

To achieve wa is certainly a major goal for any Japanese group, and it also is an essential ingredient in the attainment of other goals. In this regard, it is something like "love" in American popular culture, for it is both a major means to social improvement and an end in itself.[8]

A particular relationship between past, present, and future is characteristic of the ideology. The present generation of bank members is often reminded that the present state of Uedagin development, including the high salary level and the full array of welfare and recreational facilities, is the result of the efforts and sacrifice of previous generations. These predecessors (senpai) are in the position of ancestors for the Uedagin "great family," and to them a debt of gratitude and respect is owed by all who presently benefit from their efforts.

---

[8] It is fascinating to discover the term for human love, *ai*, being used more and more in the slogans of Uedagin youth activities. Because it is contemporary and "Western" it is appealing to them. Between Western love and the *ai* which appears in Uedagin contexts lies a profound gap of application. Unlike "love," *ai* is widely used to describe the feelings members should have for their fellow workers and for their bank. Even though *wa*, which describes qualities of relationship, and *ai*, which describes feelings toward another, are different, their use in the bank ideology is mutually reinforcing and even synonymous; they are rallying cries in the effort to forge unity and cooperation.

The symbol of their sacrifices is a fire-scorched character, one that originally was part of the signboard that hung outside the first Uedagin main office. That building was destroyed during an air raid in 1945, and the sole surviving memento of the terrible event is this single character. From those dark days Uedagin has risen to its present prosperity, and the surviving character now hangs in the president's office as a reminder of the struggle.

Stories often appear in the bank magazine recalling the trials and sacrifices of previous generations. For example, in a eulogy for his predecessor, a Mr. Katada, the president writes:

> The many stories about our former president's character and good nature are part of the early history of the bank and are already in the process of becoming legends. I would like to recount, however, a personal experience of mine with President Katada that I will always remember. Many years ago just after the war, when we first formed our union, I was chosen as one of its leaders, and in this capacity I spoke with Mr. Katada about ways of improving the living conditions of our people. At that time there was a great food shortage and malnutrition was a very real danger. President Katada talked with me in great earnestness all through one night about this. Even though he was at the time struggling with the problem of having to bring the bank out of the red, he resolved to find ways to raise salaries to meet the members' needs. That night both of us, weeping with emotion, pledged our lives to the rejuvenation of the bank.

According to the ideology, the present membership is duty bound to repay their debt to the past by working to advance Uedagin for the benefit of future generations. Conceptually, the present generation stands in an intermediate position between the past and the future Uedagin. This relationship, one that stretches over time and interlocks different generations, is fundamental to the bank's sense of history, institutional continuity, and social morality.

Such intergenerational ties are analogous to the traditional ideal conception of the Japanese household (*ie*) as a social enterprise existing in time, with each generation benefiting from its parents and ancestors and in turn having the obligation to return these benefits and increase them for their own children and their descendants.

The degree to which salaries, profits, and material welfare are relegated to a minor place in the bank ideology is extraordinary to a Westerner. The major exception is the president's idea that all are working to build a future paradise (*rakuen tsukuri*):

In order to realize our dream, and considering the fierce competition in the financial world, we must build a strong and efficient bank. To do this we must work to our full capacities as people. Each must become stronger in order to survive and succeed in the face of this fierce reality. I desire bankers who, through their toughness of body and spirit, can realize the dream of building a paradise. This paradise we all desire is definitely not something that others will create for us while we relax and watch. It is something we must make ourselves.

While most members interviewed do not take this idea of an Uedagin paradise seriously, claiming to have no understanding of what the president really means, the theme has a definite place in the ideology. This *rakuen* stands for the progressive development of the bank, a development that will bring greater personal satisfactions for everyone. Paradoxically, when the president urges the membership to strive for this goal, he also states that, for the present, ease and comfort must be postponed. The existence of a future Uedagin paradise makes today's sacrifice not a personal, but a group matter.

Not all the goals focus on the "great family." The bank has a mission (*shimei*) to serve (*hōshi suru*) the society beyond its gates. Uedagin's primary mission is to advance as a bank of the region, of the people, and of small- and medium-size industry. These responsibilities are frequently mentioned, both separately and in combination. The bank also has a mission to be socially responsible in other ways. It should contribute to and help lead public campaigns for improving the general welfare, and it should educate its young to be good members of society.

It is fascinating to note the degree to which the bank's operations are tied to even such distant goals as world peace and the betterment of underdeveloped countries. Spokesmen for the bank do not hesitate to add fashionable public concerns to the list of goals. No sooner is something announced in the papers as a pressing problem than it appears in the list of tasks to which the bank intends to contribute. That individual bank members, for example, by doing their work well, contribute to the financial and economic success of Japan, to the nation's international stature, and to world peace is not considered far-fetched. As long as the concept of interdependency remains, the bank will have no difficulty establishing its role as a contributor to national and international causes.

Something more should be said about shakaijin. As an adult member of society one has the responsibility to contribute to the general welfare. By combining entrance into the bank with entrance into adult society, the implication is clearly made that fulfilling one's duties to Uedagin serves to fulfill one's obligations to society at large. With the aid of this concept the bank takes a position between the individual and whatever aspirations he has to be of service to society.

A corollary to the shakaijin theme is that the bank assumes responsibility for the socialization of the young people it accepts. Since they are still young and not yet perfected as adults, the argument goes, the bank should educate and discipline its new members in order that they may be better shakaijin. This implies a concept of adulthood that acknowledges the need for continued growth, maturity, and perfection, and for this the bank takes responsibility.

When bank spokesmen discuss the proper attitude toward the company, "love Uedagin" (Uedagin o ai suru) is likely to be heard. Because it is their community and the source of a good life for them, and because it is made up of their fellow workers, people should naturally feel emotional attachment for the bank and express it through pride, dedication, and enthusiastic participation. Rarely will any explanation or elaboration of the phrase "love Uedagin" be offered, for its meaning, correctness, and implications, vague as they may be, are considered self-explanatory. However, that an effort is made to sponsor this attitude indicates that it is far from being realized in the breast of every member. Consulted privately, people in the bank express little interest in examining their own feelings about Uedagin in any depth, but they usually endorse the general correctness and acceptability of the idea that one should feel affection for one's company.[9]

To a large degree all of the foregoing themes are statements of one general ideal: that of a collectivity, constituted of emotionally satisfying personal relationships, working in the spirit of concord for the general interest. This ideal fits neatly with the principle of membership discussed in the previous chapter. The fellowship of effort and reward, created in the abstract by the concept of membership, is detailed and given momentum in the ideology. Images such as "one great family," harmony, and "love Uedagin" all depict the ideal spirit in which the fellowship of Uedagin membership should be conducted.

9 Aishashugi, "love-one's-company-ism" is a common phrase in Japan used to describe the programs and ideological endeavors designed to bring the individual and his company into a close relationship. This phrase, rather than a personal statement of affection for Uedagin, is central to individual explanations of the matter, an indication that personal convictions and feelings, if they do exist, are not as relevant as the fact that aishashugi is one company ideal. Emotional attachments, one person observed, are not the product of ideological convictions. They derive from such tangible experiences as close and supportive office relationships and the fellowship of company friends.

All is not sweetness and light, however. Almost invariably, the condition of the world, particularly the financial world, is portrayed as filled with threatening competition. Warnings about various economic hazards that endanger the existence of the institution are repeated often. Contrary to the fact of recent Japanese and Uedagin prosperity, for example, conditions are not viewed as getting better. Always, just around the corner, lies a most serious problem that only hard work, greater efficiency, and sacrifice will overcome. We might say that the official world view contains the assumption of an essentially hostile environment, one that requires the bank to be forever on guard. The debilitating effects of prosperity also threaten the bank, as the president notes in a New Year's letter, "Won't someone speak out, warning that the consumption mood which is recently so evident in our land brings in its wake a tragedy as it did for England? I have just said we have tasted the wine of victory, yet the real test comes after victory. Those who are misled by momentary prosperity into loosening the reins, are destined to become, as England has, a sorrowful spectacle of decline." The specter of company decline, raised within the ideology by such matters as competition, economic uncertainty, and the effects of luxury, sets the stage for the ubiquitous reminder of the need for greater effort and more efficient organization. This is the juncture, then, between an ideology focused on good human relations and the underplayed but ever-present requirements of modern business organization. Efforts to streamline operations, to boost office efficiency, to increase the collection of deposits—that is, any action taken according to the logic of business rationality—can be defended ideologically as necessary for the preservation of the Uedagin community, even if it is damaging to social relations or individual satisfactions. Those actions that are most difficult to defend, we should note, are the ones most directly in contradiction to the principle of membership—especially, laying people off for economic reasons.

THE PERSON AND PERSONAL FULFILLMENT

In all of the above, concepts and ideals focusing on the individual (his nature, fulfillment, dignity, and the like) appear, at first glance, to have little significance. In fact, considerable attention is paid to the individual, not only as a member of Uedagin, but as a human being with an inherent urge for satisfaction and accomplishment. In the official view, there is no need for a person to be independent of his institutional connections in order to achieve happiness. There is no contradiction, that is, between institutionalized work and personal

aspiration, whether it be for artistic fulfillment, social service, or even
spiritual release. What we view as the eternal conflict between man
and society is a problem that is not nearly as immutable in the Uedagin ideology. Stated simply, devotion to duty, perfected through
greater self-discipline, in time leads to a reduction of the disturbance
caused by conflicting demands. The result is an improved state of
personal spiritual freedom and a sense of joy focused on fulfillment
in one's work. This is a solution to man's problems in society based
on a preoccupation with or absorption in socially prescribed activity.
Devotion to duty, long esteemed in Japan, is the road to spiritual
growth and fulfillment. Or, as the bank's leaders imply, the responsibilities of membership and the challenge of efficient work performance
are the opportunities for what is, in effect, a particular and totally
secular form of salvation. Persons familiar with Japanese Zen teaching
will find echoes of its insight here.

This psychology is part of the more general Japanese tradition labeled "spiritualism" (seishin-shugi). Spiritualism will appear as an
important element of Uedagin training (chapter 9), and, in anticipation of that discussion, let us consider sections of an essay, "My
Thoughts," written by the president, in which he sets forth his personal philosophy on the question of the individual and the organization. Upon entering the bank all new members receive a copy of this
essay, for it is a major statement of the goals of introductory training
and also a guide to the interpretation of the relationship between the
difficulties of work and individual satisfaction.

> Since man is an animal of feeling, it is the condition of his
> spirit (kokoro) which guides his life. Two of the sayings I like
> and often quote are:
> "Respond to all situations as though they are natural and
> expected," and "Receive life's experiences correctly." The first
> quote is related to mental preparation (kokoro no mochikata),
> and the second, to the quality of open responsiveness. Happi-
> ness and sadness no doubt have something to do with motiva-
> tion and freedom, but basically these things are products of the
> condition of one's spirit.
> Buddha taught that the actions of the body are products of
> the spirit; therefore, first we must improve the spirit. A philos-
> opher of the Ming dynasty said, "If one's spirit is at peace one
> will not suffer discomfort. If one's spirit is strong one will never
> be concerned about material welfare." These teachings empha-
> size spirit above all else.
> Among the many aspects of kokoro is the spirit of my work,
> that is, my belief in the importance of the saying seiju-fuju

("correctly accepting-not accepting"). I would like to explain this further.

When I was a young man I had a passion for playing go. My opponent in go was an elderly dentist who suffered from rheumatism in his shoulders. Even when lifting a tea bowl or using chopsticks his face would show the great pain he was experiencing.

However as soon as he said, "let's play go," he suddenly forgot his discomfort. He not only smiled happily, but he could effortlessly lift the five- or six-pound go board.

All of this is easy to talk about, but it isn't so easy to think and feel this way from the beginning. Whether one can become involved in something, instead of resisting it, is related to the state of his spirit. Buddha also said, "All men live for something, that is the sum of it; however, some are mistaken and some are right in what they live for." The mistaken ones think of themselves and are employed in trying to get rid of suffering, unhappiness, ill fortune, and the like from their lives, but, in fact, they are seeking and inviting these very things into their lives. On the other hand, trouble and suffering are good medicine for people on the right road. If one begins with a mind prepared for trouble, any difficulties, no matter how great, can be faced. In the process, the problem itself vanishes, leaving the person free to pursue his goals.

It is certainly not unnatural to think life is difficult and dark, but thinking so makes it just that. Strictly speaking, I don't think there is any work in the world that is perfectly suited to our wishes. If it is work, no matter what kind it is, it is not going to match our tastes, but in spite of this, men must all do some kind of work. Thus, let's try to adjust to whatever work we are assigned, without complaint, regarding it as the best there is. The very people who complain that if only given a different job they would be happy and do well, are the ones who, no matter how often they get their wish, continue to complain and consequently never complete anything. People with seiju can live happily day after day, but for those with a fuju attitude troubles pile up. No matter what pursuit it is, failure is entirely the product of one's own making.

There is no work that can be done well if one dislikes it. In such cases, the only feeling is that of irritation and displeasure. But if one works with a positive attitude, giving his best effort, the natural consequence will be enjoyment of work and happiness. The fact illustrates the great utility of seiju.

Furthermore, society is made of people, and people are raised and educated by society. Because of this our obligations to society must be repaid. We do this through service. Our aware-

ness and delight in human existence is involved with the wish
for the prosperity of society.

Won't unhappiness and suffering disappear if we can all together adapt our lives to the spirit of seiju and end contention
and discord? In the brief time life allows us, we must establish
a life of happiness based on this spirit. There is no question
that, persisting in the face of adversity, we can attain our goals,
if we have that spirit.

I am human, I have had disappointments and been bewildered at times. I have been greatly upset and discontent, too.
However, I haven't turned from the correct road through life,
and now, I am ready to enter the final and most rewarding
stretch of the way. Isn't this because I have lived under the influence of *kokoro?*

The president's explanation that if problems are accepted and faced
cheerfully they may be overcome is squarely part of the tradition of
Japanese popular thought, and while it is hardly a sophisticated philosophical argument, its common sense strikes most Uedagin people as
undeniable. More important for our purpose, its "mind over matter"
approach is apt as the official doctrine of an institution such as Uedagin. Satisfaction or unhappiness depends on the individual, particularly on his attitude, and not on outward causes such as low pay, long
hours, boring work—all of which are relative and therefore cannot be
eliminated. Tenacity and perseverance, indications that the spirit of
seiju is alive, are among the most highly valued personal qualities according to this view. Other personal qualities (initiative, intelligence,
personal warmth, etc.) are also highly valued, but in the official ideology spiritualism and its associated perspectives prevail. The understanding of the person expressed in this doctrine is not limited, however, to Japanese companies. It may be found as a vital alternative to
"modern," "Western" views of the person in most areas of Japanese
society.

UEDAGIN PEOPLE AND THE IDEOLOGY

The question of participation in the generation and maintenance of
the ideology is an important one to examine in some detail. If only
the leaders of the company voice the official view, then perhaps it is
imposed and even alien. Such a situation would be a patent contradiction of the ideological assumptions themselves. On the other hand,
if Uedagin people in general embraced the ideology with as much
fervor as the leaders use in presenting it, then it would have to be

interpreted as a primary source of motivation and a key to our explanation of all else related to the bank. Neither of these extreme and facile interpretations is appropriate, but the actual situation must be recognized as containing a little bit of each.

Let me begin by discussing briefly why belief (*shinjiru* or *shinkō*) is not the basic issue. The term is used to apply to some religions and some political movements in Japan, but in the Uedagin case proper conduct as a participant in the group is the more important consideration. Both the safest course and the highest virtue lie in keeping still about personal opinions that contradict public ideology. The concept of belief, as we know it, places the individual in a social vacuum and implies that consistency of action with personal conviction, regardless of context, is highly virtuous. We should not bring this concept of "belief," the meaning of which is generated in an alien tradition, to our interpretation of the bank.

It is in the nature of the Uedagin ideology to be vague and agreeable. People have a hard time having a strong opinion about it either way, so full is it of conventional platitudes.

Asked whether idealism and a sense of values are necessary aspects of business management, officials and lower-ranking members alike answered that without them members of the same enterprise would have difficulty uniting and enjoying work together. This practical emphasis on the collectivity and its requirements not only provides one justification of the ideological effort, it is also an indirect confirmation of the basic idea of the company as community.

Many efforts are made to involve a wide variety of people in the formulation and expression of the official Uedagin ideals. The president has appointed a committee of people of all ranks to examine the bank's principles and offer suggestions for its improvement. The deliberations of this group have not resulted in any basic changes, but the principles are, as a result, interpreted as the product of consensus. Participation is also encouraged, one might say ordered, through the established practice of having representatives of virtually all ranks speak at ceremonies. Their presentations are invariably of the testimonial sort in which the company values are confirmed. As Thurman Arnold (1937) observed, "When one appears on the public stage to take part in some important ceremony, he should not question the assumptions on which that ceremony is based." This is a general understanding, and there is no need to "supervise" the speech making to guarantee that it is positive and optimistic. That ceremonial occasions are designed to represent unity and to kindle the fires of purpose in the hearts of those present, whether of high rank or low, is appreciated by all participants. Speakers have an obvious duty to the group to preserve this quality in their own performance. Participation and attendance are part of the work of the bank, but a sense of belonging to the production, and thus to the bank, is imparted; that is to say, the total effect is far greater than that of having witnessed a series of empty gestures.

The company's major instrument of inspiration is its monthly magazine, the Uedagin *News*. Printed on fine paper, filled with pictures, and often sporting several pages of color photographs, the *News* is a sophisticated publication that covers a broad range of subject matter. In addition to editorials, we find articles stating bank policy and messages from leaders, many heavy with ideological rhetoric. Other regular features include such diverse things as round-table discussions, reports of Uedagin events, news from the branches, a monthly child care, health, and home economics section, accounts of foreign travel, discussions of the economy, and announcements of marriages, births, retirements, and deaths. A typical issue runs about seventy pages, and, as would be expected of a company magazine, it presents a picture of happy people. Human interest stories and personalized material are two notable emphases of the news staff.

The participation of average members is encouraged through monthly "relay" articles and round-table discussions (*zadankai*).[10] In the latter, eight to twelve average members gathered by the magazine staff discuss a common problem or experience in the bank. This form of public discussion encourages a serious outlook, and the participants find themselves voluntarily indicating a strong interest in solving the bank's problems. Their printed comments, then, become testimonials of their commitment to Uedagin. For readers the result is an impression of wide involvement in bank affairs on the part of persons of all ranks. New policies are also discussed in this way, and the zadankai thus serves to maintain an impression of broad popular consideration and support for decisions handed down by management.

Also serving to publicize the ideology are such documentary enter-

---

[10] Zadankai, which are widely popular in Japan, are of a particular pattern. Each participant seeks to offer opinions to the accumulating commentary without creating too much divisive argument. It is more important that a pleasant discussion ending in general agreement be held, than a logical debate be pursued. Should there be too strong or intransigent a debate, the round-table character is lost, and the participants and listeners alike are left with a feeling of disturbance. The zadankai is a public performance and calls for expressions of publicly accepted ideals.

prises as the periodic writing of the history of the bank and the display of important historical materials. On the bank's twentieth anniversary, a beautifully bound and illustrated volume of over six hundred pages was published, and an even larger history is planned to commemorate its twenty-fifth. This publication appears to be intended to serve several purposes. It is written to intensify the awareness of and pride in the history of the institution, and its interminable lists and photographs of past personnel serve as an album of memories for older members.

Although there is no other, competing ideology in the arena of official bank communications, and none would be permitted, there are many conflicting interpretations and ideologies in the general intellectual life of modern Japan. Privately, bank members may consider these important, but such outside influences have not become more than personal convictions, and, for this reason, their total effect on behavior within the bank is slight.

Bank ideology does shift, however, with new outside developments. Sometimes it bends with the wind (such as in supporting the ecological movement), and other times it seeks to counterbalance popular change (such as in opposing the "leisure boom"), but, as a rule, individual expression within the bank context must wait for Uedagin policy shifts to move in new directions.

The outside ideology of particular significance to the thinking of most Uedagin men is what is characterized as the modern (*kindaiteki*) approach to business management, one that sees in the present conduct and organization of large American corporations an eminently efficient approach that is the pattern of the future. Particularly those at the management level are inclined to this view, especially as it defines the direction of future change for the bank. Increased "rationality" (*gōrisei*), they believe, will be necessary to meet competition; the changes they envision are in large measure aimed at the elimination of personnel policies and practices which, because they are oriented to people and people's feelings, create a variety of cost burdens not present in the American system of management.[11] "Rationality" here is set in contrast to "Japanese-style" (*nihonteki*) management, and the two are lined up with another ubiquitous polarity of Japanese

11 Much of Yoshino (1968) is a discussion of this point of view as its popularity has grown in management associations and among many managers of large companies. The crucial point is that often this perspective is voiced in contexts when being modern and progressive is expected, but seldom are changes made with the same incisiveness.

daily thought, namely the modern-traditional contrast. The result is that the concepts of "traditional," "Japanese," and "human feeling" are closely associated and set over against "modern," "Western," and "rational," a set of polarities familiar to the Western mind. The stereotypes do not, of course, account very well for the remarkable growth of the Japanese economy or the recent floundering of American industrial organization, and so it is not surprising to discover a new trend away from eulogizing the "American" and a renewed interest in the strengths of the "Japanese" approach.

Our interest here is with the fact that "rationality" is, logically at least, rather contradictory to the images and values presented in the company ideology by the bank leadership. There are four things to note in this connection. First, often the same men who present a glowing picture of the bank in human relations terms express their conviction that the human relations emphasis is not efficient and must change. Second, there is obviously a time and a place for each kind of remark: the former at ceremonies, public events, and in the company magazine; the latter in private discussion, in serious lectures to men during training, staff meetings and the like, and to outside managerial specialists. Interview research involves this latter context. Third, that the two ideologies are often viewed as contradictory does not mean that in the official ideology there is no room to emphasize efficiency and the threat of competition, just as "rationality" must acknowledge the human aspects of organization. Finally, although people dwell on the contradictions when they are the subject of conversation, most often the contradictory nature of the two perspectives is ignored and each, in the appropriate context, serves as a proper ambition for management.

ECHOES OF THE CONFUCIAN HERITAGE

The similarity between the bank's conception of social life and the Confucian world view is so pronounced as to deserve further attention. Derk Bodde (1953) has summarized the Confucian concept of social harmony in the following terms:

> The welfare of the social organism as a whole depends upon harmonious cooperation among all of its units and of the individuals who comprise these units. This means that every individual, however high or low, has the obligation to perform to the best of his ability those particular functions in which he is expert and which are expected of him by society. Thus the

ruler should rule benevolently, his ministers should be loyal yet at the same time ready to offer their frank criticism, the farmers should produce the maximum of food, the artisans should take pride in their manufactures, the merchants should be honest in their dealings, and no one should interfere needlessly in the tasks of others for which he himself is not qualified. In other words, society should be like a magnified family, the members of which, though differing in their status and functions, all work in harmony for the common good [pp. 45–47].

There is no question that Confucian thought has greatly influenced the Japanese intellectual tradition for over a thousand years (Naka-mura, 1969). In particular, the moral philosophy of both merchants and bureaucrats of the early commercial and industrial period show a basic indebtedness to this philosophical tradition (Bellah, 1957). What has not been sufficiently recognized is the persistence of this tradition in the ideologies of companies like Uedagin. While public debate, both economic and political, has been carried on during the last twenty-five years in the language of democratic society, the internal life of many institutions has continued to be influenced by a different and more traditional philosophy.

This older social morality is one well suited to the organization of modern, large-scale institutions. Certainly, it is more appropriate than the ideas and ideals bequeathed to the modern world by the French, American, and Russian revolutions. As Bendix (1956) has demon-strated, industrial and business institutions, no matter what the reign-ing political philosophy of the country, must have a hierarchy of au-thority, and this they must explain through the development of some ideology. Uedagin, and other modern Japanese organizations, have a ready-made explanation for authority within their own tradition. This Confucian heritage, as transformed in Japan into an institutional rather than familial morality, is unquestionably an asset for those businesses that succeed in adapting it to modern organizational re-quirements.

The major reason this older ideology and the public emphasis on democratic society can exist side by side is important, for it offers one key to understanding Japanese cultural continuity during the last hundred years of remarkable Westernization. The difference is essen-tially a matter of context. Inside institutions like the bank, social re-lations can continue to be defined (in part) by the principles of a so-cial order inherited from an earlier era, although in both public and private life the ideas and ideals of the West enjoy increasing popularity. These separate views may coexist without persistent conflict, although people at times suffer a poignant awareness of the contradictions.[12] The strong and inclusive life that many Japanese institutions have been able to maintain is one explanation for their ability to retain their own interpretation of society during a period of exceptional foreign influence and social change.

It must be remembered, in all of this, that large scale organization and bureaucracy are not recent accomplishments in Japan. "Modern" and "bureaucratic" are not synonymous. We are examining a tradition with deep and firm roots in the history of the Far East, and it is a mistake to see this development solely as the product of Westernization or economic modernization. In fact, premodern China and Japan witnessed several of the world's more successful bureaucracies, and their continuing excellence with this form of organization deserves our greater attention.

The "organic" aspect of the bank's world view seems so much like the western "functionalist" conception of the world that a brief comparison of the two would be helpful here. While the emphasis on interlocking roles, hierarchy, and the final, total outcome are the same for both, there are profound differences too. Our "functionalism" borrows the image of the machine. This mechanical view of organization defines relationships as essentially impersonal. Uedagin "functionalism" utilizes the image of the "great family," thus implying deep personal involvement. This important difference gives rise to two very distinct views of the place of the person in organization. In the western case, because of the impersonal nature attributed to both individual roles and the entire organization, little room is allowed for personal fulfillment and social satisfaction. These are properly ignored or even repressed in organizational contexts. Personality, so important to us, emerges full-blown only in private worlds and these are viewed as almost totally separate from work organizations. Thus individuality and the value of personal expression and growth are set in fundamental opposition to organization by our understanding of the nature of each.

---

[12] Western observers, including myself, find reason to be amazed at the Japanese tolerance for contradictory and even ludicrous explanations and meanings given by authorities to daily social patterns. We feel that each individual should examine, personally decide on, and remain consistent with a set of coherent and logical principles, and when the Japanese do not emphasize these things, we are likely to seek explanations in terms of some concept like their underdeveloped sense of self. This, however, tells us more about our own understanding of self and personhood than it tells us about the Japanese. The fact remains that in the Japanese company world doctrinal strife is not at all common, and the possible social science explanations for this are numerous and generally unsatisfactory.

The worker as a participant in a social community of work is also lost as a real possibility by the powerful draw of individual, private spheres thus established. The Uedagin image of a "family" sort of integration does not make for such a thorough opposition between the person and the organization. Rather, personal fulfillment and a community of work are axiomatic goals of the organization in the bank's ideology. How this ideological perspective meshes with the daily understandings of authority, group motivation and so forth will become evident in subsequent chapters.

How are we to place this ideological scheme in relationship to what we are about to observe of the daily affairs of the organization? Clearly it is foolish to try to tie the ideology too tightly to behavior, for although it is always available as a source of interpretation and understanding, it is not the only guide to or template for action. The nature of bank business and the general problems of maintaining order in large organizations are the foundation for another distinct perspective that is equally inclusive and general. Each, furthermore, is capable of acknowledging the importance of the other, if only tangentially. We have seen how the necessity for efficiency is built into the discussion of community interest, and in a similar manner high morale is recognized within the "rationalization" approach as valuable.

If there are several general perspectives available, is it better to visualize them as alternatives or as semi-transparent filters that may be applied simultaneously? It seems both are possibilities, but for specific situations (such as groups and organizational subsystems) we are likely to discover other versions of reality in the actions and sentiments that constitute the routines of bank daily life. How they relate to the more general interpretations is of considerable interest. In the following chapters we examine a series of the more crucial situations within the organization, and in each case we aim to elucidate the meaning of the specific context and its place in the totality.

3

ENTRANCE, DEPARTURE, AND
"LIFELONG COMMITMENT"

In his pioneering study of Japanese industry, James Abegglen (1958) pointed to the central importance of the practice of "lifetime employment" for the interpretation of the Japanese company system. He observed,

> When comparing the social organization of the factory in Japan and the United States one difference is immediately noted and continues to dominate and represent much of the total difference between the two systems. At whatever level of organization in the Japanese factory, the worker commits himself on entrance to the company for the remainder of his working career. The company will not discharge him even temporarily except in the most extreme circumstances. He will not quit the company for industrial employment elsewhere. He is a member of the company in a way resembling that in which persons are members of families, fraternal organizations, and other intimate personal groups in the United States.
>
> This rule of a lifetime commitment is truly proved by its rare exceptions, and the permanent relationship between employee and firm imposes obligations and responsibilities on both the factory and the worker of a different order than that on which personal practices and worker-company relationships in the United States are built. The difference between the two systems is not, of course, absolute, but one of degree. Reluctance on the part of the worker to quit and on the part of the firm to fire him are constant factors in the American relationship; the Japanese firm will discharge employees, employees do occasionally quit. The magnitude of the difference is very great, however, and its consequences and implications will be seen repeatedly throughout this description of the large Japanese factory [pp. 11–12].

Subsequent investigations of this subject have raised questions about Abegglen's interpretation on the grounds that his sample companies were much larger than average and thus unrepresentative of most Japanese industry.[1] The pendulum, once swinging strongly toward an emphasis on the unique qualities of Japanese employment, began to swing back in the other direction, and similarities between Japanese and American statistics on employment tenure were emphasized. The major problem, to sort out the sources of variation in both countries so that their comparison may be more precise and revealing, is still to be satisfactorily accomplished.

The factors of company size, blue collar or white collar, sex differences, region, and labor supply are all of some influence in both national pictures. Although a single case study cannot resolve such issues, it can contribute to the process by which statistical differences are clarified. Uedagin is a company close to the pattern Abegglen describes, and it therefore provides an excellent opportunity to understand "lifetime commitment" in the living context of one company. By considering the Uedagin system in detail, we will examine how the constraints on company and individual alike contribute to the preservation of the permanent employment pattern in the face of undeniable counterforces.

ENTRANCE

The selection of new members is a serious matter for the bank. An executive explained:

> We can replace machines by buying new ones, but when we bring someone into the bank he is with us for a very long time. If he is no good, we must pay him until he retires. If he is uncooperative, the work of others is disrupted and their effectiveness is reduced. Uncooperative people make work less pleasant for everyone. We make mistakes in our selection of new recruits and they soon show up, usually before training is over. In such cases, we have to work hard to improve them, and there is often a good side we can develop. If they are not so good, we watch them closely in making our assignments and in applying our counseling. We never tell anyone they have to leave, but when people we don't want—our mistakes—leave, we are privately relieved.

[1] Criticisms of Abegglen are contained in Taira (1962), Tsuda (1965), Cole (1971a and b and 1972), Karsh and Cole (1968) and Marsh and Mannari (1971).

The fact that the president personally presides at all final interviews for men is perhaps the best indication of the importance of this matter to top management.[2] Furthermore, this task is regarded by the personnel section as among its most weighty duties. The decision to include someone is not irrevocable only from the bank's point of view; men deciding to join Uedagin also expect that the relationship thus formed will continue uninterrupted until their retirement. Decisions thought to be irrevocable are seldom made without great caution, and the Uedagin case is no exception.

Recruitment is also significant because it produces a number of general characteristics of the bank's social organization. Obviously, the age, sex, and educational profiles of the bank's population are determined in large measure by its admissions policies. More importantly, the factors of age, experience, rank, and reward are first calibrated at the time of entrance. Finally, in the philosophy governing recruitment practices, we find instructive implications about the relationship between the bank and the individual.

People who become members are recruited and selected differently from people who will become quasi members or nonmembers. The latter are selected to fill specific roles in the organization, and specific job openings determine when hiring takes place. Candidates may come from another company, from the category of retired members, or directly from school. As a result, the "labor market" for quasi members and nonmembers has a broad definition, even though the actual number of available people may be small. The manner of original contact may also vary considerably. Telephone operators, key punchers, and others with special skills are usually hired directly from special schools. Custodians and cooks tend to be hired through acquaintances. Newspaper ads, incidentally, are regarded as the lowest form of recruitment. Testing, formal interviews, and other screening techniques are not standardized for these jobs, and the overall procedure seems haphazard compared to the highly regular and standardized process for hiring members.

Generalizations about the selection of members are easier to make. Only once each year are new additions to the membership category recruited and selected, and recruitment for membership is made only among university and high school seniors. There are two procedures,

<hr />

2 Presidents of large industrial firms, I am told, do not sit on selection panels. The president of the small manufacturing company (six hundred employees) I studied in 1972, on the other hand, does take an active role, not only in selection, but also in recruiting.

one for men and one for women, and each is applied in a highly regular manner.[3]

Over the last five years, the bank has accepted, on the average, approximately one hundred new male and two hundred new female members per year. About equal numbers of male high school graduates and male university graduates are now accepted, but five years ago, three high school graduates were accepted for every two from universities. All but ten or so of the 250 women employed in 1969 came directly from high school. The ten remaining came from junior colleges.[4]

In 1968, sixty university and sixty high school male graduates were selected for entrance after their graduation in March, 1969. The ratio of applicants to people hired that year was thus 4.6 for university graduates and 5.0 for high school graduates, considerably less than in 1966, when almost eight hundred men applied for a total of one hundred positions. It is not clear why this decline in applications occurred, but it is said that there are periodic shifts away from companies with highly competitive ratios of applicants to jobs. The slowdown in the rate of Uedagin growth, thus making it less attractive, and the general national decrease in the ratio of applicants for jobs are also relevant factors. Women, who have no concern with long-term career prospects, continue to apply to the bank in about the same numbers. In 1969, 630 applied, and 250 were accepted.

One quarter of the male high school graduates come from commercial high schools, but the bank regards all high school graduates as possessing the same qualifications. University graduates, with few exceptions, come from departments of law or economics, both of which have a reputation for providing a general education for students intending to enter either business or government.[5] Again, the bank makes no distinctions about special skills among them. On the special recommendation of a professor close to the personnel section, the bank

[3] Other large commercial firms occasionally accept into their higher ranks men coming from government or a related firm, and these constitute the possible exceptions for Uedagin in the near future. Because the bank is not part of a *zaibatsu* and not in financial trouble, it has not received any such lateral entrants over the last ten years.

[4] Abegglen (1969), in his report of a questionnaire survey of twenty-five large companies (primarily industrial), notes that direct recruiting from schools accounted for 53 percent of all men, and 74 percent of all women hired in 1956. Those percentages increased to 77 percent and 91 percent respectively in 1966. Virtually no top management and few middle management people were recruited from other companies in either year.

[5] The reader interested in the Japanese postwar school system and its role in the job market should consult Passin (1965), chapter 6, and also Dore (1973), chapter 2.

may accept graduates of other departments, such as education, literature, or science, but these are exceptional.[6] High school girls coming
into the bank also lack business training. They too have had a general education that qualifies them, after brief training, to do the work
of low-level clerks. With few exceptions, the bank prefers to train its
own people to higher responsibility, rather than to take in skilled outsiders. What is most important is potential.

The mechanics of recruitment follow a schedule that is adjusted to
the Japanese school calendar, which begins in April and runs until
the following mid-March. Within a few weeks after the school year
commences, the bank begins to receive applications from prospective
seniors sent through their schools. Each year, the bank notifies high
schools and university departments that it is recruiting and asks their
assistance in finding good applicants. High school students invariably
consult their teachers or a career advisor about where to apply, and
the teacher sends in the applicant's name. University students tend to
act more independently.

The written examination given in June consists of two parts, a
scholastic aptitude test and a personality evaluation test. Women take
only the aptitude test. Immediately following the test, the applicants
are interviewed by someone from the bank, usually the chief of that
office. The men who pass the test and the interview are invited to a
final interview at the main office later in the month. All women are
interviewed only the first time. As soon as the results of these interviews are known the personnel section begins a family investigation
(*katei chōsa*) and a background investigation (*mimoto chōsa*). Letters
of guarantee for each male who is tentatively selected are also collected
before final approval is made. As a rule, applicants know of their acceptance or rejection by July.

6 Although the exact figures were lost in transit from the field, I did make a
survey of the sociological backgrounds of all 120 incoming new men in 1969. The
general results of this were: first, that more than half of the high school graduates,
but less than a quarter of the university graduates, came from homes located outside a city (*shi*); and second, that there was a much higher proportion of profes-
sionals, members of large companies, government officials, and owners of shops or
factories among the fathers of the university educated. Slightly more than half
(thirty-four) of the university graduates came from private schools, including a
few from each of such nationally known schools as Keio, Waseda, Doshisha, Nihon
University, and Meiji University. Of the twenty-six graduates of public universities,
eight came from the region's national (formerly imperial) university, and the remainder from prefectural and city schools. The major differences in social background obtained between the high school boys and the graduates of private universities. One high school sent six to Uedagin that year, but most high school boys
were the only ones from their school.

Attracting Applicants

The bank does not worry about being unable to obtain sufficient manpower, but it does worry about the quality of the people who apply. The growing labor shortage in Japan is primarily a problem for the industrial sector, and naturally Uedagin would like to select from as large and well qualified a group of candidates as possible. Though in the final analysis its ability to attract applicants of high quality depends primarily on its reputation as a fast-growing and dynamic organization, Uedagin does send out brochures advertising the bank's attractive qualities, and people from the personnel section do travel each spring to branch offices to tell interested students of the advantages of an Uedagin career. Efforts to find good people also focus on connections with teachers and business associates.

Connections

Most new members of the bank are selected without special connections or outside personal intervention on their behalf, and the great majority of entering university students reported that their decision to enter the bank was essentially their own. Unlike their high school graduate counterparts they were not appreciably influenced by their teachers, parents, or others. Some high school teachers, on the other hand, have the responsibility of finding good jobs for their students, much as they are expected to get their better students into a university. Their reputations and promotions can be closely tied to these functions, especially in rural areas. Some university teachers may feel such a responsibility, but unlike high school teachers they are not expected to provide employment advice or help. Today, the traditional responsibilities of teachers to guide and aid their students (often in place of parental supervision) are emphasized primarily at lower levels of the educational system.

Every high school senior who entered Uedagin in 1969 reported consulting closely with a teacher or employment counselor about which companies to apply to and which finally to select. Over three-quarters of the new male members entering from high schools, in answer to the question who (if any) had influenced them to select Uedagin, named their teacher. Particularly in the country, where parents are not in a position to know much about companies and recruitment procedures, teachers, who perform this service year after year, serve a crucial role as go-betweens in the recruitment process for the high school graduates. One consequence of this system is that the high school boys know surprisingly little about the nature of bank work or about Uedagin when they arrive to begin training. Clearly, their teachers find them an institution, not a job.

There is no evidence that the bank makes gifts to teachers to curry their favor, but some reciprocity exists, for the bank is often willing to select a candidate primarily on the basis of a teacher's recommendation. This amounts to a favor to the teachers, for they are often under pressure from parents to obtain good positions for their seniors. In turn, such schools and teachers are likely to guide their better candidates to Uedagin. This is but one example of a pattern of reciprocal obligations and favors found throughout Japanese society, wedged in between the expanding sphere of formal, impersonal processes and the shrinking world of family and kinship.

Another source of influence comes from business connections. Business dealings are often reinforced by the exchange of favors between companies. Among the favors good customers of the bank may ask is that a job be found for a son or daughter of the management. It is a hard favor to deny if the business relationship is an important one or if a close relationship with a top Uedagin executive is involved. How many people enter with some sort of connection (abbreviated *conne* in Japan) can only be estimated, but of the 120 incoming men, only three or four of the high school graduates (less than 10 percent) and eight or nine of the university graduates (about 20 percent) were observed by others to have connections. How significant these connections were to these men is not easy to gauge, because many are able individuals in their own right.

In 1969, the rule against employing any close relatives of members was breached in only two instances: the son of a director and the nephew of a branch manager.

Perhaps because they will not stay long with the bank, women are more likely to be employed according to connections, yet these figures are not readily available, and even those informants in the bank who were normally well informed about personnel matters could not say precisely. Conne as an element in the selection of new members is too vague, private, and subtle to nail down. It was agreed that employing daughters of business acquaintances is a useful and not uncommon practice that costs the bank little in the event of incompetence.

While the bank will certainly attempt to utilize the informal system whenever advantageous, it must also suffer the consequences. Having to cope with the pressure to accept people with conne is one of the more unpleasant aspects of personnel work, particularly when the answer should be, or must be, no. Connections involving the best customers of the bank and those introduced by directors are usually too powerful to resist. The real headaches come in the cases of less over-whelming influence: a branch manager's good customer's son, for example.

Parenthetically, the head of the personnel department, in a private chat, criticized young people for their reliance on a teacher's advice or on conne because this sets a trend of excessive dependency. In theory at least he prefers an open and competitive system that rewards more independent, self-motivated behavior, a perspective characteristic of the bank's top leaders. They express determination to develop more aggressive individuals within their company and imagine their efforts to be opposed by the persistence of informal patterns of relationship that provide security (*antei*) at the expense of self-reliance. Beginning with recruitment and extending throughout personnel matters the themes of overdependency and security are tied together and opposed to the themes of self-reliance and open competition. Ironically, the same leaders also take pride in the security their company offers, and they criticize independent action that ignores established hierarchy. Context makes a big difference for such expression, and it is best to understand management as inherently ambivalent on such issues.

Selection

The formal recruitment process is, in effect, a series of screenings designed to separate the desirable candidates from those that are not wanted.

The first step is a written aptitude test based on the curriculum of the national educational system. There is no particular need to study for the exam since it is quite general and rudimentary. University students are not really examined in what they have learned at university, but they are expected to do considerably better than the high school seniors. The results are used only to eliminate the more inadequate applicants. When the time comes to evaluate the mental capabilities of university graduates, judgment is made according to the rank of the individual's university. In Japan, university entrance exams are of much greater significance to future employment than the exams given by the companies themselves.

On the same day, male applicants take two personality tests. The results of the tests are only significant when they indicate a serious deviation from established norms. The number of people actually appearing as deviant and eliminated on these grounds is small, but the tests are retained as part of the selection process as added assurance that the bank will not accept and be stuck with someone psychologically unfit.

After the written exams the applicants are interviewed. His or her interests, studies, and family situation are discussed, and the interviewer is expected to make a general evaluation of the person. Is he or she personable? Too forward, or too shy? Healthy? Attractive? Serious? The personnel section wants answers to these questions. On the basis of the interview and the test results, a group of men are invited to a final interview, and final decisions are made about the women to be hired. Of the men who apply, approximately two-thirds pass on to the final interview. Failures at the first stage result primarily from unsatisfactory interviews.

The final interview is considered important enough to be conducted by the president and a few other top officers of the bank. It lasts, however, only about fifteen minutes and is admittedly a matter of general impressions. Of late, the question of student activism and left-wing politics has been added to the usual discussion of studies, sports, and hobbies. An outspoken defense of student demonstrations would insure rejection, it is said, but such a naive presentation at a crucial interview is most unlikely. Generally, the executives make up their minds on other grounds. What kind of young man do they like? It was explained that serious but congenial men, preferably with a sense of humor and an interest in sports, are preferred. An energetic manner is another valuable attribute. The term *majime,* "serious," is the one most often applied to favored candidates.

By assuming a central role in the final selection process, the top executives accomplish several goals. They demonstrate the importance of choosing good people; they relieve the personnel section of ultimate responsibility in this weighty matter; and they place themselves in a position to oversee the direction of any change in the profile of the bank's personnel. They work, for example, to prevent university biases from influencing the selection process by maintaining a balance among numerous contributing schools. University cliques (*gakubatsu*) have control over a number of well-known companies in Japan, and there is always the possibility of their development in Uedagin unless measures such as this are taken.[7] The executives also guarantee the continuity of their rather traditional sense of good character. The men they select will run the bank long after they have retired.

The candidates selected are not formally accepted until the investigations of their family (*katei chōsa*) and background (*minoto chōsa*) have been completed.

---

[7] See chapter 6 and also Nakane (1970) for a discussion of university and other cliques.

These investigations are particularly revealing aspects of the bank's selective process because the criteria for rejection are more explicit. Actually there are four separate investigations, namely, a visit to the applicant's home, inquiries about him and his family in the neighborhood, an interview with his teacher or teachers, and an investigation of his personal health. All are conducted by people from the branch office closest to the applicant's home, insuring familiarity with the local situation. Obviously, those at the local level are in a position to learn a great deal more about the applicant and his family than a formal interview alone would reveal.[8]

A representative of the personnel section explained the kinds of things they were most interested in learning from these inquiries. The following is a paraphrase of the list of major considerations he mentioned:

(1) The health of all members of the family. In particular, have there been any hereditary, mental, or other debilitating diseases among the relatives of the applicant?

(2) The cleanliness and order of the house itself. If the household is not orderly, then the applicant's character and the thoroughness of his socialization are in doubt. One favorite technique is to visit the bathroom to see whether it is clean as a test of whether the mother is a good housekeeper and, by extension, a good mother.

(3) The nature of family relationships. Is there trouble between members of the family? If so, the applicant comes under strong suspicion. An agreeable family is one of the best guarantees that the person in question will be an agreeable member of the bank.

(4) Whether the son will eventually be expected to succeed to his father's position. If the son is likely to return to take over either the family farm or his father's business, it is unlikely that he will be accepted by the bank. Membership in the bank should not be interrupted. The large amount of training that the bank will have given the new member will go to waste once he leaves.

(5) The parents' character. Do one or both of the parents seem particularly egoistic (*wagamama*)? This again would be a reflec-

8 While we might think such investigations to be appropriate for banks and sensitive government work, we would not expect them of manufacturing firms, but at least one large one, Hitachi Electric, investigates its applicants in this same general way (Dore, 1973:50).

tion on the kind of training the applicant had received from his family.

(6) The parents' attitude toward employment in Uedagin. If the father, for example, criticizes the bank for having low salaries, this is a minus for the applicant.

(7) The father's social reputation. If the father has changed jobs several times or been involved in some kind of minor scandal, the applicant is placed in jeopardy. The bank wants to be assured that its new members come from families with a tradition of being good members of society.

(8) Religious affiliation. Specifically, the bank does not want to employ any members of the "new religions" which require considerable time and effort on the part of their members. This is not because these religions are viewed as intrinsically bad; on the contrary, the bank sees many of them as positive moral forces in Japanese life. But the bank does not want its members to divide their loyalties. Furthermore, the possibility that members of some new religions will attempt to proselytize within the bank or with the bank's customers is enough to justify exclusion of people belonging to the more aggressive new religions.[9]

(9) The applicant's and his parents' political views. Extremist activity or opinions rule out applicants. This is particularly true of students active in left-wing affairs. Having simply participated in some demonstration during a university career, however, is not regarded as serious enough to rule against the applicant.

(10) Parents' religious behavior. If they are religious zealots of some sort (literally described as "chanting-all-night types"), then the bank is not interested in having their children, for this is a reflection of both the instability of the parents and the social reputation of the family. The bank does not want its reputation tarnished because some of its members' families are poorly regarded.

(11) Does the candidate go out a lot on dates? The bank has two things in mind here. First, it is rather unseemly for people to be openly interested in the opposite sex, if they are just gradu-

[9] The term "new religions" (shinkō shukyō) refers to a variety of active, popular religious movements which have developed during the last century. Among them, the largest, most aggressive, and best known is Sōka Gakkai. For further information about these by no means insignificant religions, see McFarland (1967), White (1970), and Norbeck (1970).

ating from high school. Girls who wear too much makeup or who dress in a flashy manner are not wanted. Secondly, an unusually strong interest in dating creates a conflict of interest because the bank expects its new employees to be devoted to their work.

In essence, all of the above relate to three basic criteria upon which applicants are judged at this point in the selection process: character, involvement in other institutions, and family reputation. Adverse information from these background investigations have occasionally caused the rejection of candidates accepted in the interview.

To conclude, the recruitment and selection process goes a long way to establish the character of the Uedagin membership. People from an unstable background, those with strong affiliations to either religious or political organizations, those with rebellious or deviant qualities, and those who are inept during interviews are virtually excluded. Furthermore, the ratio of men to women and the ratio of university to high school graduates for each entering group is set by admissions policies.

Most importantly, the number of men of any given age is determined annually by that year's recruitment policy. We shall see how the pattern of "lifetime employment" coupled with the age-orientation of the promotion system invest this number with great significance. Each year the admissions process creates an age set of men who begin and end their careers in the bank together, and who find the speed of their promotion greatly affected by the size of their age set as it relates to job openings above their level in the organization.

DEPARTURE

Of the various ways people may leave the membership of the bank, some are regarded as regular and normal, and others as irregular and abnormal. Retirement, in the case of men and spinster women, and resignation for the purpose of marriage in the case of all other women, are regular forms of departure. Quitting and being fired are irregular and abnormal. Unlike regular departures, which are honorable and enhance the reputation of the bank and departee alike, irregular terminations often have a scandalous nature about them and cause both parties to feel embarrassment. The issue reflected in these distinctions is the quality of the relationship between the individual and the enterprise. If the relationship is a good one, it is assumed, it will end in a regular manner, by retirement or resignation, and the member, instead of severing his ties completely, will continue to be associated with the bank, at least in spirit. But when someone quits or is fired there is the strong implication that the relationship has failed. A general feeling exists that both parties must share responsibility for its failure. As a rule, both suffer some loss of reputation because of it. Irregular departures are embarrassing and unhappy affairs similar in atmosphere to marital divorce. Although in a few cases gains could be calculated by one side or the other (e.g., a better job, or the loss of a poor worker), it is usual for both sides to experience a sense of failure as parties to an important relationship that collapsed. The expectation of continuity and the emphasis on the integrity of the company-member relationship establish this.

After Prolonged Illness

One form of termination does not fit neatly into the above scheme. The gradual severance of the relationship due to prolonged sickness cannot be judged either regular or irregular. When a person becomes unable to work due to illness, he is placed in one of two special categories. For the first six months he is assigned to the jurisdiction of the personnel department (jinjibu-kitsu), and his salary and bonus continue to be paid to him. If his illness continues, he is placed on leave of absence (kyūshoku).[10] Gradually his salary and bonuses are terminated. He remains a member of the bank, however, for other purposes, such as calculations of seniority. The usual limit on leaves of absence is one and a half years; after that if a man is still unable to return to work, he is released from the company. The length of time allowed for recovery is reportedly extended in some cases, and some people are returned to work even though they are unable to do regular tasks. The reason this form of termination is special arises from the fact that neither party has transgressed or broken the relationship, nor wishes it to end. The bank, considering its obligation to support its members, reluctantly, and usually after much hesitation, determines that it can no longer keep the sick person on its rolls. Postponement of this final and painful decision is not uncommon. Instead of labeling this a termination, similar to the other kinds included in this chapter, we could better describe the process as a gradual slipping away in which both sides wish the trend to reverse. Without recovery, however, the course of illness eventually forces a separation.

When tuberculosis was the major illness sending people into the

[10] Midway in my study the number of people in jinjibu-kitsu was six; there were eleven people in the kyūshoku category.

categories of jinjibu-kitsu and kyūshoku, the bank paid considerable attention to its members who were hospitalized together at bank expense. The president even called on them annually to cheer them up. Now that the incidence of TB is lower, the situation is more ambivalent; each variety of illness creates a separate situation in terms of hospitalization and the possibility of recovery.

Informants on several occasions used the situation of long illness when they contrasted "rational" (gōriteki) with "Japanese" (nihonteki) management styles. They characterized the former as "dry" (dōrai) and the latter as "wet" (wettō), implying the difference between rational calculation and the emotional response to human needs. The Uedagin policy on such issues as illness, they felt, will vary with the "dryness" or "wetness" of the man in charge, and also with the state of the bank's business.

Retirement

The one regular form of departure for men is retirement. The standing rule is that all must leave Uedagin following their fifty-fifth birthday, and throughout the year older men pass quietly out of the bank at the rate of two or three a month.[11] The small number reflects the low numbers entering during and shortly after the war. There are no individual retirement ceremonies, and the only recognition most can expect is a brief notice in the company magazine and a few parties given them by office mates and Uedagin friends who happen to be nearby. It is customary to spend the last few days calling on former associates to thank them for their support, to say goodbye, and to promise to get together again soon. These farewells are seldom happy occasions.

The retiree is leaving behind his friends and the organization he has served for many years, but he is not exchanging them for a life of leisure. Still only fifty-five, able and usually anxious to continue working, and almost invariably unable to support his family on his Uedagin retirement pension alone, the retiree must spend perhaps ten years at another job.

The man about to leave Uedagin has a limited number of possibilities before him, and they are, to a significant degree, beyond his con-

11 Some industrial companies facing labor shortages during the first years of the 1970s responded by moving their retirement ages back from fifty-five to fifty-eight or even sixty, but Uedagin as of 1972 had not changed from fifty-five. Some younger men in 1969 said management was probably looking forward to the departure of those old people who were holdovers from the early postwar period of confused hiring and this could explain why fifty-five is still the retirement age.

trol. At least, they have become so by the time he is fifty-five. His fate rests heavily with the personnel department and the top management of the bank. The bank has the option of retaining him or reemploying him as a commissionee, and it is also the primary agency by which he may expect to find a job in some other firm or organization. Exactly how many people find postretirement work without the assistance of the bank is impossible to calculate, but some figures compiled in 1966 concerning retirees provide considerable insight into the matter. Of the 378 men in the Uedagin retirees' association,[12] thirty-four are still working in the bank. Fourteen are top officials who had been retained as such, and the rest are reemployed in a commissionee status. Another thirty-one people are employed by Uedagin *kogaisha*, "child companies," small, dependent firms managed indirectly by the bank and staffed almost exclusively by former Uedagin people.[13] Another seventy-eight people found jobs as white-collar workers in small companies or organizations not directly related to the bank. Just how many of these jobs were acquired with the help of the bank is unknown, but an estimate of one-half would be conservative. The number of people who unquestionably found work on their own comes to sixty-five. Nine are operating pawn shops, thirty-four have their own store, restaurant, or sales agency, seven own small companies of some sort, three are in local government, and twelve are farming. The remaining 170 are either not working or their work is unknown. Thus, of the 191 accounted for, 30 percent owed their jobs to the bank, and, as an estimate, at least another 20 percent obtained their jobs with the help of Uedagin connections.

It is interesting to note in this regard that a major "weakness" of the Uedagin system in the eyes of its own people is the relative lack of postretirement pasturing places. Usually one of the more significant aspects of the greater security offered by large, older firms is their superior ability to provide jobs for retiring members. The bank is reasonably large, but it does not have a large network of related firms through which these problems could be solved. Uedagin people wish they could be more, not less, dependent on their company when it comes to getting a job at fifty-five.

If he is lucky, the bank will save the retiree the effort and embarrassment of having to seek work himself. Established procedures now exist that enable retirees to ask personnel for assistance. This, how-

---

12 This to my knowledge includes all retired members of the bank.

13 Broadbridge (1966) offers several accounts of dependent manufacturing companies which primarily do subcontracting for large industrial companies and mentions their acceptance of men retiring from their large patron firms.

ever, is only a recent improvement. Before, if a man knew the president or another top executive he could approach him for help, but otherwise he was on his own in a world in which almost all jobs for retirees are distributed through connections. Even today the number of jobs the bank can find is limited. Most are in small companies that are dependent on the bank for loans. The more dependent the company is on Uedagin, the more likely it is to respond to a request to find a place for a retiree. Yet, generally, the more dependent it is on the bank, the smaller and less stable the company is likely to be. Large companies, including the bank itself, usually refuse to take retirees from outside.

Job openings in these dependent firms are, in effect, controlled by the directors, and their extensive business connections permit them to find a few more jobs through private ties. To obtain these jobs the retiree must depend on his superiors, and since such jobs tend to be given as rewards for personal loyalty, there is a definite, if indirect, social control factor in this situation.

Only men considered especially valuable or necessary are given a reprieve from forced retirement. Men at the director level automatically stay on for five extra years, and some remain longer. A few chiefs may remain for two or three years, if requested to do so. The bank may keep them if their expertise is required or if they deserve special reward. Obviously, this decision can be strongly colored by company politics.

For those not retained, retirement and new employment at fifty-five tends to be a bitter experience. The new job almost invariably represents a step down in life. The retiree loses the security of his company and friends. After many years of service to Uedagin, he must enter on unfamiliar world where he is unknown and where he will probably never feel at home. His salary will be less than before, although with his company pension he may be as well off. Ironically, he must work equally as hard or harder, even with the lower rewards, because he no longer enjoys the security of membership, with its assurance of job continuity and material welfare. Just like nonmembers in Uedagin he becomes expendable, and his position in his new, smaller company is more in jeopardy. He can expect to be laid off or fired before many others with whom he is working.

Compare this state of affairs with the growing income, prestige, and responsibility of those men of much the same age who attain director rank and remain in Uedagin. Until sixty they sit at the top of the organization and never face the embarrassment of reemployment. It is no wonder that they appear so blessed and so grand. It is helpful to keep in mind, however, how long after entering the company this glaring discrepancy in rewards and status between men of similar age emerges.

Resignation of Women

Women must resign from the bank at the time they marry. This rule is as old as the bank and has no exceptions. Few women feel they are "forced" to leave, however, because the great majority are anxious to establish their own households and begin their careers as wives and mothers. Continuing to work in the bank is not consistent with these goals in middle-class Japan. Some, tired of the long hours and monotonous routines of bank work, are even inclined to agree to a marriage urged by their parents, primarily because it will allow them to leave the bank. It is not unusual for parents to object to their daughter's quitting unless marriage plans are made.

Married women are not considered unqualified (there are many conspicuous cases of women working alongside men in small family businesses, for example), but the effectiveness of women is thought to stabilize or even diminish after they pass their mid-twenties, while their salaries continue to increase, and the proper place of a married woman is believed to be the home. Japanese middle-class morality demands that a married woman accept and fulfill her roles of mother and wife completely. Those women who do work outside the home when their children are young do so out of economic necessity, and to do so on any other grounds is to ignore domestic responsibility. Uedagin informants added that if married women worked in the bank full time they would do a bad job, either at home or for the bank, and this would eventually be disruptive to both places. In the final analysis, the bank is run by older men, and it is a universal opinion among them that married women belong in the home. Only an extreme labor shortage could change their minds.[14]

The policy of employing no married women has the serious consequence of creating a high female turnover rate. Each year two hundred new women must be trained to replace those who leave for mar-

[14] Since 1971 some of Japan's largest banks have been experimenting with more flexible policies about women and marriage, allowing those that can and want to stay on after marriage to remain until they become pregnant, rehiring skilled women after their children are grown, and evaluating upwards the importance of experience and skill in the case of older women. All of this is of significance as it implies a further lessening of the men's-club aspects of lifetime commitment, but friends also report that the constraints imposed on women by marriage remain extremely powerful, reducing greatly the effects of these policy changes. For a more detailed discussion of marriage, work and the woman's role see Perry (unpublished paper).

riage. This represents an annual turnover of one-quarter of the female work force. Although the costs of training are high and the problems of utilizing throngs of inexperienced women exasperating at times, this high turnover allows the enterprise to enjoy the women's labor during the period they are, by the relative standards of the Uedagin salary scale, underpaid, without subsequently having to pay the higher salaries that accrue based on years of service.

Another less consequential result of this policy is the age homogeneity of the women in the bank, allowing for easier planning and organization of women's activities. When planning recreation, for example, one need only consider the interests of those between the ages of nineteen and twenty-six.

As already mentioned, because they leave the bank upon marriage, women are less inclined than men to feel a close alliance of interest with the bank. They never have much chance to enjoy the increasing wages and bonuses that come with years of service, and they have no chance for promotions. If they are loyal and enthusiastic, it is because they like the people and their work, not because the system is designed to reward them for such contributions. There are no public and few private complaints about this, probably because most expect to be married soon and regard work as an interim activity between school and becoming a housewife.

Dismissal

For someone to be fired, he must have committed a grave offense.[15] During 1969, two such cases occurred, both involving theft or its approximation. In one instance a man took a small amount outright, and in the other a man arranged to lend money to a relative in an irregular fashion with the intention of correcting the irregularity later. When these offenses were discovered, the bank dismissed the men following an investigation. That two members were dismissed in the same year seemed unusually high to everyone, but it is also a fact that such cases are usually hushed up.

Only when there is no recourse short of firing will a man be dropped from membership. This situation arises when an individual steals, breaks a major law, or becomes so unruly that even assigning him to an obscure position will not end his disturbance of others. Incompe-

15 Abegglen (1969) finds dismissal to be virtually inconsequential as a factor in turnover of twenty-four of the twenty-five companies he surveyed in 1966. One company suffering severe economic problems dismissed a rather large number of middle management people and found them jobs elsewhere. See Dore (1973:34–35) for a revealing comparison of Japanese and British attitudes toward dismissals and layoffs.

tency, however, is no excuse for firing someone. People unable to do their jobs are normally transferred to posts of little responsibility. Nor are members of left-wing groups, including the Communist party, fired when their membership is discovered. Instead, they are excluded from all authority in the bank and watched closely.

There is an obvious cost in retaining people who do not contribute or who are potentially disruptive, but serious problems of this sort are exceptional since few people are totally useless. It is the overall psychological effect, rather than the conspicuous infractions, that worries management. Admiration for the American system, one understood to permit dismissal on a wide variety of grounds, is sometimes voiced by leaders who also mention a belief that lethargy, bred by an overdependence on the company, could never develop in America. They quickly add that there is no reasonable hope of adopting American procedures in the bank, for morale would be destroyed, and the company union (see chapter 8) would become active. Apparently, while encouraging an official ideology of lifelong membership, many leaders are not ready to accept the unattractive consequences of such an approach. Their awareness of its inefficient aspects, however, is balanced by an awareness of how much more inefficient a situation would arise if they were to ignore the ethic of community and baldly adopt an impersonal policy on layoffs and dismissals. Finally, many executives take a personal satisfaction in bearing the burdens of their ideals.

The possibility that economic failure could force the bank to begin dismissals for cost-cutting reasons was not present in 1968–69, nor in the short history of the bank can one find this kind of action. At some date in the future, however, this could become necessary. There have been bankruptcies and near bankruptcies of moderately large companies during the several mild recessions which have occurred periodically during Japan's postwar boom. Takezawa, in Whitehall and Takezawa (1968), describes the pattern of successive steps that might be taken by a company to trim its personnel in such emergency situations, and there is reason to believe that Uedagin, should it ever be forced to such a policy, would act in much the same manner.

> In the case of such a business calamity in Japan, the first victims to go are temporary workers and workers provided by subcontractors and labor bosses. For regular workers, the first sign may be a cut in overtime work. Then, work assignments may be reshuffled to cover vacancies created by the non-regular workers who have left. At the same time, negotiations may be held by company representatives in an attempt to obtain governmental

subsidy, market-share agreements from other firms in the same industry, and/or pledges of further bank support. Within the company, cost reduction programs will be put into effect with greater intensity. Midsummer and year-end bonuses may be partially cut, and annual wage increases may be cut or suspended. Consultations will be constantly held with the labor union representatives to prove the necessity of management's various moves. When wages and salaries must be cut, those who have received a greater income in the past, i.e., longer-service workers, managers, and supervisors, must give up a large percentage.

Finally, reduction in force of regular workers may become inevitable. At this stage, a complete overhaul of top management may be undertaken before the drastic surgery is contemplated. The labor unions stage fights against "incompetent" management, but they probably know what is likely to happen. The first move to reduce regular personnel usually takes the form of soliciting volunteers for resignation with the incentive of additional severance allowances. Often, certain eligibility requirements may be specified and, for example, older workers approaching normal retirement, fathers whose sons have started in the same firm, and working housewives may be given general encouragement to accept early retirement. Older management personnel nearing retirement age may be expected to set "examples" for workers by cooperating with the reduction program. Since they have benefited more by working for the firm, they should also be willing to sacrifice more for the company at the time of crisis.

When the management finds that the predetermined quota for reduction of regular workers cannot be met by voluntary resignations alone, individual persuasions may be undertaken by management representatives with workers who belong to various "eligible" groups. At this stage, also, a secret list of workers whom the company management considers "undesirable" or "unnecessary" may be prepared and used as a guide in approaching individual workers for "resignations." The union's struggle against reduction in force intensifies, and often it attracts national attention by accompanying violent strikes.

Then comes a critical time for both management and the union, since the next stage involves the official announcement of the secret list. When it is done, it is likely that ill feelings are developed which may take years to cure. Furthermore, those who find themselves excluded from the list may withdraw from the original union to form another, and indicate their willingness to cooperate with management in the reconstruction of the business. It is only at this final stage that specific individuals may be simply "told" not to report to work because of lack of work [pp. 149–50].

The power of the tacit understanding of membership (here the company-regular employee relationship) can be clearly seen at every stage in this scenario.

Quitting

Quitting by men is one of the most important phenomena to interpret correctly in the description of the Uedagin organization, and consequently this section will be longer than the small number of cases of quitting would seemingly deserve. The time a man spends considering whether to quit or not is one of the most poignant moments in his relationship with his society, his company, and himself. It is a time when a myriad of factors intersect and are weighed relative to one another. The stakes of a man's career, his dreams for the future, his sense of personal strength and justice, and the web of personal ties and obligations are all placed on the line.

From another point of view, a high male turnover rate would upset the foundations of the bank's salary, promotion, training, and other subsystems, and the expectations about the company-individual relationship expressed in the ideology would be made groundless. Quitting is, indeed, a crucial matter all around.

Only the rare person in Uedagin has never considered quitting. Most consider it seriously enough to speak to others about it. Few, however, actually quit. The problem then is to consider not only why people quit, but also, and more significantly, why they do not quit. To say that the number of people quitting is small because people are basically content would be an oversimplification that would preclude any thorough comprehension of the matter as it is understood by people in the bank. It would be equally misleading, however, to conclude that overt suppression or manipulation explains the low rate of quitting.

The proper starting point for a detailed discussion of this subject should be a presentation of statistical material indicating how many quit, who they are, and what the circumstances surrounding their action tend to be. This information, unfortunately, is among the most closely guarded secrets of the bank. In fact, only the top executives and some members of the personnel section appear to have access to the figures. This sensitivity is due to the bank's desire to protect its reputation. If Uedagin should earn a name for having people quit, its attractiveness to customers and new recruits would suffer. Morale within the company might also decline. Naturally, management would like to appear to have sponsored a well-ordered and successful organization. This image fosters confidence and admiration, two attitudes on the part of outsiders without which the bank cannot survive.

Even without the actual statistics, however, it is possible to make a general outline of the problem in percentage terms, based on interviews, overheard conversations, and the impressions of Uedagin people themselves. My estimate is that ten to fifteen men quit each year to take other jobs, and perhaps twenty to thirty women quit without marrying. If we round off our estimate to forty members quitting per year we have a rate approximating 1.5 percent of the total membership.

There is a saying in the bank that if a young man is going to quit he is most likely to do it after three days, three months, or three years. Knowledgeable people indicate that their impressions of the actual pattern agree with this. Whether the peak times are precisely on these occasions or not, it is agreed that the majority of quittings do take place during the first four years and that quitting for men over thirty is almost unheard of. Men who quit, therefore, tend to be young, unmarried, relatively inexperienced, and low ranking. They have had the least time to adjust to Uedagin life, and they are in the age bracket for which quitting is the least harmful to their career prospects. In the early years, quitting is a gamble: later it can be a disaster. The longer one is out of school, the older one is, and the more dependents one has, the less a change of companies offers a chance of success. That is, unless a good position has been found in advance. The reasons this is unlikely will be taken up shortly.

More high school than university graduates quit the bank. Their alternatives are different. University graduates can go back to school or offer their limited talents to another company. Most high school graduates come to the bank rather than continuing their education, either because they are poor in academic talent or poor financially; for them the alternative of further education has been ruled out by these circumstances. Even so, high school graduates, for whom the gamble is more risky, quit the bank more frequently. The reasons appear to be related to the fact that they enter at a younger age and are more prone to loneliness, disillusionment, and fantasy, three of the most notable factors in cases of men quitting.

Why do young men wish to leave? While I am unable to provide a statistical breakdown of their relative significance, I can outline the variety of reasons with some thoroughness. Case materials collected and observations of Uedagin young men can be catalogued into six major causes:

(1) Dreams of a more interesting or more exciting life and work.

Though the bank offers prestige it does not fulfill ambitions for such things as travel, social service, and adventure. One university graduate quit to become a lawyer, feeling that to be a more relevant career. A high school graduate quit to study on his own in the hope that he could eventually join an airline and go abroad. Another said he often thought of quitting to become a newspaper reporter, his "dream" career abandoned on his father's advice that banking was more secure.

(2) Bad relations with one's superiors. Being unfairly accused, or in some other way suffering at the hands of one's boss, becomes intolerable in some cases. When redress is absent, the individual feels he must quit to preserve his dignity and honor. When the anger and resentment fade, these people often regret having quit, it is said.

(3) A general sense of unsuitability for banking work. One man who now works as a bartender, for example, explained that he quit Uedagin, even though it meant a step down in status and salary, because he was unsuited for bank clerking.

(4) Loneliness. Those just out of high school, in particular, are susceptible to terrible loneliness if they cannot find friends in the organization. They may quit in order to return to their family and home town.

(5) A special opportunity for advancement elsewhere. There are some cases of men in their twenties leaving to assume good positions in much smaller firms where their banking experience would be of special value. In such instances connections are important. If the company making the offer is small, even a promise of being made an executive may not be as promising in terms of security, salary, and status as a normal career in the bank.

(6) Unsatisfactory social relations. Some people become unhappy due to their failure to get along with others in their office or dormitory. Excessive introversion may be the reason, but a more serious source of difficulty is an inability to conform to group norms. Nonconformity receives little support, not even lip service.

Salary, we should note, is an insignificant factor.[16] Moving elsewhere is never prompted primarily by the promise of a larger pay check. Nor is the chance for promotion and career advancement very significant, although a few cases do exist.

Three factors obviously contribute to the decision *not* to leave. They are: the small probability that an equal or better job can be found

---

[16] Because all who quit are young workers, who are universally paid low salaries, the issue is not salary but rather career advancement and ultimate status.

after quitting, the stigma, and the supportive and yet dissuasive response of friends and associates.[17]

Quitting necessarily involves the question of being hired again. As mentioned, large companies rarely, if ever, hire white-collar people from other firms. Those who quit must find positions in small firms where, unless there are special circumstances, their status will be lower. They can expect to drop to the bottom of the years-of-service totem pole. Just as a divorcee can never remarry with a fine ceremony, so people who have worked in the bank rarely attain first-class citizenship in their next company. Even satisfactory rank, salary, and promotion arrangements cannot totally erase the problem of being regarded in the new company as an outsider.

A professional career, involving a return to school, is almost impossible for high school graduates for reasons already mentioned. And the road to professionalism is also difficult for university graduates, due to peculiarities of the Japanese educational system.[18] Another alternative, employment in local government, is characterized by low pay, low status, and little upward mobility. No foreign companies, one of the places where white-collar job changers are often welcome, are located in Aoyama.

Few who quit can escape feelings of doubt about their own character. No matter for what reasons he leaves, a man who quits has failed according to the simple test of perseverance (see chapter 9), and his character can be judged accordingly. It is typical for doubts about personal worth to grow. Someone who has quit tends thereafter to live down his past either by hiding it or by trying extra hard to prove himself. It is not that he will be openly criticized: many people may

[17] The literature of scholarly opinion about why people do or do not quit Japanese companies is briefly reviewed in the most recent consideration of this general topic by Marsh and Mannari (1971). They argue on the basis of questionnaire results that the lack of alternative satisfactory jobs, not Japanese values about company loyalty, best explain the lower rates of job changing in Japanese industry. This is not an interpretation I would argue with except for its persistent use of an either-or analytical framework, one that makes values and job prospects representative of two totally separate kinds of motivation and two contradictory philosophies of social science explanation. It seems to me that a question of why people do not do something cannot help but be complicated. Looking at the history of the question, it is probably fair to say that the first oversimplifications came from those ready to emphasize cultural relativism (i.e., uniquely Japanese values), but this is no excuse for others to misconstrue or ignore cultural factors. It is inappropriate, for example, to use attitude questionnaires as representative of the relationship of meaning to behavior.

[18] These include the necessity of majoring in the proper field at the same university at which one intends to do professional study, and the difficult national qualifying exam for future lawyers and judges.

say they admire the man's courage. Yet gossip and stereotyping will thereafter dwell on this matter. The possibility of being judged unstable or irresolute, serious matters among Japanese businessmen, will follow the quitter.

The self-criticism of several who did quit helps clarify the situation. Few actually have feelings of resentment against the bank. They leave friends behind and tend to feel appreciation for what the company has done for them (the term *on,* "beneficence," is used). Two university men who left are described by an acquaintance as feeling mild guilt over their failure to realize their obligations to the company. In letters to friends, they characteristically apologize for their selfishness (*wagamama*) in leaving and add that they must continue to pursue their personal ambition. One who has had a change of heart and now wishes to come back to the bank does not attempt to arrange it, for that would make him act in a selfish and ungrateful manner toward his present company.

When a man says he thinks he will quit, his boss does not say, "Go ahead and see who cares." Nor do his friends congratulate him on his daring and independence. Instead, everyone becomes worried and concerned, for quitting is a serious matter, particularly for the individual himself. What has happened to make him feel this way, his associates wonder. What can be done to overcome his distress and return him to a normal place in the company? Questions like these are preliminary to their attempts to encourage him to reconsider. Most associates do not do this for the company's sake by any means, but rather out of a sincere concern for the individual. Only the office chief, whose reputation could suffer, has a strong personal interest in dissuading the person.

Rather than direct argument, more subtle approaches are usually attempted. Some may ask about future plans, and thereby emphasize the hazards involved. Some may discreetly seek redress for the wrongs the individual feels he has suffered. He may be challenged to show fortitude in the face of present difficulties, implying that things will soon get better. As a rule, the person's close advisors will suggest that he try to stay on a bit longer, another six months or a year, just to be sure that quitting is the right step. Most often, acceptance of this advice postpones the crisis, and the impulse begins to fade.

As noted, most incidents of quitting involve young people. The role of a slightly older friend (a *senpai*) in the "quitting crisis" is often crucial. Two personal acquaintances, both unusually active leaders among the young men, have, by my count, a combined total of over twenty they have helped pass through such crises. A senpai, they explained, has the responsibility to act as a guardian, which means keeping the junior person from quitting in the heat of emotion so they will not wake the next day to regret their decision. Older friends have the duty to point out the risks and, thus, to counter youthfulness with a more sober, mature attitude. If, once the junior's emotions subside and his appreciation of the consequences approaches a realistic level, he should still wish to quit, the senpai should not disapprove. He should, in fact, offer to be of help.

It is curious to note how many people at one time or another indicate to friends that they are thinking of quitting, but never actually quit. My impression is that this phenomenon has some similarities with weakly attempted suicide in that attention and sympathy are important latent goals.

The most determined know that talking it over with friends will probably result in dissuasion, so they are likely to decide independently, yet to remain silent about such a momentous decision requires a degree of self-assurance that is rare among Uedagin young men. Those wishing for sympathy and those lacking confidence talk it over, and most of them end up changing their minds.

What happens to personal relationships after a man quits the bank? While formal connections with the organization end, communications and get-togethers with Uedagin friends often continue. There are numerous examples of Uedagin people continuing to give support and comfort to those who have quit. The bartender just mentioned, for example, is patronized by his old friends from the company dormitory. This never fails to cheer the man, who, incidentally, continues to bank with Uedagin. In another case, a very bright university graduate who quit to enter graduate school now indicates he would like to return to the bank—a rare, but not impossible move. On occasion, personnel will even help young men who have quit to find subsequent jobs.

The rate of quitting is undoubtedly higher for women than for men, yet in this account we have concentrated on men. The reasons are: my material on women in general, and on their quitting in particular, is, unfortunately, not complete; also, informants usually discussed the bank and its policies as if Uedagin was constituted only of men; and with so many departing each year for marriage, quitting by women causes much less stir. In fact, few people know the details, for unlike the young men living in a company dormitory, women living at home have more limited acquaintances in the bank. When a man thinks of quitting, it is not unusual even for friends in out-of-town branches to become involved, but this is rare for women.

Unquestionably, officials are disturbed when women quit, particularly when the rate increases and appears higher than in other banks, for they have been trained at considerable expense. It is less the principle, and more the cost that worries management when women quit.

The ideological emphasis on concord and satisfying social relations described in the previous chapter contributes to a situation in which different ritual interpretations are placed on regular and irregular departures. The most obvious example is the difference between responses given when a woman leaves for marriage and when she quits. In the case of marriage, the bank and union congratulate her, give her monetary gifts, offer her the bank's facilities for the ceremony, and make comments much as satisfied parents might, saying such things as "in her husband we are gaining a new member of the Uedagin family." Her office will hold a party, and her boss will, in many cases, attend the marriage ceremony.

But if a girl plans to quit, her supervisors and office seniors, and perhaps even her friends, will feel obliged to try to dissuade her. Personnel may also talk to her with the object of showing official concern. If, even after all of this, she does quit, the fact will be covered up to the extent possible. She will be given a farewell party during which her office mates say good things about her and wish her well, but the mood will be far from happy. If several women quit from the same office, it is possible that its chief will be transferred and demoted. These different responses are not governed by considerations of personal qualities or work efficiency. The differences arise from the distinction between regular and irregular form as it reflects an essential interpretation of the meaning of bank membership.

THE IMPLICATIONS OF ENTRANCE
AND DEPARTURE FOR THE ORGANIZATION

A young man, upon entering Uedagin, can expect to spend the next thirty-two to thirty-six years working for the bank. This sobering prospect certainly influences his response to life in the bank. The realization that Uedagin will be "home" for a long time may not be accompanied by a thorough comprehension of the implications of this fact, but neither is it as sudden or as shocking a realization as we might expect. True enough, the Japanese socialization pattern today is discontinuous in the sense that neither the family nor the school are consciously designed to prepare young people to assume their eventual positions in the life of such organizations as Uedagin, but the expectation of a long and extensive involvement in a single institution is not lacking. Japanese traditions teach the opportunities and ethical propriety of just this kind of career.

What, we might ask, are the implications of such a long relationship? Caution, compliance, a highly developed sensitivity to relationships and emotional states, a smothering sense of no escape, and the gradual development of a close identification with Uedagin are all, it would seem, fostered by this situation. With change only a remote possibility, it is natural that great attention and effort will be directed to getting along well in the bank. Some persons come to depend overly much on Uedagin, and others develop the self-confidence to operate aggressively within its confines, but generally, social conformity and a sense of immersion in the institution are fostered by "life-long employment."

Personnel is charged with the responsibility of matching the requirements of the organization with a supply of talent. Given the manner of entrance and departure, the supply can only be manipulated at the two ends. Untrained graduates may be accepted in greater or lesser numbers, and retiring members may be retained in the service of the bank in greater or lesser numbers. The ratio of university to high school men, and the ratio of men to women may also be altered at the point of entrance. Under normal conditions these are the only areas of direct control. New requirements for a special skill can be temporarily filled by hiring outsiders, but soon members are trained to do such work in order to guarantee labor continuity and to provide maximum work opportunities for members.

According to my estimate, any group of entering men will only be diminished by about 15 percent by the time it reaches mid-career, and it will change in size very little after that. The quitting rate during the first four years is predicted to average about 3 percent annually. Past that point, the group may lose, in total, another 4 percent due to quitting, illness, and other factors. This is not a large amount, and the causes for such departures are outside the control of management almost entirely.

If, for some reason, a particularly large group of men enter one year, they remain to overload the supply of their age group throughout their climb up the ladder of ranks. If all work was the same, or if people did not care what rank they held, this inflexibility might not be so serious, but the rank system, which contains minimum age limits for all but the highest ranks, defines the shape of personnel requirements. For the system to work smoothly there should be an acceptable ratio between the openings within each rank and the number of people qualifying in terms of age and years of service. No one expects every qualified person to receive high rank, but opportunities for promotion (defined as some ratio of job openings to men of a certain age) should be as good as or better than in other large companies.[19]

This arrangement is affected by the course of the bank's business. If the rate of expansion slows down, for example, then openings for new deputies and chiefs do not increase. If there is no growth, then men hired in anticipation of future expansion come to constitute a serious oversupply when they reach the age to qualify for positions of leadership. Conversely, if expansion accelerates, the need for talented leadership may outgrow the supply, in which case the minimum age for ranks such as deputy and chief may have to be lowered.

Obviously, the low rate of mobility between companies is the source of a strong drive for expansion, for once growth begins it is ever more necessary for it to continue in order that places in the middle and upper ranks be created for the increasing numbers of young men hired. Presently in Uedagin the time lag between entrance and reaching the qualifying age for deputy is slightly over ten years, and it is the personnel director's job to judge correctly what will happen in that period.

There is one important release mechanism from the situation just described. That is the substitution of women for men in lower-ranking jobs. Because women are short term, it is a much less difficult and complicated matter to increase or decrease their numbers. The inclusion of women in the membership brings other problems, but it does provide an important degree of flexibility, and it allows the personnel section at least partially to avoid subsequent imbalances in the upper ranks by permitting the bank to meet the short-term changes in low-level work requirements with adjustments in the acceptance rate of new women. Men may then be admitted according to the long-range development plans of the bank.[20]

We should also note that by retaining directors past the normal retirement age the bank extends the close relationship between age and rank into the highest echelons. At the top of the rank pyramid sit a group of men most of whom are past fifty-five and therefore older than any of their subordinates. Of all the members of this executive group, the president, at sixty-six, is the oldest. He is the most senior person in the entire bank, as was his predecessor. Since the next presi-

---

[19] All of this is clarified in chapter 6.

[20] The flexibility that comes with a larger proportion of women in the company is generally replacing the flexibility of temporary employment as the primary form of adjustment to shifting needs at lower levels in Japanese companies.

dent will probably be selected from among the present directors, and since directors older than him will be encouraged to retire shortly after, the pattern will continue. This contributes to the overall integration of rank, authority, and age, creating what is in outline a pattern of gerontocratic rule.

Uedagin clearly does not correspond to the usual assumption made by theorists of Western economic organization that individuals possess a strong capacity and inclination to change from organization to organization. Of the people who wish to leave at one time or another, few actually do. As we have seen, the reasons for this are complex. It is symptomatic of a general situation that makes intercompany movement unrewarding and of a set of values that emphasizes continuity of group membership and endurance in the face of problems. Dwight Waldo (1963) has observed that among the European biases in Weber's thinking on bureaucracy (and in the more recent theorizing in the same tradition) is the notion of voluntary participation, particularly, that it is always possible to reverse the original decision to participate. This assumption has been part of utilitarian social philosophy from at least the time of Adam Smith, and it is a crucial part of the ideology of American companies. The Uedagin material highlights the fact that the notion of individual volition and the companion idea of the central labor market are only to be understood in the context of specific socio-cultural situations. It has been shown that economic prosperity, increased communication, and easier transportation, for example, do not result in interorganizational mobility rates for Japan nearly as pronounced as those in America.[21] Such gross comparison is not really at issue here, but it is instructive. If anything, the foregoing material illustrates the point that joining a Japanese firm is not the same as taking an American job.

There is considerable variation within the Japanese picture itself. Smaller firms and blue-collar elements show higher changing rates than large firms and white-collar elements. Clearly Uedagin stands among those firms that have especially low rates of job changing. It is important to note that these low rates in Japan are associated with companies and career types that occupy the pinnacles of prestige. Rather than being interpreted as evidence of stagnant individual ambition, few alternative opportunities, or the like, the low changing rate among white-collar workers in large firms is taken as an affirmation of the hierarchy of company and educational status. It also confirms the notion that the larger the company the more satisfied the workers. This

21 See Tominaga (1962 and 1968) and Cole (1972).

constitutes a neat complex, for precisely such attitudes contribute to the persistence of this general pattern by making those who quit large firms look strange, and by encouraging large firms both to keep quitting rates down and to conceal them from the public. The association of permanent employment with high status is one of the most prominent characteristics of the Japanese company scene, and it colors the entire statistical spectrum.

Most significant is not the question of which factors are more powerful—economics or values—in such situations, but rather the fact that there is a strong coincidence between the two, at least in Uedagin. As we noted at the beginning of this chapter, it is not in the nature of ideology to be true or false, nor is it necessary that ideology explain behavior. What is of significance is the general fit, and the fact that events, no matter how mundane in motive, have elevated significance at the level of general interpretation.

Finally, I wish to emphasize that high turnover and the expectation of job changing have a profound impact on any organization: diluting human relations, emphasizing the impersonal, sharpening differences of background and interest, sponsoring individual competition, and generally fostering alienation from the organization and its goals. In America today these qualities are widely viewed as the results of large-scale organization, but studies of Japanese organizations remind us that all of these undesirable qualities derive also from the pattern and degree of individual mobility in large organizations, and this is a quality that undoubtedly varies with culture and with time.[22] Like it or not, we must recognize that our cherished sense of individual independence from organizations greatly accounts for the unpleasantness of social relations we experience within them.

[22] Tominaga (1968) and Abegglen (1969) both see the permanent employment pattern as increasing for large firms. Tominaga compares the prewar and postwar periods to reach this conclusion, while Abegglen compares the same companies over a decade from the late fifties to the late sixties.

Also, job changing seems to be on the increase among young blue-collar workers today (Cole, 1972), and this is best explained as the result of a shortage of skilled, semiskilled, and middle-school graduate labor making the ease and the rewards of changing companies relatively greater than in the past. This situation will not arise for Uedagin in the foreseeable future because the labor shortage is least severe in the highly educated, white-collar group, especially for large firms with good records.

4

Nothing is clearer from interviews with Uedagin people than that their primary experience of company life centers on their daily work in an office. Individual reports of satisfactions and dissatisfactions tend to focus on two things: the nature of the daily routine and the morale of the office group. Working hours are long, the average being ten hours a day during the week and another six on Saturdays. It is taxing work too, considering the tedious repetition and the pressure to avoid mistakes. Only the rare individual is not exhausted at the end of the day. Many complain of these conditions and look forward to the time when computers will lighten their burdens by reducing office record keeping and when Uedagin growth will bring greater security to the overall enterprise and thus lessen the general pressure on performance.[1]

The question of satisfaction, however, hinges essentially on whether pleasure can be found working as part of one's particular office group. It is virtually axiomatic that some offices enjoy good working relations and others do not. At its best the office group can make this hard work exciting and meaningful, at its worst it is a cancer in the organization and the source of great individual unhappiness.

Many of the terms used in the bank's ideology to describe the ideals of good relations, including "harmony" and teamwork, tend to be part of the vocabulary used by average members when discussing the morale of office groups.[2] In fact, it is the small group, not the overall

[1] Parts of this chapter are contained in Rohlen (forthcoming) in which I compare the Uedagin material with data subsequently collected on office and factory work groups in a medium-size manufacturing firm.

[2] One of the most common phrases used to describe good relations in the group is *matomari ga aru*, "the group is drawn together," "it has unity." A major dimension of Japanese popular thought about small groups is represented by the contrast between this state and its opposite, referred to as *bara bara*, "scattered," "fragmented," or *matomari ga nai*, "lacking unity." The term *morale* as used here refers to a general sense of enthusiasm within the group for common tasks and for

company, that can actually be measured by the criteria of good relations presented in the ideology. Finally, because Uedagin is a company
constituted primarily of branches, the question of the office group is
of particular centrality to our analysis.

A TYPICAL BRANCH WORK DAY

The following account attempts to portray the activities and atmosphere within an average branch office. It is based on notes made during a particular day of observation in an office of twenty people. The
second half of the account, a description of a meeting and an office
party, occurred on the same day, but these events are not to be understood as daily occurrences. Meetings occur on the average of once
every month or two.

Branches open their doors promptly at 9:00, but for the people on
the inside the day necessarily begins earlier. The standing rule is that
people must be in the office in time for the morning staff meeting at
8:30. They have safes and files to open, cash boxes to check, adding
machines to set up, and desks to arrange in preparation for the rush
of business that begins when the doors open.

Until 9:00, there is an air of genial informality as people exchange
greetings and make small talk while they go about their own preparations. The activities of the night before, the weather, bank gossip, and
details of office procedures are discussed. The women finish their own
preparations early in order to serve cups of tea to the others. The hot
brew and cheerful attention bring smiles. Several younger men, sitting
on top of their desks, enjoy a funny story.

The responsibility for presiding over the morning meeting (chōrei)
is rotated daily. Everyone gathers toward the back of the office, forming a circle in front of the chief's desk. The proceedings begin with the
leader bowing to the others and saying, "Good morning." They bow
and in unison return his greeting. Still standing, they recite together
the principles and teachings. "We, constantly abiding by the ideas of
cooperative banking, will, together with the general populace, advance
in our mission to serve as instruments of small and medium business
enterprises," and so on. Occasionally, they sing the bank song.

With the formalities over, everyone sits down, and general announcements from the main office are read. The chief is called upon
to make any remarks he may have. In this instance, he speaks about

---

the group itself. This is something felt by participants, and it is also verifiable for
them in the continuation of cooperative acts, expressions of enthusiasm, and the
like.

the regional meeting of branch chiefs and explains the coming month's goal for the collection of deposits assigned to their branch. He has his own reservations about the target the main office has set but asks all members to consider what they might do to improve the branch's record. He concludes by announcing a party after work to kick off their drive to meet the new goal. Next, the deputy in charge of the office reads a report on the number of clerical mistakes made by each branch. Everyone is relieved to learn that their branch has a relatively low monthly average. He urges them to work for an even better rating. Since there are no other announcements the meeting is closed. All stand once more and go through the morning exercise routine. These are of the stretching and loosening-up sort and are directed by a cheery girl's voice and piano accompaniment coming from the record player. Altogether the meeting has lasted about fifteen minutes.

The entrance of customers transforms the entire mood and orientation of the group. At 9:00 sharp someone steps outside, winds up the metal door, and unlocks the entrance. Moments before, like backstage at curtain time, people scurry to their desks, adjust their posture, and assume businesslike expressions. Soft music is turned on, and attention is directed to the door. Until three in the afternoon the people at the counter and those located behind (who give record-keeping support) are totally occupied keeping abreast of the day's flow of business.[3]

The young men and women working as tellers greet the customers as they enter with a "good morning" or "good afternoon." When possible they stand to greet them, showing added respect. In the smaller branches, many of the regular customers are well known, and, while they wait for the record keeping to be completed, the teller often engages the customer in friendly conversation. The stiff competition among banks for even small depositors has made the quality of counter service important, and everything from the greetings to the polite bow and "thank you" as the customer leaves is drilled repeatedly during initial training. The more enthusiastic tellers appear thoroughly to enjoy these brief encounters. During training they have learned a few impressive tricks, such as counting paper notes by fanning them in a half circle, and then, with a flick of the wrist and fast finger ac-

---

[3] Argyris (1954:54–56) comments that contact with customers in banking adds a human element to work and reduces coworker interaction. Both of these are points made by Uedagin tellers, but there is also a counterinfluence in the case of Japanese branch banking, for it draws the office group together and creates isolation from others of the same company. The reduction in interaction during the hours a branch is open is balanced by more interaction in the "off hours."

tion, giving each bill a loud snap as it is counted. Impressing visitors with a sharp performance is part of a teller's job.[4]

All but the largest branches function primarily to collect deposits. In this office, there is an almost equal division of personnel working inside and those who spend most of their day circulating through the neighborhood seeking new deposits. Known as salesmen, these men have undergone a special course in sales techniques. Their work is among the most trying, for salesmen are constantly under pressure to find more deposits.

One deputy supervises the work of the inside staff. His desk is located directly among his record-keepers, and it faces the line of tellers, keeping him in close contact with the people he supervises. Much of his work is to review and approve the transactions and reports completed by his subordinates, and he seems forever to be applying his personal stamp to a flow of office documents, most of which he has no time to consider.

The branch chief's desk is not in a separate room, but at the back and center of the office. He, too, is close to his subordinates. During some part of each day, however, he is absent, for his responsibilities require that he attend numerous conferences with his superiors and fellow branch chiefs, as well as call upon leading customers.

Activity is usually so brisk that only one or two workers at a time may go upstairs to the meeting room to eat lunch (usually delivered from a nearby restaurant). The tellers can enjoy a long smoke at this time. On duty they must abstain, for it is inconvenient and unseemly. The bank has no system of coffee breaks, but the women pass out cups of tea when they have free time, and after the doors close at three people may take breaks whenever they wish.

Even though a few customers may still come in the side door, after three o'clock one can sense a gradual unwinding as attention shifts away from the counter. The metal shutters cut off noise from the street, and, with visitors gone, the office suddenly seems quiet. No one stops work, but conversation increases and people walk around more. There are hundreds of calculations to be done, checked, and recorded

---

4 Role fulfillment as a virtue and roles as highly crucial aspects of individual identity in Japan are topics discussed at great length in DeVos and Wagatsuma (1970). Because this account does not focus on individual job performance, the striking perfection of and involvement with work roles in the daily operations of the bank are not sufficiently emphasized. Let it be noted, then, that proper role fulfillment, specified and done to an extreme by American standards, permeates the nature of work routines. Perhaps for this reason matters outside the specified scope of an individual's role are disturbing and can be paralyzing. The leader must provide guidance in such situations. We might label this "role inflexibility."

before the day's work is finished. Sometime before five everyone stands, stretches, and does the afternoon exercises. By 6:15, an hour and a quarter later than scheduled, all stop work, clean up their desks, lock the safe, and go upstairs to the conference room for the meeting. However mundane this daily routine may appear, it does provide the setting for a variety of meaningful interactions among members of the group. The closeness of working relations and the repetition of procedures serve to intensify individual sensitivity to slight alterations of expected conduct. People expect, for example, to be served tea. For this act to encourage a cheerful response, however, it must be done in a personalized way, with a smile and some pleasant comment. Tact and attention to the proprieties of simple interaction, such as acknowledging each other with appropriate greetings, are crucial for the maintenance of good relations. An outburst of anger (never personally observed, but reported by a few informants), a failure to lend a hand, or an unusual reserve receives immediate notice and often leads to interpersonal problems that take a long time to resolve. During the course of daily work, then, there is ample opportunity for subtle variety. Some actions contribute to the goal of improving team spirit, while other actions may bring its very existence into question.

Two other occasions are central in the life of the group. These are discussion meetings and joint recreation activities.

AN OFFICE MEETING AND PARTY AFTERWARDS

On the second floor numerous folding chairs have been arranged in front of a long table. The chief and his two deputies sit behind the table, and the rest arrange themselves in front. The women sit together in the rear. As usual, all stand to recite the principles and the "President's Teachings." The chief next discusses the branch's record for the last six months and reads a formal announcement from the president regarding the next half-year campaign to collect deposits. This document, filled with expressions of the difficult battle ahead, is listened to impassively. The deputy in charge of sales next stands to explain his ideas for improving the collection of deposits. Both presentations have been rather formal, and no one has interrupted or asked questions. People have been listening seriously, it appears, for soon a discussion involving about half of the men develops around the issue of how best to deliver the bank's monthly advertisements to households in the area. The chief enters only to ask questions. In no way does he dominate the conversation. The topic shifts several times, but always the same people offer opinions. All along, the women and several of the men have remained silent. When talk seems about to end, one deputy stands and announces that the meeting is for everyone and those that still have something to say should speak up before it is closed. The silent members indicate they have nothing to add, and the meeting ends. It is seven-thirty and time to start the party.

While some bring in the food and beer, the rest arrange the tables into one large rectangle. The chief, flanked by his deputies, sits at one end. The other men sit along each side (in no apparent order), and, as before, the women sit at the back. Although the general arrangement has been changed from the meeting, the three divisions (leaders, men, and women) has not.

The party, known as a *teiki taikai* (periodic meeting), is expressly held to initiate the new campaign to collect deposits. Numerous bottles of beer are passed out and opened, and glasses are filled. All members stand with glasses in hand as the chief offers a toast to the success of the coming months' work. For the next fifteen minutes everyone settles down to a meal of Japanese and Chinese delicacies. A relaxed atmosphere with much animated conversation and laughter spreads over the group. Turns are taken filling each other's glasses, and the two deputies circle the room, large bottles in hand, making sure everyone is drinking heartily. Only the women are permitted to refuse the repeated offers to "have another glass."

When things seem sufficiently enlivened, the chief raps on the table for attention and suggests that singing begin. Everyone claps in agreement, and someone calls out Mr. Ono's name. Clapping erupts again, and he stands, sings a brief folk song, and then sits down amid much applause. The chief calls next on Kato, another of the younger men, who, because he is a bit of a wiseacre, is regarded as the black sheep of the group. Kato makes an excuse, drinks a full glass in one swallow, makes more excuses, but fails to stand and sing as requested. An awkward silence follows. Everyone sympathizes with Kato's embarrassment, but he must sing like the rest, for the solo performance is an integral part of office parties.

Suddenly, the older of the two deputies stands and begins telling a story to relieve the silence.

> The other day I was riding on a trolley, and unfortunately it wasn't very crowded. You know, I like crowded trolleys because the girls bump into me, but this time I was just sitting reading the sports page. Two young girls were standing with their backs to me. They looked a lot like Miss Maeda and Miss Kondo over there: one was rather thin and the other a bit chubby. Well, they had these new mini-skirts on that come down no farther

than here. Since I enjoy looking at girls, I was sort of sitting there contemplating the scenery, when I noticed that one of them had forgotten to take her laundry tag off the bottom of her skirt. I debated for a long time whether to tell her about this or not. I am a firm believer in helping others [turning to the framed copy of the "President's Teachings" on the wall beside him, he recited the section on sincerity], but there are times, you know, when it is difficult to know just how to be kind. Finally, I threw caution to the wind, and tapped one of the girls on the rear like this with my paper, and pointed to her friend's laundry tag. She understood and reached down to pull it off. Unfortunately it had been stapled and wouldn't come off. Her friend turned in surprise and started trying to get the staple out too. Well, this caused quite a commotion and everyone in the trolley turned to watch the proceedings. When the tag finally came off, the girls looked up to discover that they were the focus of all eyes, and they turned red as beets. It just goes to show how good intentions can sometimes make things worse.

The deputy's style and gestures develop every risqué element in his story, and the room is filled with laughter from beginning to end. The women, embarrassed to be laughing at such a story, hide their faces in their hands.

The other deputy next stands and recounts discovering in public that his fly was open. He graphically demonstrates how he leaned over to close the gap in his pants and then, using his briefcase as a shield, attempted to zip up discreetly. The story is pretty much a failure, but the rest laugh and clap generously at the end.

During this time Kato has been swigging down glass after glass of beer and puffing on a cigarette. Attention turns to him once again, and everyone claps at the suggestion that he now try to sing. Finally ready, he hurrys through a popular song and sits down amid thunderous applause, obviously relieved. Then everyone in the group takes his or her turn singing a solo. With much giggling and hand holding, two women pair off in a duet. One young man sings a song filled with taboo sex words disguised rather transparently as puns in the midst of an otherwise innocent story. Another offers a fine rendition of a soulful ballad. The deputy who told the funny story ties his necktie around his head in the homespun manner of folk dancers and proceeds to sing and dance an exaggerated rendition of an old folk song. He has everyone in stitches again. Finally, the chief, in a polished and charming manner, sings a traditional song and then its modern counterpart.

By nine, when the meeting closes with a final toast to the success of the branch, over twenty large bottles of beer have been consumed, and the men are gaily drunk. The women are urged not to clean up, since their parents are probably waiting for them at home. After they leave, the men sit down to polish off the remaining beer, and then, at the chief's invitation, they head off as a group to a nearby bar. The singing and drunken calling back and forth continue during their walk through the dark, empty streets. Several of the more euphoric stagger along arm in arm with a steadier companion.

Sitting along the bar, there is much effusive exchange of compliments and revelations of personal feelings. The chief and his deputies allow themselves what seems to be nearly uninhibited expression, but their subordinates appear to check themselves from reciprocating with as complete a degree of intimacy.[5] Beginning with the younger men, people start going home about eleven, and only the chief is left talking to the owner of the bar at eleven-thirty.

To the American observer accustomed to the homeward rush of employees at quitting time, these office meetings and parties that last long into the night seem at first profoundly exotic and inexplicable. In Uedagin offices, there is no set time when work ends, no time clock, and a reluctance to leave before the rest. Staying late is a common quality of office work. In some instances, the whole office will stay until the last person is finished. This remarkable degree of cohesion is best understood through an examination of the main facets of Uedagin office groups.

THE OFFICE AS A COMPETITIVE UNIT

Branches are placed in competition with one another in numerous ways. In the collection of deposits, each is assigned a quota based on a certain percentage increase in performance. The standard of success is well understood to be relative to the record of other offices. Branches with good percentages of increase are held up to public notice in announcements. At the awards ceremonies gold, silver, and bronze awards (actually certificates for the office wall) and four other classes of recognition (for effort, cooperation with other branches, enthusiasm, and office efficiency) are distributed to the most successful branches. Awards to deputies for outstanding individual performance go almost invariably to men from the fifteen top offices. While a branch chief is seldom rewarded individually, any honors his office receives honor

---

5 On other similar occasions I have often seen leaders more reserved than their subordinates, and I tend to view the intimacy displayed by this particular chief and deputy as exceptional.

him and indicate that he is looked upon with favor. Obviously, the
career chances of chiefs and deputies hinge to a large extent on the
successful performance of their offices.[6]

Reportedly, there is another reward for good performance. Offices
that do well are said to receive larger amounts for miscellaneous expenses. This means that they can afford more sumptuous office entertainment, and in many cases it means less out-of-pocket expenditure
for the chief who likes to treat his men to a drink after work.

Sections in the main office, because they do not collect deposits,
are left out of this competition, but they are included in other comparisons. The morale of each office, for example, is measured by an
annual survey. The answers to a long set of questions about satisfaction, office leadership, and personal problems are tabulated to give a
profile of the morale level in each office. Personnel also pays close
attention to the complaints and quittings for each office. A chief is
judged by these standards as well as by rates of deposit collection and
office efficiency.

SEX, AGE, AND RANK COMPOSITION OF OFFICE GROUPS

No matter how large the branch, the ratio of men to women remains
about three to one. Important roles, such as supervisor and salesman,
go exclusively to men. Only the positions of teller and record keeper
are occupied by both men and women. Essentially the hierarchy within
the office parallels the system of ranks. The youngest and least experienced men and women are assigned to either the front counter or
record keeping. It is part of the official philosophy that all careers
begin at the bottom and that training for later responsibility should
include all of the fundamental jobs within a branch. For this reason,
young men coming out of introductory training are automatically sent
out to a branch to gain basic experience.

Most salesmen working out of a branch office are men in the twenty-
eight to thirty-five age bracket. It is not unusual to find one or two
much older men destined to work as salesmen until their retirement.
They are regarded as tragic examples of wartime dislocation, because
they tend to be people who lost their original jobs during that period
and were subsequently employed by Uedagin as commissionees.

Close friendships within the salesman group are not particularly

6 Cole (1971a:92–100) contains a description of a group-oriented incentive wage
system in a small manufacturing firm that is interesting for comparative purposes.
The Uedagin wage system, one that does not offer commissions or other wage in-
centives either individually or on a group basis, is described in chapter 7.

developed. The men are almost all married and self-sufficient in their work. They do, however, often befriend younger people in their branch, offering them counsel and accompanying them on pleasurable excursions after hours. Because they are married and removed in age, they may also assume the role of big brother toward the younger women in the office. The duty of serving as sponsors and chaperones for youth-oriented activities within the office usually falls on their shoulders.

The age range among deputies is pronounced. Promotion begins at age thirty-three, and the average age of deputies is thirty-nine. There are almost as many deputies of forty-five as thirty-five, and this wide age range is a major factor in producing variation in office relations. The ideal office is characterized by an even distribution of ascending ages within its rank hierarchy. Large age gaps and reversals of the usual parallel between age and rank are seen as potential problems for group relations.[7] In reality, it is possible to find deputies in their fifties supervising people in their early twenties. One may also find a thirty-eight-year-old chief in command of a regular or deputy ten years his senior. To remedy such age disjunctures, a young deputy is usually assigned to branches with an older chief. Little more can be done short of a major change in promotion practices.

What are the consequences of age-rank disjunctures? Many said that younger men placed in positions of authority over older men can cause resentment and a refusal of cooperation, but few actual cases were encountered. Older men apparently can accept leadership from their juniors if it is polite and considerate. Offices with an older deputy and chief, and thus an age gap, are liable to morale problems emerging out of a sense of distance and boredom among the young. Young people complain that men in their late forties and fifties cannot understand their generation, appreciate their humor, approve of their views of the world, or lead them in appealing recreational activities, such as bowling, hikes, and swimming. A sense of separation can be strong, and few older office chiefs are able to cope with this problem without the aid of a young deputy.

Problems in the main office occur less from disjunctions of age and rank than from other sources. Because all young men are sent to

---

[7] It is possible that the bank's normal age range for the men in an office group is rather great compared to that of small task-oriented groups famous for high morale in Japan's recent past. Certainly, military units (with the exception of the latter half of World War II), youth groups in rural areas, and bands of late-Tokugawa samurai did not have to cope with the kind of age-gap problems some Uedagin offices have. The ideal image of high group morale is often, although not invariably, exemplified in Japanese history by groups more age homogeneous. The forty-seven *ronin* included a man sixty-nine and a boy fifteen.

branches for their initial tour of duty, there are few men under twenty-five, but a large number of young women, in the main office. In the computer section, with its many key punchers, this shortage of young men is particularly acute. More characteristic of central-office problems, however, is a reduced sense of group involvement resulting from the availability of many activities and people not connected with the office group (most of which, however, are within the Uedagin framework). Bank-sponsored sports, hobbies, dormitory life, and the like do not replicate office group interaction in the case of the main office. Branches are like small islands in a sea of strangers, whereas offices within Aoyama have little of the outpost psychology.

Women occupy a place within the office only slightly different from the place they have in other areas of middle-class Japanese life. They are subordinate to men not only in rank, but simply because they are women. They never rise above the position of ordinary and never have supervisory powers. The only exception to the general rule that they occupy a position in the group analogous to their place in marriage is the nature of their work. At home the division of work by sex is almost complete, whereas in the office women work alongside and do almost precisely the same tasks as the youngest men. Both serve as tellers and record keepers, and in cases where the women are more experienced or more skillful they will be recognized for their ability. But no matter how valuable a worker she may be, a woman must play the part of a woman. This includes showing deference to men (even those younger), serving them tea, preparing food for parties, taking responsibility for brightening up the office with flowers and other decorations, and being cheerful. Women leave drinking parties early, act as hostesses for guests to the office, are expected to arrive at the office early, and are permitted to go home before the men. In all of these examples, they act the conventional part assigned to women in the home. At times the fact of working at the same tasks as men is rewarding, but just as often women report taking comfort in the womanly aspects of their place in the group. Making others happy and brightening up office life are tasks many mention as being the most satisfying.

Commenting on women in the office, men stress how sensitive and hard to manage they can be. A chief or deputy cannot get mad at them as he can at men, it is said, and the slightest friction may cause them to become upset. "Women's feelings are delicate, and we must be very tactful," they say. It is also felt that their presence at office parties and on trips interferes somewhat with the essentially male practice of getting drunk together.

These complaints are part of a general set of difficulties arising with the increasing utilization of women by the bank. Because they are as efficient, yet considerably less costly than men (they leave before their salaries get very high), women have since the war come to have considerable importance in banking, one area of Japanese business that has learned to use women efficiently in clerical positions.[8] Problems center on the fact that they are not inclined to respond to the company and to their work with the same involvement as are men. Women have no career at stake in the organization and can always turn back to their parents. Office morale problems are quickly apparent among the women, and a great deal of effort is expended these days trying to find ways to keep the Uedagin woman happy. She has come to have a special kind of leverage because she is more willing to show her dissatisfaction and even to quit.

It must be emphasized that the chief assumes particular importance because he is the one responsible for the group's performance, a matter understood to depend in large measure on good group relations. When morale is poor, office performance is poor, and almost invariably the leader is blamed. The people in the office may feel that responsibility falls on everyone's shoulders, but the personnel department views the situation differently. For them, the prime variable in performance is the character and ability of the chief. When a branch does poorly the chief is likely to be transferred and demoted in responsibility.

TRANSFERS AND OFFICE GROUP CONTINUITY

Although the average man retains a long association with the bank, his participation in any particular office group is interrupted by periodic transfer. In 1968, four hundred people were moved from one office to another. This figure, representing over 10 percent of the total personnel, applies primarily to men. Transfers involving women occur only within Aoyama, where it is possible for the woman to commute from her home to a different office. The continuity of office group membership is also affected by women who leave to marry. One of four leaves each year for this reason. Combining the two factors, we

---

[8] The increasing utilization of women in the face of a growing labor shortage is a much-discussed trend, yet according to government statistics most categories of employment did not show significant increases in the percentage of women over the decade 1958–68. Only the category of clerical work showed a marked increase in female participation, from 36.9 to 49.3 percent, and this lends support to the observation that banks, one kind of organization that pioneered in giving women greater clerical responsibility, have been leading a trend of some significance (Office of the Prime Minister, 1970).

can estimate an annual turnover of 15 percent for the average office, and the personnel department offers the additional information that the average time in an office is 3.75 years. Continuity, so characteristic of the individual-bank relationship (for men at least), is not particularly characteristic of relationships within an office group. It is useful to keep this picture of steady change in office group membership before us as we consider the efforts undertaken to unify the group and to sponsor good personal relations within it.

INTERNAL ORGANIZATION

Several general patterns of relationship are characteristic of office groups in the course of their normal activities. These patterns are manifested in the adjustments of the group to two basic requirements —work output and group maintenance. Both are the interrelated concerns of all participants, but especially of the chief.[9]

The two fundamental configurations are the formal pyramid and the informal circle. The arrangement of desks within an office reveals much of interest in this regard. An aerial view of any branch office reveals a system of hierarchy with the lines of command beginning at the chief's desk at the rear center, proceeding through the deputies' positions immediately before him, and terminating at the desks along the front counter. Set on end, this picture fits the typical pyramid pattern. The fact that branch offices must be oriented to customers means that little internal facing can occur. Desk arrangement takes a somewhat different and more revealing form in the main office, where there is no need to face a front business counter. Typically, the chief's desk is at the back center of the room. To his sides and a bit forward we find the desks of his deputies. The rest of the staff is gathered around in front, with many of them facing inward creating a ring. Whether an actual circle is formed or not is less relevant than the fact that desks are arranged to face one another. The exact pattern is determined by the space available and the preference of the chief, but never will one see a section arranged so that people are looking at the backs of others in the same group. Invariably, there is the

9 These two primary aspects of small work groups, production and maintenance, are also fundamental aspects of the PM (production/maintenance) approach to small group leadership (Cartwright and Zander, 1960). It is fascinating to note that at the level of abstract scientific language the commonalities of leadership style regardless of culture can be demonstrated, and yet the actual practices, interpretations, and nuances of small group leadership can vary remarkably from culture to culture (as well as from group to group in the same organization), as this chapter hopefully illustrates.

sense of an in-looking circle, yet the positions of importance are easily determined at a glance. The chief, at a slightly larger desk, is clearly the focus of the arrangement, and his location permits him in a single glance to take in all that transpires within his domain.

In all cases chiefs work in direct contact with their subordinates. They have no separate private offices. Partitions, cubicles, and small side rooms are only used to set off special areas for conferences with visitors or for small discussions within the staff.[10]

The structure of work follows the office hierarchy, but there are qualities that distinguish it from a simple hierarchy. First, the general interrelationship of persons within the group is expressed by the desks' facing inward. Secondly, vertical ties within the office are direct and close, for no barriers are set up between the leader and his followers. There is little sense of individual isolation or of mechanical relationship in this pattern. The group, of course, is oriented to its work, but to the degree possible it is also oriented to maximize the sense of being a group. Interferences, such as noise, are not considered serious enough to justify separation or seclusion.

An informal circle is used for social relaxation and for other times when fellowship is the primary focus. Morale is sponsored by activities of the circle kind, in which differences of rank, age, and even sex are diminished while common membership in the group is manifested. If a pyramid represents the essence of the organization of work, a circle symbolizes the essence of the group principle.[11]

Considering all of its activities, there is no sense in describing the group as having but a single structure. Each activity and context calls forth slightly different arrangements based on a combination of the two principles, and the group finds it normal to shift from one to another. In the preceding description, the morning ceremony, the work routine, the staff meeting, and the party were all arranged differently. In the abstract, there are contradictions between the two principles, but in practice they depend on one another. In fact, one

[10] This and much else in this chapter exemplifies my assertion that in Japanese office groups distance and impersonality are not characteristic nor necessary for control in the way discussed, for example, by Johnson (1968) for American situations. See Dore (1973:230–251) for a similar view of authority in Japanese work groups.

[11] The pronunciation of the character for circle and that for harmony are the same, *wa,* and this coincidence, if that is what it is, is utilized by some spokesmen for traditional morality. One Zen priest speaking to bank trainees expressed the opinion that the circle was the ultimately meaningful form, and a traditional artist in Aoyama, founder of a public association known as *wa no kai,* once spoke to me about the beauty of the almost completed circle as it reflects the dynamic and the ideal in social relations.

key to maintaining an efficient office is to make frequent, but orderly, shifts from one arrangement to another so that the spectrum of relationship possibilities within the group, official and personal, may be realized. It is, of course, imperative that the pyramid regulate daily affairs. This makes the shift to informal, group-centered activities the direction that requires more effort and time. The general expectation of good group relations results in the fact that the working order will begin to break down, or at least lose motive force, unless discussion meetings, parties, and other maintenance gatherings of the circle type are forthcoming. It is part of the chief's job to be sensitive to this need.

Group maintenance requires effort and time. For the group to coalesce, for the potential cooperation and team motivation to be realized through informal activities, opportunities must be available after work and on weekends. This is why the administration and the office leaders plan, conduct, and usually pay for a heavy schedule of office social affairs. Individual members take time to participate, some out of obligation and others out of interest. Some feel coerced by the group pressure and resent having to go along, but whatever the reason few decline.[12]

DECISION MAKING AND ORDERS

The chief is empowered with the authority to make all decisions, and, if he wishes, he may maintain a strict order in which he alone decides. On the other hand, because the entire group is involved in the work of the office, most chiefs submit problems to discussion and, if they wish, to the rule of group consensus; or, after discussion they may decide the issue themselves. Of these possibilities, the last is the most common on major issues, whereas group decision making is characteristic of minor matters. Group processes require considerable time, and to push for an early consensus or to fail to involve everyone can lead to resentment and opposition. One simple rule influencing office decision making is: the more urgent a decision, the more likely it will be made according to hierarchy. Another basic consideration, however,

12 This issue is of serious concern to Americans (and to some Japanese) who see in the American practice of a strict separation of work and leisure protection of the private right to spend one's "free" time as one pleases, and there is evidence that the younger generation of Japanese have a comparably greater inclination to affirm this idea than their seniors. The company's recent shift to more peer-group recreation is significant in this light. See Plath (1964) for a general discussion of leisure patterns in Japanese life, and Dore (1973:207–213) on recreation patterns in a large industrial firm.

is that people favor group discussions wherever possible and have an expectation of participating in considerations of office affairs. This includes consideration at the office level of new bank-wide policies and directives.

This is also true of policies to which the chief has been committed by higher authorities. Office discussions, in this case, can transform an imperative into a solution endorsed and shared by everyone.

The question of delegating decision-making power is in all of these cases a subtle one. A chief, anxious for the positive effects of group discussions, may hold many meetings but submit issues of minor significance. He might choose to discuss his own decisions with the group. He might also introduce a question only when certain that his opinion will prevail. The conclusions may be foregone, but the fact that discussions have been held is most important, for a chief is expected to share his opinions, ask for advice, and permit dissenting voices to emerge. His trust and respect for the others and his acknowledgement of the group's importance, both symbolized by this process, are what count.

OFFICE SOCIAL ACTIVITIES

During Japan's most important holiday week, New Year's, almost the entire office visits the chief's home for a party. These gatherings are pleasant but far from carefree, for it is the chief's house, and circumspection is expected. Some men bring their wives along, and this too contributes to the restrained atmosphere. The holiday season is a time for women to dress in their most gorgeous kimono, and the brilliance and warmth of the occasion parallel that of Christmas in the West. Next to family visiting and strolling about in public, the most characteristic event of the holiday for Uedagin people is the party at their boss's.

The calendar of office social events for the year includes two overnight trips at company expense. These excursions, known as *ianryokō*, "rest and recreation trips," are usually made to a scenic resort, where the entire group stays together at a hotel or large inn. Hot springs and famous tourist spots are popular. Planning of these trips is a group effort that provides pleasures of anticipation for all.

When the selected Saturday afternoon arrives, all typically board a bus and commence drinking and merrymaking. Excursion buses are especially equipped for onboard parties with microphones that can be passed from passenger to passenger, making the each-sing-for-the-group arrangement possible. Bus companies also supply uniformed hostess-guides, who help the partying get underway by singing and telling stories themselves.

Seldom is there much time to sightsee before taking a bath and joining the group for dinner. Hotels and inns specialize in elaborate group bathing facilities, and, divided into sex groups, office mates bathe together before changing into the inn's gaily patterned robes. After feasting on good food and consuming considerable sake and beer, the familiar pattern of singing and joke telling followed by an inebriated flow of emotional conversation is repeated. Japanese skill in this sort of group self-entertainment is remarkably developed, and bankers who in daily life seem formal and uninteresting prove to be talented contributors to the life of such parties.

Group drinking parties are obviously an important part of office social relations. The reasons can be appreciated from an analysis of the dynamics of the simple ritual involved. At first stage everyone becomes relaxed and happily inebriated. The gesture of filling another's glass is a convenient bridge across strained relationships. No one is forgotten. No one need pour his own drink. Support and attention for all revolves within the group, and a swaying, relaxed fellowship is created. This prepares the atmosphere for the round of solo singing.

It is no easy thing to stand before a group and sing. Trembling hands, shaking voices, and nervous faces reveal the stress many experience at the moment they are selected. The group responds sympathetically, however, clapping encouragement, and sometimes by actually joining in the song. When the ordeal is over, it is normal for the performer to experience a rush of relief and a feeling of gratitude to the others for their help. From that point he is deep into the group emotionally, for he has revealed his humanity and been accepted by the others; what occurs is much like a confession-forgiveness sequence. The round of performances should end on a high note, and the chief, because of his position and experience, is the likely last act. A lackluster job from him would be embarrassing for all and cause the session, which has been of mounting intensity, to falter at its most poignant moment. To insure against such a disaster, many men of chief rank take singing lessons on a regular basis.

With the solos over, a final stage has been reached. Restraint further decreases, and the men arrive at a plateau of drunkenness. The entertainment may proceed with group singing, games, or intimate conversations, and at this point women in the group usually depart, for it is a men's affair. The process of uniting the group has ended, and there is no further obligation for full participation. Those in the mood are left to continue the party.[13]

Office groups experience six to a dozen such drinking parties a year. The ianryokō and teiki taikai, already described, are typical occasions, as are the traditional year-end party (bōnenkai), welcome and good-bye parties (kangeikai and sōbetsukai), and parties that develop out of the Saturday afternoon recreation program. The importance of the drinking party is strikingly illustrated by the observation of Uedagin friends that a man who could not or would not drink is at a great disadvantage in the achievement of leadership. Not to drink means to be unable to utilize the drinking party to win the affection of followers, to solidify the group, and to improve office morale in general.

Sleeping arrangements on an ianryokō place the men together in one or a few rooms and the women together in a separate room. Group sleeping arrangements are pleasant and preferred, for the intent of the trip is cozy relaxation, and this can make for similarities with the American teenage slumber party.[14] Sex, it must be emphasized, is totally out of bounds. During the drinking, suggestive joking and humorous comments often occur, but sex has no place within the office group, and even a secret romance between two young people in the office must be forgotten for the moment.[15]

Although the trip is ostensibly made for rest, the marathon drinking party that ensues leaves people dazed the following day. Similarly, in the planning stages scenery and places of special interest are considered, but in fact there is little time for sightseeing. Some people complain of this and find ianryokō a necessary, if disagreeable, chore that takes time from their personal pursuits. For one with this attitude, such trips involve a submission to the group that can be rather humiliating. Objections, however, are rarely voiced to the group. The individualist, if he is to succeed in the bank, must overcome his resistance to office group social rituals of this sort.

Once each month, under the cosponsorship of the union and the welfare section, each office spends a Saturday afternoon in some form

---

[13] A party of this sort epitomized what Nakane means by "tangibility," a quality she characterizes as "the essential element in organization for the Japanese [1970:139]."

[14] See Caudill and Plath (1966) for evidence that the young commonly sleep together with their parents in urban families.

[15] See chapter 11 for further discussion of office romance. I might add here that the common theme of illicit sex in the office found in popular magazines directed at white-collar workers appears to be 99 percent fantasy according to my experience.

of physical recreation. During the warmer months interoffice softball tournaments are held. An astute observer of bank social relations commented that the inversion of the usual hierarchy during sports events created by the athletic superiority of the younger men makes such recreation a useful means for reducing office tensions. That every strike-out by a normally demanding boss is a home run for office relations sounds funny, but certainly such recreation does intensify office solidarity.

A field day with relay races, children's entertainment, games, humorous skits, and other pageantry is held each summer by the offices within each region. A great deal of imagination and effort goes into these affairs. The focus is on entertaining the family, a departure from the usual pattern in which only office personnel are included.

With the overtime load so variable and the degree of informal socializing among office mates largely dependent on personal inclination, a precise estimate of the average time spent each week in social activities with others of the same office is impossible. Clearly individual variation is significant, yet an estimate should be attempted. My figures are intentionally conservative.

(1) Average work time in the office: 56 hours a week.

(2) Office parties and Saturday afternoon recreation: 4 to 6 hours a month.

(3) Office trips: 60 hours a year (two overnight trips).

(4) Informal gatherings of friends and small groups in the office: 2 to 4 hours a week.

Thus, a typical individual spends fifty-six hours a week working with and four to six hours socializing with office mates. The point that the work group does considerably more than share an office and a set of tasks is evident. The contrast here with the recreation patterns of American firms is striking in at least three respects: overall time, the work group (rather than hobby, family, or other) focus, and the degree of intimacy obtained through drinking, singing, and the like.

DEVIATION AND THE RESPONSE TO DEVIATION

Actions at variance with the expected and required behavior within the group seldom if ever take the form of open confrontation with authority or refusal to perform required work. Numerous factors, including the ethic of cooperation, inhibit direct confrontations, and deviance takes more private and qualified, yet quite discernible forms.

The individual unhappy with his boss or with relationships in the group is likely to set himself at odds with group norms where matters of personal preference intersect. Wearing excessive makeup, drinking too much, joining a leftist youth group, avoiding office social activities, and remaining notably silent during discussions are examples. These are actions that disturb others but cannot easily be labeled insubordination and dealt with in a direct way. Along the narrow line where private inclination and public involvement join, creating ambiguity of interpretation, one finds much of the nuance of group life.

Conformity and full participation can thus be viewed as voluntary offerings to the common existence. They should not be forced from individuals. Disagreement and criticism, as well as unhappiness, can be expressed through acts of subtle nonconformity. In "resistance" (teikō), both unhappiness and disagreement are merged. The understanding is that resistance is analogous to the rebellious behavior of children toward their families. The individual's natural state of existence, it is assumed, is within some group, and resistance is interpreted as essentially a sign of unhappiness and personal need. Thus, with few exceptions, acts of nonconformity are answered with sympathy and with special efforts to bring the individual back into the fold. The group's members, especially its leaders, may experience considerable irritation and anxiety, too, but these reactions should be repressed. Though some chiefs assert their authority and attempt to control the situation directly, particularly if it involves a man, the more typical response is a general group effort to pay more attention to the recalcitrant member and thereby overcome his feelings of resistance.

A notable exception occurs when most of the group object to their chief. Certainly the fastest way to bring relief from an oppressive or otherwise undesirable chief is to protest to the personnel section, an agency usually responsive to serious trouble at the office level. Personnel constantly reviews office performance, the results of its morale survey, and other indicators of trouble (such as quitting) in its decisions about which chiefs to transfer.

Schisms and personal animosities within the group can also have an alienating effect, and we find revealed in one office leader's attempts to cope with this kind of problem a third response to deviation, one utilizing the personal influence of deputies and others intermediate in the hierarchy. In this example, a branch is experiencing difficulty with relations between three small cliques of women. They go out separately after work and are unfriendly to one another in the office. Each is led by an older women (in her mid-twenties). The most serious aspect of the matter is the fact that one clique, including the most diligent workers, has recently followed its leader in attending weekly meetings of the Communist Youth Movement (*Minsei*). A deputy in the office explains:

> Our chief has asked us men to engineer better relations among the girls and improve our own relations with them too. I have been taking groups of them out driving on weekends and invited them to have coffee with me after work. My approach is to invite girls of the same age and thus cross-cut the age vertical cliques. By bringing members of the separate cliques together I hope to break down their sense of separation. When some have complained to me that I did not ask other friends of theirs, those in their own clique, I have explained that I am operating on a same age principle and will invite a different age group next time. This apparently satisfies them.
>
> The chief has also asked us to keep an eye on those in Minsei, to report what we can find out about their activities and the degree of their involvement. Of course, the bank can't say anything directly to the girls, nor can we go to their parents. That sort of thing would be criticized as unwarranted interference in individual politics. Some of the girls' parents, however, have come to us for consultation and advice on this matter.
>
> We can do several things to make it difficult for the girls to get deeply involved. We can invite them out on evenings when there are Minsei meetings, if we know when that is. It is hard for the girls to refuse our invitations since we work in the same office. Another possible countermove would be to reassign the girls to other offices in Aoyama far from their homes, so that so much time must be spent commuting that they can't attend meetings. Fortunately, girls marry and leave the bank. If our young men got involved in a left-wing group to the same extent, we would have a much larger problem.

In this and other instances it is often necessary to live with internal problems for a long time, and the chances of success often hinge on such separate factors as transfer and marriage. The departure of those who do not fit in or the arrival of a new chief or deputy able to draw the office back together often characterizes the final redemption of group spirit. Efforts to engineer cooperation and full participation through focusing increased attention on those withholding themselves from group life are highly predictable, and partly because they are expected, their success is not as predictable.

OFFICE GROUPS AND THE LARGER ORGANIZATION

The general nature of work groups is acknowledged by the treatment they receive from above. We have already noted the common practices of encouraging competition between offices and of judging chiefs according to their group's performance, and the result, that rivalry is often strong among men of that rank. The team form of motivation is relied upon, even in cases where the lack of comparability makes intergroup competition impossible. This complex has the following general correspondences with the larger organizational set up:

(1) The rank of chief has special significance. Its status is high; it is crucial to most operations, particularly nonroutine ones; and careers are either made or destroyed primarily at this level.

(2) Individual forms of reward do not receive strong emphasis in the salary and promotion systems, at least by American standards. For example, no commissions on deposits collected are offered to salesmen.

(3) Work groups, because they are recognized as independent social entities, are allowed considerable autonomy.[16] Experts are not utilized to solve operational problems for specific groups. This would be regarded as outside interference, and the result would be to undermine morale and leadership. The bank does have an inspection team that visits each branch once every few years, but basically the work group is entrusted with full latitude to handle its own daily affairs.[17] When it cannot do this well, it is likely that a new leader will be found. Nor do policies announced by the central administration concerning the conduct of groups necessarily have binding force. One year after the bank made 5:30 the official quitting time (on Wednesdays only), for example, most offices still were ignoring the policy. On matters of this kind, each office is encouraged to comply, but not forced to do so. Management watches the performance of work groups with a keen eye, but is reluctant to interfere. When a radical change is necessary, however, the intervention of central authority can be thorough and swift. The sense of domain and the expectation of discussion and consensus in small groups mean that much of the normal effort at changing work methods is directed at gaining voluntary participation. Management frequently calls for branch-level discussion of company problems, and new programs are often initiated at a ceremony attended by representatives of each office. The basic rule appears to be

16 Vogel's observation that "the section chief in the large organization has none of the independence in imposing arbitrary patterns upon his underlings that the old middle-class boss had in his narrow social microcosm [1963:263–264]" is also true, indicating a different parameter for the term *autonomy*.

17 Contrast this with the situation in America as described by Argyris (1954:164) of a cadre of officers any of whom is a boss for the general group of clerical personnel. Even in the Uedagin main office the criteria of group limits override that of rank alone in defining authority relationships.

that goals come from above, and the means of implementing them are
decided at the office level.

(4) The office group is constrained by the large organization in
various other ways, however, such as the absence of office-level control
over recruitment and promotion. Transfers may be caused by office
problems, but no chief has much power over who will be assigned to
his unit. In fact, chiefs' requests are discouraged as a rule. Furthermore, the size of office groups is not determined by considerations of
group dynamics, but by the work load and other external factors, with
the consequence that some offices are too big to be easily organized on
a small group model.

(5) The company does not have a written set of rules defining the
procedures of decision making for any level, but it is assumed that
collective consideration is proper and necessary.[18] Obviously, the
hierarchy of ranks and the establishment of central authority define
much of the process, but, even above the office level, group discussion
and consensus are acknowledged, although their significance varies.
Even at the top many of the small group procedures are the same, and
the same kinds of alternatives in decision-making patterns characterize
the interplay of leadership and group discussion within the realm of
management.

(6) The intense internal life of work groups, based on such factors
as joint effort, common competitive position, and the elaboration of
relationships, contributes to a sense of separation between them that
is often accompanied by cliquishness and difficulties in cooperating
with one another. Loyalties directed inward tend to make relations
with other units reserved and occasionally even hostile. Mutual suspicion and criticism are common between groups in private, and occasionally they surface in one form or another. Chiefs, set in competition with one another, find lateral lines of communication tenuous
compared to vertical ones. Without firm direction and coordination
from executives of the department-head level, these difficulties can get
out of hand.

These manifestations of how the large organization and the work
group are related are perhaps of secondary importance compared to
the influence the ideals of small-group conduct have on the manner
of administering the entire company. The image of a company comprised of people dedicated to the same goals, personally involved, and

---

[18] It is necessary here to distinguish between written rules and formality, for
though the former are lacking there is a high degree of formality of procedure
based on routine, precedent, and common expectation.

united by interest and common spirit is, we have seen, the common underlying theme of company ideology. Executives, rather than consciously concocting such an image, appear to take the model of the company as a small group for granted when human relations matters are considered.

The fascination here is that any organization over a certain small size will find it exceptionally difficult to preserve a sense of personal, emotional connectedness that extends beyond the work group and other face-to-face relationships.[19] While the nature of work groups is best approached from the question of their fundamental conceptualization, it is less likely that an ideology emphasizing small-group values will have the same significance for the larger organization. Company leaders may be devoted to such values, but they are not in a position to unite the entire personnel in the same immediate way group leaders can. Uedagin has been able to elaborate a wide range of activities of symbolic participation (ceremonies, gatherings of representatives, company-wide outings, and civic and charitable programs) but none of this guarantees a sense of connectedness to the whole.

DYNAMICS OF THE OFFICE GROUP SITUATION

We have come full turn, from considering the office group as a competitive unit that ideally should have a high degree of teamwork (wa) and satisfy many of the personal needs of its members, to a discussion of the established means to realize this conception, and finally to an understanding that problems of disunity and dissatisfaction are as constant to the situation as are the methods adopted to overcome them. Solidarity in work groups is something to be achieved, and, compared to the ideal, groups are likely to be viewed as imperfect. Basic understandings and values not only point to goals, but also highlight existing inadequacies.

Acknowledging the various qualities of small groups to be matters of degree compared to a set of ideal expectations creates the basis for examining the dynamics of the situation in terms of shifting conditions

[19] It is precisely on this point that Nakane's (1970) general characterization of company organization appears weak, for while she is basically correct about the way small groups should work she recognizes neither how often the ideals only highlight the lack of involvement and morale nor the basic differences between the small group and the large organization. Nakane's approach does have the virtue of describing the informal cliques and personal ties often in the background of high-level influence, but companies are far more rationalized and impersonal than her account recognizes. It is as if her primary focus never leaves the small group, and thus factions, cliques, academic circles, and other small entities within larger organizational spheres dominate her analysis.

within the group. When the sense of solidarity is down, for example, hierarchy is less agreeable and more apparent. The reverse is also true. Solidarity itself is essentially a mood related to the emotional aspects of the group, particularly the relationship between the group leader and his subordinates. When things go well, when the leader is followed out of affection and respect, the internal structure of the group appears useful and proper. The three basic factors—positive emotion toward the leader, solidarity, and structure—are thus interrelated in crucial ways. When structure comes to imply distance and difference and morale is threatened, then the able leader invokes activities of the circle kind. His style is thus crucial, particularly as he must be able to create a mood of fellowship.

The most poignant sources of stress in this situation are the requirements of work. Pelzel (1970) is justified in underlining the importance of the task orientation of Japanese groups. Without a common task, office groups would have nothing to justify their existence, and enjoyment of one another informally would become frivolous and soon terminate. On the other hand, the demand for greater production, the problems of sharing the work and the responsibility, and the fatigue of strenuous effort most tax the emotional ties and the sense of mutuality within the group. This pressure falls particularly on the chief, for he alone faces the full force of demands and criticisms from top management.

It is interesting to note the response of people in the bank to the characterization of their organizational life in terms emphasizing close personal relations and a sense of unity. These, they say, are qualities a foreigner might choose to emphasize, but such a description ignores the daily problems and inadequacies of Japanese organization. When these problems are discussed, however, the same people's comments imply the existence of models of close relations and solidarity. Outstanding groups, ones with good working relations of the sort described in this chapter, are standards of comparison. A cultural approach, we may conclude, is of significance because it highlights the standards and expectations taken so much for granted by insiders. As cultural outsiders we must penetrate to this level, for otherwise we will be unable to understand the conceptual unity underlying the dynamic flux within any selected single group.

THE CHARACTERIZATION OF AUTHORITY

A central issue in any cross-cultural comparison of bureaucratic organizations will be the question of authority. Recently Crozier (1964), citing cultural difference as significant, has suggested how authority problems in French bureaucracy are closely related to various themes and patterns of French culture. Face-to-face dependency and warm primary group relations in work are difficult for the French, and the result is a high degree of impersonal authority and a reliance on rules. Crozier's general approach, one that views the nature of authority as varying with such things as dependency, is one that receives support from this material.

To begin, legalism, such things as explicit rights and duties, is not characteristic of Uedagin hierarchical relations. Instead it is assumed that short of leaving the organization entirely the subordinate has no recourse to contend directly with his superior. Open argument with him, refusal to obey orders, and other forms of insubordination are all possibilities so rare as never to have come to my attention, and there are no rules that condone or permit such actions. People with exceptionally strong grievances usually hide them behind a screen of silence. In this sense the superior has absolute authority, but it is not legal in basis. Nor does the company union stand between a superior and his ability to exercise authority.

The acceptance of dependency (with limits) is a definite part of successful personal relationships in Japan, and there is much evidence that dependency is often regarded as a positive aspect of social relations.[20] But dependency does not automatically lead to the "acceptance of most arbitrary discretion," another of Crozier's preconditions for bureaucratic success. We have seen that work group discussions and situations of informal intimacy are regular aspects of the program designed to maintain participation and acceptance. Without such efforts the group ideal of mutual interest would soon disappear.[21] For the office leader, the ability to be arbitrary one moment depends greatly on his readiness to be highly responsive to the group the moment before and the moment after. This shifting emphasis is supported by official company policies and is therefore institutionalized and expected to a large degree.

Although Japanese procedures indicate much the same authority-compliance complex as that discussed by Bernard (1938) and those after him, the practices of American and Japanese work groups are quite different. For the Japanese, the procedures of discussion and participation are institutionalized, office groups are far more sensitive

[20] See in particular Caudill and Plath (1966), Caudill and Weinstein (1969), Doi (1962, 1963, 1967, and 1971), and Kimura (1972).
[21] Nakane (1970:135) refers to the frequency of meeting as a basic measure of the closeness and firmness of the relationship.

to the process of inclusion, and their leaders are far more inherently equipped to manage this form of direction than their American counterparts. In fact, the term for authority (*keni*) is not used in common thought to describe the dynamics of group activity. Acceptance (*nattoku*), participation (*sanka*), resistance (*teikō*), and opposition (*hantai*) are the dimensions of the problem, and impersonal rules and formal position are of little significance in adjusting behavior from the negative to the positive sides of these dimensions.[22] Instead, the leader's virtue, his concern for others, and the general esprit within the group are the most effective means to individual acceptance and participation. Involvement and trust, once established, permit considerable "arbitrary" discretion. Pelzel attributes essentially the same qualities to authority in Japanese household groups. He writes, "The tolerance for authoritarianism is perhaps higher in the Japanese than in many Western or Chinese situations, but in Japan no head can expect well-motivated action on any decision that has not been deliberately accepted by members who have the right by interest or competence to be heard [1970:246]."

The patterns we have described are characterized by involvement, an emphasis on feeling, and little capacity to separate the people from their roles.[23] Definitions vary with the people involved, not with some legal or rational formula. The energetic, warm leader creates for himself great power, while his opposite commands no more than a mechanical authority based on his position alone. Pelzel (1970:247) also asserts this view when he writes, "I argue that no attention is in fact paid to what may be called the social personality of the individual member. It is the emotional aspects of the personality that are instead

22 Consider here David Riesman's observation during his extended visit to Japan, "People refer to organizations as 'undemocratic' if there is no harmony or consensus. Thus, democracy and politics would seem antithetical [1967:202]." Nakane (1970:144) also emphasizes the particular democratic nature of small Japanese groups.

23 It is natural for American social scientists to ask about the conflict between "instrumental" and "affective" aspects of the leader-follower relationship. This distinction is not of primary importance to the Japanese, although it is recognized. Crucial personnel decisions (promotion, transfer, and firing) are made at the personnel department level to avoid excessive personal influence. The small-group leader will often use intermediaries, such as his deputies, to scold or caution his subordinates when their personal influence is stronger, an illustration of how "affective" ties are used to support "instrumental" ones. Argyris (1954:154) describes "weak authority" contacts between officers and subordinates in the U.S. bank he studied, and there are, in Uedagin, leaders who also avoid almost any open expression of authority. The Japanese office situation allows much latitude here, but it does not allow the leader to withdraw to an impersonal distance. The marked centralization of crucial personnel functions in Japanese companies could well be interpreted as a counterforce to the strong "affective" pull at the office level.

~~given outlet in the procedures of the Japanese small group, and a wealth of standard behavior patterns can only be interpreted in this light.~~" Loyalty to an immediate leader is obviously a crucial aspect in the flux of motivational levels. ~~The more important motivation is to the work at hand, the more important leadership becomes.~~

It helps to keep these qualities of "authority" in mind when we consider such things as the union and the official ideology, for the vocabulary of both revolve around this and other key understandings.

5

A FRIEND AT COURT

In Japan many valued relationships involve a difference in age. Those between parents and children and between teachers and students are the most prominent, and they provide models for other relationships. Strong personal bonds between people of different ages have, for example, been noted for those working together in labor gangs, gangster outfits, village communities, and factories.[1]

We have also seen how intergenerational ties are emphasized in the bank's ideology. Finally, the most recent and prominent analysis of modern Japanese organization (Nakane Chie, 1970) gives a central place to the importance of what rather unfortunately must be termed senior-junior relations. It is Nakane's conclusion that this relationship is crucial to our understanding of the uniquely Japanese qualities of modern organization. Clearly this aspect of Uedagin interpersonal relations deserves our close attention. And in fact, a detailed look at senior-junior relations will permit us to understand a great deal more

1 Because they are so prominent a part of Japanese society, nonkin relations based on age differences have received considerable attention from scholars of various fields. Among the more notable works on this subject are Benedict (1946), Kawashima (1948), Ishino (1953), Norbeck and Befu (1958), Bennett and Ishino (1963), Nakane (1967 and 1970), Whitehall and Takezawa (1968), and Cole (1971a). Only the last four are addressed to the problem of senior-junior relationships in industrial and commercial organizations. Bennett and Ishino document the importance of such personal ties between a work boss (oyabun) and his followers (kobun) among temporary workers in many kinds of labor gangs. Whitehall and Takezawa note the importance of senior-junior relationships among factory workers, but they offer no details. Cole discusses the foreman-worker and other personal relations of a hierarchical sort among blue-collar workers. Nakane generalizes over the range of vertical relationships found in modern Japanese organization. Her work will be discussed briefly at the end of this book. The general topic of the patterning of non-kin relations on kinship patterns, of which the senpai-kohai relationship could be viewed as an interesting example, is taken up by Kawashima (1950), Wolf (1966), and Hsu (1970) among others. Drucker (1971) has noted what he calls a "godfather" relationship within Japanese management. His account contains inaccuracies but is an attempt to pinpoint informal senior-junior relations within modern management. For Chinese examples of a similar pattern see Folsom (1968).

about the daily reality from which the ideological image of hierarchy is taken. It will also help us understand leadership style, and it will illustrate the crucial role seniors often play in the process of fully joining the company.

By way of introduction we should note that an awareness of relative age is a constant necessity in the proper use of the Japanese language.[2] A person will converse with those older using a more polite vocabulary and set of grammatical forms. This is quite the reverse of the American tendency to minimize age differences in a search for the intimacy of equal status, and it seems that an appreciation of the satisfactions of senior-junior ties is not one we come to easily. The Japanese, it will help to remember, have a generally positive attitude toward relations involving age differences, and, as in the work group, the hierarchy of age not only serves organizational purposes but can be a matter of intimacy and emotional involvement. This point will help us to grasp the underlying character of senior-junior relations in Uedagin.

GENERAL DESCRIPTION

Discussions among young men and women of personal affairs and reactions to working in the bank generally lead to the mention of a senior person who has offered help and advice. The term for senior, *senpai,* is a compound of two characters, the first meaning "before" or "ahead," and the second meaning "companion." *Senpai* may be understood to mean a person who proceeds or leads, with the implication that those that follow are his or her companions in the same pursuit, career, or institution. *Kohai,* literally "companion that is behind," expresses the other half of the senior-junior relationship. The complete image created by the characters is of companions, one leading and the other following, passing along the same road.[3] Senpai-

---

2 For an incisive and revealing study of the linguistic components of status differentiation and some of the psychological consequences see Niyekawa (1968).

3 The concept of *michi,* translated as "way," "road," or "path," as it symbolizes an institutionalized course for the attainment of skill, personal cultivation, and even enlightenment, is of some relevance here. We are familiar in the West with the "way" of Taoism, of Zen, of judo, and the like. In such michi and others like them, the senpai-kohai relationship, like the teacher-disciple relationship, is significant. Whether it is credited with the appellation of michi or not, any institutionalized pursuit, including the career of an Uedagin banker, carries for the serious Japanese something of the same significance that the concept of michi bestows on more philosophically rationalized pursuits. Senpai-kohai relations in Uedagin and other institutions with common goals have special weight among senior-junior relationships, for they are between persons sharing the same institu-

kohai relations are present in the bank's informal organization at all
levels, but it is during the first four or five years of work in the bank
that they develop and are notably influential.

In the most general sense, all people in the company are senpai
to those younger, and all people younger are kohai to their seniors.
Usually, the application of these designations is limited to persons of
one's own sex. Women are senpai for women, and men are senpai for
men. One never hears a young man refer to an older woman as his
senpai, and when women use the word they mean an older woman.
Among the reasons for this division along sex lines is the implied
comradeship between senior and junior, a form of comradeship that
does not cross the boundaries of sex.

We will distinguish several different kinds of senpai-kohai relationships in Uedagin. All of them share the following basic characteristics:

(1) The senpai is older than his kohai, has worked longer for the
    bank, and is in a position of power relative to him. This power
    enables the senpai to assist the kohai in one or more ways. It
    also means that the senpai is secure and established compared
    to his kohai.[4]
(2) The senpai is beneficially disposed toward the kohai.
(3) The kohai accepts the benefits bestowed by the senpai.

---

tional path through life. Lest this invocation of traditional Japanese thought be
misunderstood as a statement that no change has occurred since the days when the
concept of michi was central to most Japanese morality, it must be added that men
in Uedagin do not think that they are interrelated to the same degree as men pur-
suing the same formal michi; however, the concept of a businessman's michi was
mentioned once by a middle-aged banker. He wished for such an idea as the basis
of a moral framework meaningful for modern Japanese.

4 Like the relationships between parents and children, older and younger siblings,
teachers and pupils, superiors and subordinates in an organization, boss and follower (a special relationship in Japan called oyabun-kobun), and teacher and disci-
ples, the senpai-kohai relationship is, in the words of Nakane Chie, "a vertical one"
involving a relationship between people of different age, status, and power. Of these,
the senpai-kohai relationship is the least institutionalized, and yet among the most
common. That it is not mentioned more often in the literature on Japan stems I
think from the fact that detailed studies have not been made of institutions and
groups where it is particularly significant, such as student groups, sports teams,
iemoto (professional and semiprofessional organizations for the study and teaching
of a particular art form), business and industrial organizations, alumni groups, and
the like. Another reason is that the senpai-kohai relationship, being quite personal
in most instances, is liable to great variation, making generalization difficult without considerable direct experience. In villages and urban residential groupings,
where the most detailed studies have been done by non-Japanese, the senpai-kohai
relationship is not as pronounced as kinship, landlord-tenant, neighborhood, and
other relations.

(4) These acts and related feelings are the basis of the relationship, though no explicit agreement is stated.

(5) Ideally, the kohai feels gratitude to the senpai for his beneficence, and this feeling is accompanied by a desire to return the favor along with a commitment to become, in turn, a good senpai for someone younger.

A chain of relationships of "good turns" is thus created. This is not, however, between equals, nor is the exchange "balanced," in the narrow sense of the word. The senior is more powerful, and he gives more than he receives, but when the junior (who has received) occupies the position of senior (who gives), balance is introduced. Over time this becomes a general structure, much like a chain letter without the multiple. In time, the kohai may also have opportunities to repay his senpai through personal loyalty. The time may even come, as it does with parents and their children, when the power to assist and the need for assistance are reversed between the two. We have, therefore, an exchange relationship between unequals in which time is a factor of great significance in the establishment of a semblance of balance. However, developing as it does over time and involving numerous acts of unknown relative value, balance is impossible to compute. It is a vague ideal and an ultimate goal. No one is so naive

5 Benedict (1946) and Kawashima (1956) mention the interrelated concepts of *on* (benefit), *ninjo* (human sympathy), and *giri* (obligation) as being of central importance to the character of interpersonal relations along a vertical axis. Kawashima corrects some of Benedict's misunderstandings about this. The most thorough discussion of on in terms of social transaction is Lebra (1969), in which she clarifies how various procedures or mechanisms operate to establish balance in the relationships involving on. Her entire article is well worth reading carefully in connection with this chapter.

In the postwar period, partly because of the association between these terms and prewar "feudalistic" social relations, the expressions *on* and *giri* have dropped from normal daily speech to a large degree. They are only infrequently heard in conversation in Uedagin today, but it is not unusual for on to be included as part of explanations of feelings of obligation to pay back some other party, even the bank itself. The willingness of seniors to befriend and assist those younger than themselves out of sympathy for them is certainly part of the pattern of interpersonal relations that Benedict and Kawashima have described as the manner on is given and received. It seems that there is less emphasis today on strict fulfillment of felt obligations and less expectation of it. The specification of relationships in these terms is vague, and the range of variation in degree of sensitivity to these considerations is large. To others in the bank who take such issues less seriously, some Uedagin senpai-kohai relationships appear quite old-fashioned in their degree of involvement. The old-fashioned versus the modern is one way people evaluate such personal relations. Another is to look on interpersonal involvement and a strong sense of obligation as a reflection of good character. Uedagin people see from both of these perspectives.

as to be unaware of the many long-standing imbalances. Nor, however, are people encouraged to be cynical about commitment to this sort of relationship. Juniors may forget their obligation to be in turn good seniors. Seniors may demand too much of their juniors. Some kohai are ungrateful. The system of interrelationship, however, continues to follow the form set by the ideal of unselfish sympathy and involvement. Mood, that is feelings of attachment-disaffection and satisfaction-dissatisfaction, ultimately serves as a measure of the balance.

The similarities between this relationship and that of parent and child or older and younger sibling are more than coincidental. In fact, family relationships provide analogies, as in the statement, "Senpai are like older brothers." These analogies are instructive if we examine the ideology of the Japanese family. First, interdependency and continuity, rather than individual independence, are the family ideals. Second, the emphasis on continuity translates into a prescription of gratitude to past generations and obligations to assist future ones. Third, affection and hierarchy, rather than being contradictory, are understood as mutually reinforcing. Last, the dependency of the younger, weaker party is not only accepted, it is the focal point of the relationship. These are, one can say, basic ingredients of one major Japanese code of interpersonal relations. And this code can make seemingly dissimilar situations and involvements, such as a family and an office group, comparable. Because of this code, the patterns of Uedagin senior-junior interrelationship receive powerful reinforcement from comparable relations throughout the society, since they all repeat essentially the same message.

Ideally, senpai will represent, advise, console, teach, and discipline their kohai. Kohai, in turn, will confide in, listen to, depend upon, follow, and respect their senpai. The senpai is older and therefore has more experience and knows his way around better. He has contacts in the age groups above him. Probably he can call on his own senpai for help. Thus, seniority, particularly as it stands for the relative length of time in the institution, is the major source of the senior's power to assist his kohai. This will be even clearer in chapters 6 and 7.

While everyone who is older is, in a general sense, a senpai, the term usually connotes a specific older individual who is particularly close and protective. It is seldom advisable or necessary to have close relationships with more than one or two seniors, although there are a number of people in the bank who, as senpai, have more than a few kohai.

These highly personal relationships are, almost by definition, formed between people who grow to like each other. They must be able to enjoy each other in a relaxed and intimate manner, and this is based on trust and respect. Typically, senpai and kohai drink together often. Drinking and drinking places create for Japanese men a special situation in which formality and other constraints are relaxed and sometimes forgotten altogether. In this atmosphere, it is particularly easy for people to discuss personal problems, offer criticisms, and exchange feelings and opinions frankly. It provides an opportunity to be more "human."

The most common place for this relationship to originate is the office. Besides sharing the same daily work and group affiliation, men from the same office often stop off together for a drink or a snack on their way home. This provides a fine opportunity for the requisite familiarity to develop. In other instances, a young man will find a senpai from among the alumni of his high school or university, or in the bachelors' dormitory, or in some bank extracurricular group, particularly a sports team. In the case of women, office and high school ties are the basic sources of the relationship.

No matter what the initial opportunity for contact, the relationship develops by a process of increasing reliance by the kohai and increasing assistance by the senior. The deepening of the relationship follows a course similar to the development of friendships as we know them.

It is impossible to be precise about the time and energy seniors put into this kind of relationship. In critical matters, such as the total disillusionment of a kohai, a senior may devote days to the problem, but normally the usual opportunities for interaction in an office, dormitory, or team setting, coupled with a night out together perhaps once a month, suffice. I have recorded numerous instances of seniors devoting an evening or a Sunday afternoon to discussing a kohai's problem with him. Several I know have helped kohai locate a prospective bride, a time-consuming and delicate task. Senpai may use their contacts with more influential men in the company to remedy an office situation that causes the younger man grief. There are stories of seniors helping to cover the mistakes of their juniors, but most typically assistance comes in the form of consolation and encouragement when the younger man is discouraged. Often this is all that is needed, and this sort of attention lies at the heart of the relationship.

Since senpai appear to give much more than they receive, it is important to discover what encourages their willingness to befriend and assist those younger. Rather cynically, I originally presumed that, in the case of men at least, an obligated and loyal subordinate would be a conscious goal explaining senpai motivation. The senior calculated to gain power in this way, I thought. Another motive that seemed plausible was that seniors would assume the responsibilities of a senpai to impress their superiors and thus gain promotions. Informants, however, rejected these suggestions of blatant self-interest, saying that while the observations of possible advantages were not incorrect, they were hardly the reasons motivating senpai. Instead, they mentioned *omoiyari*, "feelings of sympathy and compassion," and *kawaigaru*, "to have affection for a weaker or helpless thing; to find something adorable," as basic to the explanation of senpai action. The essential ingredients in any person's motivation to befriend and help a junior are emotional, they argued. People who rationally calculate self-interest would hardly choose to assume the burdens of a senpai since the possible benefits to one's career are hardly guaranteed. Furthermore, they pointed out that men who lack emotional involvement would not make good senpai, and, thus, would be avoided by younger men.

An illustration of the degree of intimacy sought is the value placed on perceiving the implicit needs of the other before he must openly ask for assistance. Sensitivity is generally valued in superiors, and a senpai is expected to be the most perceptive. Assistance of this kind expresses concern and greatly contributes to the satisfaction of the relationship. The gratitude of the kohai is greatest when he has been given help without having to ask for it, and it is important that he learn to return such favors by anticipating the desires of his senior.

Proximity is the key ingredient in all forms of close personal association. When a transfer forces separation it is likely that the relationship will begin to fade even though letters, telephone calls, and periodic visits are common. In time, new relationships develop as the old ones enter a dormant period. The general influence of a large organization, particularly one with a high transfer rate, is to reduce the chance for long lasting senpai-kohai ties. Assignment together at a later date, even decades later, can, however, be the occasion for a reiteration of mutual involvement.

Of the Uedagin men in their thirties, there are many who do not befriend younger men. Some do not want the burdens involved, and others have difficulty establishing rapport. Some are definitely avoided by younger men because it is apparent that they are failures, misfits, or incapable on some other grounds of offering assistance. Attractive, energetic, personable people make good senpai, and they are also likely to be regarded as natural leaders when the time for promotion comes. Only among the youngest men (those in the 18–25 bracket) is the importance of a senior almost universal, although the more introverted and those living at home may never find a senpai. In the case of women, there are many without close ties of this sort.

Obviously, some senior men have more than one kohai. A few have regular groups of devoted followers, calling on them for assistance and coming around for company. These senpai are so busy with their followers that they have little contact with people their own age. It is not necessary that close relations with kohai preclude those with one's contemporaries, yet senpai-kohai ties do orient people in this direction. It is also evident that a senior's marriage is a likely watershed in the relationship. Those senpai who continue to be active do so at a certain cost to their new marriage. To thus give priority to company relationships makes one appear a strong personality, the kind destined for company leadership. In chapter 11 we will review the place of family relations in company life; here we only need to note that career success is related both to being a senpai and being willing to spend less than an average amount of time at home.

SENPAI-KOHAI RELATIONS IN THE BANK'S IDEOLOGY

The responsibility to be a good senpai is a common theme of bank training. People who have been around for a few years are often reminded of their senpai's warm assistance, and they are urged to view becoming good senpai themselves as a most important responsibility. Memories of first year difficulties are made fresh by organized discussions, and empathy is cultivated for newcomers. The logic is the same as in the ideology, that as a beneficiary of the hard work and generosity of one's predecessors, it is proper to work hard for the benefit of one's successors.

The senpai who built the bank and carried it through the difficult formative years, the "ancestors" of the organization, were the direct and tangible senpai of the bank's present managers, even though to younger members they are only a vague image conjured up in speeches.

Retired members are in a position analogous to living ancestors. Twice a year they have a meeting of their association, the *Uedagin Kai* or "Ueda Bank Club." The president and several of the top officers represent the bank membership at these functions. The spokesmen for the retired men wish the bank well and urge the present generation to greater accomplishments. They also express a desire to be of assistance to their juniors if possible. When the president speaks, he thanks the former members for their service to the bank and tells them how grateful the present membership is for the benefits they have received. The bank gives each person who attends these meetings a present and assumes the expenses of the banquet as a further expression of its gratitude. The meetings invariably end with all persons present joining together in a series of banzai cheers for the future success of the bank.

In another ritual symbolic of this "ancestral senpai–descendant kohai" relationship, each year the bank holds a commemorative service for the spirits of all deceased members on the anniversary of the air raid that destroyed the bank building and killed many Uedagin people working there. Expensive decorations and the employment of a high-ranking Buddhist priest are involved in this solemn ceremony, attended by almost all of the bank's top executives. Relatives and descendants of the commemorated individuals are invited, and after the ceremony they are treated to a banquet. About one hundred people attend each year, and the event is reported in the company magazine. It is a ritual the older people, at least, take seriously.

More fundamental, perhaps, is the fact that many Uedagin people, particularly the older ones, say they take considerable satisfaction in the knowledge that their individual endeavor is part of a much greater effort. The various ceremonial recognitions of ancestral senpai extend this sense of weight, significance, and broad participation.

The present leaders of the bank are themselves old, and they appreciate very well the desire on the part of retirees to be recognized and respected. They must often feel this need themselves. Their connecting position between past and present gives them a special interest in continuing the rituals of gratitude and respect for earlier generations, and as long as old men occupy the highest positions in the bank, it will not be difficult to appreciate why the past continues to be a prominent part of the official ideology, and why it is understood in personal terms.

SENPAI AS CONNECTIONS TO THE ORGANIZATION

The most apparent significance of senior-junior relationships is their contribution to the socialization of new members. Good senpai are a steadying influence on young men and women not fully adjusted to the burdens of work and the intricacies of social relations within the bank. A most common interpretation of individual difficulties asserts that the person in question lacks a senpai to guide and succor him. Conversely, a large measure of credit goes to the senpai of those who work hard and seem well adjusted, and the relationship is generally appreciated as an important means of preventing alienation among the young. By taking newcomers into their confidence, warning them of their superiors' idiosyncrasies, offering corrective advice, giving encouragement, and generally befriending the person, senpai obviously serve the interests of both the individual and the organization. It is important to understand that the two are not separated.

It is no wonder that their efforts are appreciated by officials of the bank. The personnel department, in fact, often seeks to remedy personal problems among the young by finding a good senpai, and the men and women who come to bear the burden of such responsibility are appreciated and often rewarded from above.

When introductory training ends each newcomer is handed a small black leather handbook detailing useful information including the name of their "office senior" (*shokuba senpai*). This person is expected to teach them how to do their job efficiently and to offer any other assistance necessary to assure a smooth transition into bank life. The person assigned to this task is the only exception to the rule that the senpai-kohai relationship is *not* official.[6] "Office seniors" are selected with care. They must, of course, be the same sex as the newcomer, a little older, gregarious, and knowledgeable. Most importantly, they should be models of good work habits and proper attitudes.[7]

Senpai, both those assigned and those personally discovered, teach their kohai much of what they must learn to operate successfully in Uedagin. Special knowledge, such as the unstated rules and obligations of group membership, as well as the technical details of their work, are usually taught by them. They also teach their wards how to cope

[6] In both Uedagin and the medium-sized manufacturing company I studied in 1972, the attempts by management to foster senpai-kohai ties achieved success only when the ingredients were right. There is no way a company can force personal relations of this sort. The fact that fostering them is now a common managerial practice reflects both the importance of the relationship and the fact that an increasing number of young people are not becoming involved with a senpai in their place of work. This lack of relationship was much more prominent among the blue-collar workers studied, particularly those who lived at home rather than in a company dormitory.

[7] One aspect of the image of the ideal leader that is not underlined by the parallels with the senpai image is the quality of strictness. The truly outstanding leader is a man gentle and understanding, but also strict and demanding.

with the many irritants of organizational existence. The senpai more than anyone else, except perhaps the chief, is involved with the process by which an individual accepts the bank, for acceptance depends in large measure on the availability of good examples of acceptance by others who are intimate or admired. Safe passage through the period when the desire to quit is strongest is an important aspect of Uedagin socialization, and this period coincides with the time when reliance on the advice of a senpai is heaviest. As noted in chapter 3, there are countless cases of young people deciding not to quit through the influence of a senior.

Senpai, particularly those in the same office, often serve to cushion the effects of hierarchy and authority. An office chief, for example, may pass advice to his youngest subordinates through their senpai. After work the senpai may take time to explain management's position, or he may confirm the correctness of a superior's action. Senpai are also known to intercede on behalf of their kohai to explain their mistakes. In all of these instances, the personal relationship between senior and junior mitigates the more impersonal organizational hierarchy. The result in many cases is that the young person comes to accept organizational necessity as the result of personal influence. If he has affection and respect for his senpai, he will be encouraged to accept the general constraints of the system. No cases of a senpai advising a kohai to contradict established authority ever came to my attention There are people in the bank who might do this, but they have no influence, precisely because they cannot be trusted to play the proper senpai role. In serving the interests of his junior to help him avoid trouble, the senpai sponsors acceptance of Uedagin and its requirements, and in the process he comes to represent a special form of virtue, one appreciated by those above and below.

SENIOR-JUNIOR RELATIONS IN MANAGEMENT

What has been said pertains primarily to young people for whom the problems of adjustment to Uedagin life are central. Senior-junior relations are also of significance for some people past the period of initial adjustment. There is the expectation that kohai will continue to be involved with their senpai for a long period. Out of obligation, gratitude, personal attachment, and perhaps ambition, he is usually anxious to return the favors he has received and to be a loyal follower. He may have little chance to do this immediately, but if the relationship is a good one and continues for many years, then opportunities for the kohai to be of assistance increase. There are occasional references to senior-junior ties within management levels of the bank. I could not collect first-hand data on these, but a general outline of this kind of connection and its significance can be drawn from the explanations of others.

Many senior-junior relationships recede with the passage of time as the younger man adjusts and attains greater independence, and as transfers separate one from another, but the sense of relationship often continues, particularly between capable people who can rely on one another in matters of work. Not all senior-junior ties are founded during initial socialization. Some develop between the more dynamic young leaders in their late twenties and thirties and their counterparts ten to twenty years senior. A few such relationships eventually assume great significance to the overall organization when one or both men reach high office. At the higher levels, informal and highly dependable ties of this kind can be of considerable assistance in the conduct of authority and the pursuit of personal advancement. At this point a kohai is able to assist his senior in practical ways, and their mutual affairs become more cooperative. The hierarchy based on age is not altered, nor is the personal bond forgotten, but the association does assume some of the qualities of a political alliance, one that will be likely to conflict with the organizational ethic of impersonal procedures, not to mention rival alliances. The senior may request that his kohai be assigned to work for him. If this request is granted, the two will be able to combine their personal regard with the requirements of their work, creating what they would regard as an ideal working relationship. Most requests for kohai are regarded with disfavor by the personnel office, however, because of the threat they represent to established impersonal procedures. Students of large organizations are familiar with the desire for personal associates in high level staff situations.

Senpai-kohai working in separate offices constitute important informal channels of communication and influence that operate behind the scenes. A network of such relationships is known as a clique (batsu), some having their origin among alumni of the same school and others developing around an important person. The senior-junior relationship is undoubtedly the foundation of these cliques, found at the management level of many Japanese companies. Rumors of them in Uedagin and stories of the efforts of the president and the personnel department to restrain the formation of cliques are regular topics of company gossip. The general consensus is that Uedagin is not yet riddled with cliques and factionalism, "as are some other companies," but that constant efforts to prevent them from emerging must be made.[8]

A special set of ties among a group of chiefs and directors is, however, acknowledged. They all came to the bank from various overseas government operations following the war. Their leader is the man who found jobs for them in Uedagin and afterwards looked after them. As in this example, senpai-kohai bonds begin usually from the best of human sentiment, and they are officially encouraged, yet as part of clique factionalism they may threaten the rule of formal procedures and the unity of the company.

AS AN IDEAL OF LEADERSHIP

The influence of the senpai-kohai pattern on feelings about official superior-subordinate relationships is worth noting. The pattern of close involvement between an older and a younger man, between a more experienced and a less experienced man, between a more established and a less established man, describes one ideal working relationship, one that is secure, beneficial, reciprocal, and selfless (to a degree). This ideal is often applied to the relationship of superior and subordinate in the official system of organization roles. Company leaders are occasionally referred to as senpai, and there is an implication that leadership should be as sympathetic, protective, and unselfish as are good senpai. In other words, the relationship is to a significant degree the basis for the ideal of superior-subordinate relations, and while this ideal of course often goes unrealized, it does establish a set of expectations about proper leader and follower conduct.

The superior finds his authority strongly limited by the general expectation that he will look after the best interests of those who work below him, that he will be their guardian or patron. The subordinate, on the other hand, finds that he should be submissive because of inexperience and out of gratitude.

It would be erroneous to view Japanese superiors simply as pseudo-parents or their followers simply as docile believers in the faith. These two extremes, neither totally contradictory nor totally allied, create between them a fluid context rich in ritual gestures, maneuver, and subtle intrigue, and here daily reality is to be found.

[8] Nakane (1970) has discussed such cliques at great length. The academic and political worlds often mentioned by her appear to contain stronger personal ties and more factionalism than the normal company. Such things as the high transfer rate and the requirements of efficient cooperation within the organization make companies less fertile ground for the development of powerful cliques based on personal ties.

Gratitude, loyalty, beneficence, and sympathy are but the most prominent and readily appreciated aspects of particular hierarchical situations. Other realities (promotions, personal animosities, business necessities, and the like) are interwoven with and often translated into this more elevated language of personal relationship. The senpai-kohai code, is, in effect, a sacred language for discussions of vertical relations in the bank.

As dissatisfactions with leaders or followers mount, the credibility of the conceptual scheme may come into doubt. Private skepticism is far from unknown. But gestures symbolic of the coherence and vitality of the senpai-kohai model are almost inevitably forthcoming in times of trouble, and their acceptance reiterates the fundamental premises of this relationship. By such things as self-sacrifice, magnanimous gestures, and intimate contact, superiors (including management in general) can represent their commitment to the scheme, just as patience and self-sacrifice symbolize commitment on the part of subordinates. These gestures must of course be accepted and at some point reciprocated for the preservation of the total orientation, but it is virtually impossible in normal circumstances to withhold acceptance for too long. As gestures continue to be made, resistance is both a disregard for the other's humanity and an antisocial act, for it threatens the existence of the group or the total organization. A rise of cynicism or a complete breach of relationships would lead necessarily to the establishment of a new order, one based on impersonal rules, power, and the assumption of conflict. That this has not happened in Uedagin is testimony to the powerful Japanese dislike of cynicism and to the power of symbolic redress provided by the senpai-kohai ideal.

6

GETTING AHEAD

From considering personal relationships founded on a difference of age, we turn next to questions concerning the promotion system, another aspect of Uedagin strongly colored by considerations of relative age. As noted, Uedagin is organized into a hierarchy of ranks, and this hierarchy is the major source of difference in such important matters as the allocation of status and authority. Salary differences, too, are influenced by this consideration, one that is of consequence only for men, since only they advance upward in the system. We must know how men move up, which men move up faster, and what the organizational factors influencing promotion are before we can characterize Uedagin according to a number of key sociological issues.

The promotion system is of equal significance to our general concern with the meaning of basic matters throughout the organization. In the official ideology we are told that all members share a common relationship to the bank, that the efforts of older men deserve appreciation, and that "spiritual" strength is the basis of personal achievement, to name but three assertions related to promotion matters. On the other hand, the business and organizational requirements of the bank speak out for an emphasis on individual ability, and the nature of the office group demands that leadership qualities be recognized. Not only are these diverse requirements brought together, adjusted, and compromised in the course of actual promotions, but the promotion system itself provides a major perspective on the matters of age, ability, and personal worth. It too offers implicit definitions of these things in relation to the division of labor in the organization.

Because the bank brings men into its organization at the bottom and at the bottom only, all men begin their careers at the same starting point. On the surface, at least, they appear to enjoy an equality of opportunity; originally they are equal in rank and are assigned basically similar tasks. Does this common starting point imply that members of each entering group will remain on a par in terms of rank throughout their careers, or are differences among them soon translated through differential promotion into differences of rank? Obviously, considerable differentiation occurs. To describe this process of differentiation is to offer one more perspective on hierarchy, one that defines upward mobility for the white-collar workers of Uedagin. We must remind ourselves at the outset, however, that some 40 percent of the personnel (nonmembers, quasimembers, and women) work in Uedagin without concern for promotion. Their status is low and static.

THE MECHANICS

A major event of the autumn is the announcement of promotions and transfers.[1] Although advancements to chief and department head are treated separately and announced in the spring at the annual chiefs' meeting, for most men the fall announcement is the moment when their own fate and that of their office mates may suddenly and dramatically be changed. It is also the time when evidence of change in the policies governing promotions may be discerned and deciphered. These possibilities and the coincidental announcements of transfers invest this season with enormous suspense. Rumors abound, and even those who are certain that there will be no change in their own lives find themselves drawn into the speculation and discussion. For those in line for transfer or promotion, the anxiety and preoccupation interrupt their office performance, but fortunately the people around them appreciate their predicament.

The number of people promoted each year varies according to the number of empty positions in each rank, and these are opened up through the combination of promotion, retirement, reorganization, and expansion. The retirement of a department head, for example, means one person may be promoted from each lower rank. The division of a section in two creates new chief and deputy positions. Be-

[1] In our examination of the promotion system and the principles upon which selections are made we will rely on information from interviews with responsible officials in the personnel section, discussions with other informants, a statistical compilation of the relationship of rank to sex, age, and total numbers, provided by the personnel section, and a compilation gleaned from the Uedagin *News* of biographical data on men reaching chief rank and above during the last seven years. The inner sanctums of the promotion process and matters of influence and intrigue which may be of significance remain essentially unknown to me, as they are to all but a few Uedagin people. My informants have offered speculation on certain points which will be reported but cannot be confirmed. I have found no fully adequate discussion of the general characteristics of the promotion system for white-collar workers in Japanese companies, in English or Japanese. The better brief accounts are to be found in Glazer (1969) and Whitehall and Takezawa (1968:276–314).

cause the bank does not promote men to ranks such as deputy or chief unless a specific position in some section or branch is available, there is a strict limit on the entire process. During periods of rapid growth in company operations, new leadership positions are created and the opportunities for advancement improved. Expansion is understood to bring the sweet reward of more rapid promotion for more people.

The first thing the personnel section must do in preparation for the selection proceedings is to make an assessment of the general requirements for additions to each rank. It then compiles a list of persons who are qualified for promotion to each level. Finally, it selects those to be promoted.[2] It is a simple set of procedures, but the factors involved are considerably more complicated.

We must first distinguish between those factors that qualify an individual for consideration and those criteria upon which final selection is made. The pool of qualified persons is established on the following basis:

First, the person must presently occupy the rank immediately below the one under consideration. No one is promoted by jumping a rank.

Second, the individual must have spent the requisite number of years in the previous rank. That is, before promotion to the rank of regular, a high school graduate must spend a minimum of seven years and a college graduate a minimum of five years serving as an ordinary. Theoretically, a high school graduate may be promoted at age 25 and a college graduate at age 27. In a similar manner, a four-year period as a regular is required before promotion to deputy is possible. Someone promoted to regular at age 27, therefore, could expect to qualify for promotion to deputy at age 31. Finally, individuals must spend at least three years as a deputy before further promotion.

The number of men who qualify by the criteria of time and rank outnumber the openings in the rank above by a considerable amount. The exact proportions will be different each year for each rank, depending ultimately on factors that include such variables as the number of men admitted in previous years, the growth rate of the bank, and the number of men reaching retirement age. The higher the rank, the more competition there is for each new opening. My estimate of the ratio of those promoted to those qualified in 1969 is:

2 Exceptions to this are chiefs and department heads, whose selection often involves the directors of the company as well as the personnel section. Or the appointment of chiefs may be left to the head of the personnel department, with the approval of the president and other directors.

Regular	1 to 3
Deputy	1 to 10
Chief	1 to 30
Department head	1 to 100 [3]

This kind of consideration, however, does not fully represent the promotion system as it is understood and analyzed by people in the bank.

AGE SET COMPETITION

The standard of comparison for the interpretation of promotions is the age set consisting of all those men of like age and years of service. Uedagin people and outsiders alike have a keen interest in knowing, "At what age do the first of the age set attain each new rank? When does the bulk of the age set get promoted to that rank? What percentage of the age set is left behind? And, after what age is there no hope for promotion to a given rank?" These questions dominate the speculation about and analysis of both promotion policy and individual careers.

The personnel section also utilizes this perspective, juxtaposing the age set and the rank system, in its decisions of who should be promoted. "The group of university graduates that entered in such and such a year, and the high school graduates that entered four years before that" is the usual definition of an age set. This concept conditions the promotion pattern in a particular manner, for the decision makers have a predisposition to favor people of certain ages within the pool of qualified persons. According to the rules, for example, it is possible for a man to qualify for promotion to deputy by the age of 31, but in fact no one under 33 has advanced to that rank in many years. The lower age limit of 33 for deputies is thus an unstated, but fully appreciated, policy. Should the age be lowered in the future, it would be interpreted as an indication of a significant increase in the number of openings for deputies—a sign of bank growth. Conversely, if the lower limit should go up to 34, it would be a discouraging sign that Uedagin was declining or had hired too many men ten to fifteen years previously. People comparing companies often ask the age of the youngest deputy and youngest chief, for these are

[3] As will be explained, appointments to department head do not occur before the individual is forty-seven or forty-eight years old. The ratio of 1 to 100 ignores this fact and uses the total number of chiefs (130) as a base. Since somewhere between one and two department heads are created each year on the average, we arrive at a ratio of 1 to 100. The same overstatement of the actual competitive ratio holds for the estimates for the lower ranks, too.

crucial indicators of a company's growth, its rate of promotion, and
the nature of its personnel situation. Morale is understood to be
higher in companies where promotion comes early.[4]

In a related effort, the personnel section also applies limits on the
number of people promoted from the upper age brackets of any pool
of qualified persons. To promote very many of these older men, ones
who have been passed over time after time, is to ignore more capable young men, it is felt. These two age-oriented considerations establish a promotion pattern of the basic shape indicated in Figure 5.
Men fortunate enough to be promoted during the years their age set
is in the A position (that is, during the first years the group qualifies
in terms of age) are regarded as the outstanding members of the age
set. They have the brightest future ahead of them. Those promoted
during the longer B period, when the probability of promotion is
highest, are not considered outstanding. The men promoted late
while in the C position escape the disgrace of being totally passed
over, but their careers are likely to end in this rank.

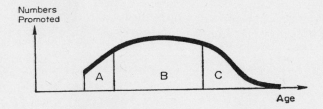

FIG. 5. Relation of age to numbers promoted in an age set.

Retaining the image of the curve just described and the concept of
the age set, we may consider the situation in 1969 for each rank
(Figure 6). Although these figures are not diachronic, the basic
situation facing age sets, as they move up and face specific promotion
situations, may be discussed. The youngest men promoted to regular
are three men 28 years old. They represent about 5 percent of their
age set. Among the 29 year olds, twenty-five men have become regulars, better than 50 percent of the age group. By age 32, 71 percent,
or all but fifteen men, have made regular.

4 One of Japan's most rapidly growing large industrial companies has many
chiefs in their early thirties and a department head thirty-eight years old. This
places their promotion schedule six to ten years ahead of the bank's, something
that is possible only in organizations with exceptional recent growth records. It is
also true, however, that many smaller firms promote early as a form of status
compensation.

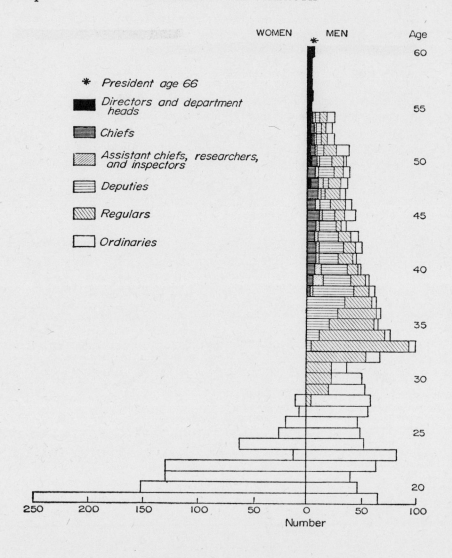

FIG. 6. The relationship of rank to age and sex of members.

Promotions to deputy begin with 33 year olds. Five are promoted that first year and six the next. Among the 35 year olds, one-third have become deputies. This is the group within the age set that is marked for special attention, and most of those promoted to chief will come from this accelerated group. The period of maximum opportunity for promotion to deputy is from age 36 to 38. During those

1. The main office.

2. The counter area of the main office.

3. The training institute (foreground) and Aoyama bachelors' dormitory (in back).

4. An older, small branch office.

5. Greeting customers.

6. A typical branch office scene.

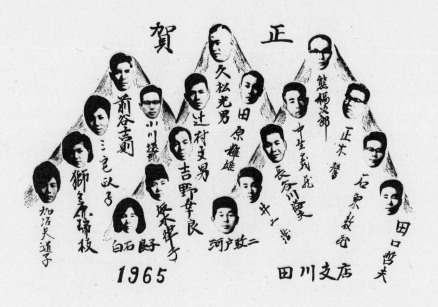

7. The New Year's greeting cards of two office groups (printed in the Uedagin *News*). Each card graphically expresses the principle of office group structure. The character in the middle of the circle is *wa*.

8. A twelve-man *han* of trainees (minus the author) during a break in introductory training. That day we were working in tangerine orchards to appreciate farming.

9. New women practicing proper phone speech.

10. A new man doing *zazen* as part of another training experience.

11. Morning exercises in front of the training institute.

12. New men playing a physical contact game, "war of the horsemen."

13. The graduation luncheon: the executives give the trainees a party to celebrate the end of the introductory course.

14. A union meeting.

15. The president (left) leads the Uedaginkai (retirees' association) in a banzai cheer for the bank.

16. Executives (president in the foreground) lead off a relay race at an Aoyama company field day.

17. Dancing during the bachelors' dormitory picnic.

18. The Aoyama apartments.

19. A typical Uedagin young family.

20. The ceremony to commemorate deceased members.

21. A meeting of a company hobby group
(the calligraphy club).

22. The union's arts and crafts exhibit.

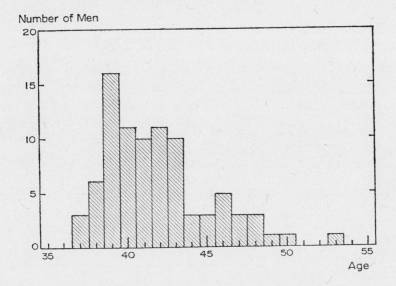

Fɪɢ. 7. Age at promotion to chief (1963–1970).

three years about thirty more reach deputy, leaving approximately 20 percent behind with very diminished chances of ever making that rank.

When an age set reaches 37, it witnesses its first promotions to chief and assistant chief (virtually the same rank, for chiefs of small branches and assistant chiefs of sections and larger branches have the same level of responsibility). In 1969, five men (7 percent) from among the sixty-seven people in the 37-year-old age set (including thirty-eight deputies) advanced to chief and assistant chief rank. About the same number are promoted from the 38- and 39-year-old group, and the total promoted to chief from the age set reaches 30 percent.

Let us consider in detail the promotions to chief for the period from 1963 to 1970. The relationship of age at promotion to numbers promoted in ninety cases is summarized in Figure 7. On the average, eleven men were promoted to chief annually during the period, although as many as twenty and as few as four were promoted in a single year. It is apparent that the largest number of promotions (64 percent) are of men in the age range 39 to 44. This is the period offering the best possibility for advancement to chief. The assistant chief rank, a recent and still very minor addition to the rank system, has had the effect of bringing earlier recognition to a few young men.

The best candidates are promoted at 37 and 38, but their numbers are small.

Those who reach chief rank after age 45 appear to be exceptional cases. Evidence that such late promotion is unusual comes from a closer examination of individual histories. Most of these men entered the bank late in terms of age, due to special circumstances following the war. Several were war prisoners in Siberia who were not returned to Japan until around 1950. The C section of our hypothetical model (Figure 5) is best understood as containing many such exceptional cases involving men of the wartime generation.

Age is also an important factor governing promotions to the rank of director. Of the fifteen directors appointed since 1964, the youngest was 48 and the oldest 57. Their average age was 52 at the time of promotion, and more than 50 percent were made directors between 50 and 54. Since they stay on until 60, the result is an age grading among the directors that closely parallels the rank hierarchy within the board.

Enough has been said to indicate the importance of age in the decisions of the personnel department. Not only the criteria of years in rank, but the division of each age set into something like the A, B, and C subgroups of the hypothetical diagram are fundamental aspects of the promotion pattern. The ramifications of this age orientation are:

(1) It places limits on how fast any individual may be promoted, thus stretching the process of advancement over many years for even the most qualified.

(2) It establishes general limits on the number of people from each age set who will attain each rank. Rather than competing with the entire compliment of Uedagin men, an individual is judged essentially against his own age mates, although the higher the rank, the more competition we find among men in neighboring age groups.

(3) Since only a limited number of men are left behind in each rank, a majority of the age set can count on promotion as far as deputy. The speed of promotion is the primary variable.

The term *nenkō joretsu*, literally "the procession according to the merit of years of service," is commonly cited as a description of the Japanese company promotion system. It emphasizes seniority of company service, the caricature of which is an "escalator." Such descriptions are not adequate, however, for as we have seen in the Uedagin case, competition is evident, the "merit of years of service" is no absolute guarantee of advancement, and from the beginning the ambitious must work hard to achieve a place in the A subgroup of their age set. Nothing is so automatic in this promotion system that people are encouraged to sit back and let the "merit of years of service" take care of their future advancement.

CAREER PATTERN AND PROMOTION

Competition within the age group is the crucial measure of a man, and this competition begins early, long before any promotions. In Uedagin, the first evaluation of entering men is made toward the close of their three-month introductory training. Everyone in the two separate groups of high school and university graduates is ranked in comparison to the others in his group. Those receiving high marks are given better assignments, usually to the most important and best-managed branches in the bank. They are marked as men of promise. Those judged the least capable, along with problem cases, are usually sent to smaller, more rural branches. They begin at a disadvantage, one that only especially hard work will overcome.   *no such thing in St. Louis.*

Each year chiefs write evaluations of their subordinates' work. The head of the personnel department is reported to have observed that within a few years of joining Uedagin a man's reputation with the personnel section is established and rarely do their subsequent promotion patterns verge far from this early estimate. After a few years of work the group of outstanding men has been tentatively identified. During their years as regulars and deputies, it is not unusual to find them in positions within the personnel department or with choice assignments to the most active branch offices. They are befriended by more important men and given special responsibilities. In this way, distinctions within an age group are established and maintained before any rank differences appear. Resignations during the early years also eliminate some of the most dissatisfied and unsuited newcomers.

The differentials inherent in the first assignments are important in subsequent career patterns. While a talented young man must wait a long time for his first promotion, and although his salary remains uniformly low, hard work and thorough application will allow him to establish a competitive advantage over his age mates during this period. Once he gains informal recognition for his talents, he will be assigned more challenging work, and his position as part of the A group will be secured. Much later, the important reward of promotion to chief will be granted, but only if during the preceding fifteen or so years he has continued to do well. Gratification, in the sense of promotion to high rank, is delayed in this arrangement, although gratifying signs of informal recognition are forthcoming earlier.

PERSONAL CHARACTER AND PROMOTION

Quite patently, the goal of the system is to promote the best men from each age set into the ranks of leadership. The question, what constitutes "best" in the eyes of management, is the next we must consider. Two facts of Uedagin life appear to be of particular relevance here. First, because of the long apprenticeship in each rank before promotion and because there is no career pattern of change from company to company, all men are judged according to their performance over a long period of time. Qualities of personal charm and persuasiveness are of little significance in this situation, compared to the value of persistent, dependable, and careful work. The single most common term applied to those who succeed is *majime,* "serious," the same term applied to favored applicants by the interviewing bank directors. In practice, seriousness is demonstrated by hard, loyal work, courtesy to others, and moderate behavior, all displayed over an extended period.[5]

Supervisors of the training program are quick to observe and discredit those new recruits possessing flamboyant charm, but lacking in persistence or modesty. Several trainees who by American standards would be marked for leadership because of their self-confident manner were warned on numerous occasions that they lacked "seriousness" and would soon have a reputation as undependable. Certainly, there are charming people who have succeeded in Uedagin, but a crucial measure of character is the requirement that hard work and impressive performance not be transitory. The delayed promotion pattern, the value placed on persistence, and the "lifetime employment" situation, thus, reinforce one another. The bank's leaders, men who view their own success as reflecting these standards continue the same system of judgment when they evaluate today's generation.

A second fact of Uedagin life that influences promotions is the organization of work into branch and section units. This places a premium on persons who are able to work well in groups and eventu-

---

5 Adams and Kokayashi (1969:103) note this emphasis on the long haul in the evaluation of ability when he observes, "The Japanese consider that not before the age of about thirty-five will a man's abilities be fully demonstrated." This is not a uniquely Japanese attitude, as evidenced by the characterization of promotion in the small U. S. bank Argyris studied. One employee said the general situation implied "work hard, have patience, you'll be advanced [1954:65]." It is worth speculating about the existence of a universal tendency for banks to have relatively slow, but steady promotion systems. See for example Murry (1958).

ally to lead them. *Kyōchōsei,* "cooperativeness" or "harmoniousness," is the term used to generalize this quality. It appears as a regular item on the personal evaluation sheet. Most people are judged adequate by the standard of group participation, but there are a few who are particularly outstanding, and there are others who are notably deficient. Those who are deficient in kyōchōsei, no matter how intelligent, creative, or serious, are unlikely to be promoted very high in Uedagin. As leaders of office groups they would be likely to fail, and since there are no middle management positions which do not involve group leadership, their chances are slim. *Ningen kankei,* "human relations," is a phrase often heard during discussions of promotions and individual character.[6] In Uedagin, to ignore human relations is a disastrous mistake, and to be particularly inept at them is a personal tragedy.

A person's health, intelligence, industry, and vitality are all important qualities in promotion deliberations, as we might expect. Evaluations are, in essence, the product of a relatively undifferentiated set of impressions of the whole person. Those considered top leadership material are generally men with a surplus of energy, intelligence, and ambition, qualities they must learn to control and discipline in order to survive the long years of subordination to the organization, their superiors, and their office groups. For the average man this subordination may not be particularly difficult, but for talented and vital people it can be a struggle.[7] Uedagin's leadership is formed from this crucible of organizational discipline, a fact that may help to explain the leadership's special interest in Zen and other aspects of Japanese spiritualism (see chapter 9). Learning self-control and accepting the limits and burdens of a particular situation are goals of such training. Young men of energy and intelligence have great difficulty accepting organizational constraints, but their personal growth in the face of such problems makes them excellent leaders, according to the common view. Company changers, no matter how talented, are suspect by this perspective, for they appear to be avoiding the challenge of organizational discipline. Obviously, the promotion system produces a

6 Most popular books on personnel management for supervisory and managerial-level people stress the importance of ningen kankei. Emphasis is placed on close relations outside work and utilization of group discussion to draw everyone together.

7 In the training of new members, the tests of endurance are viewed as affecting different personality types differently. Men with ambition and energy are to learn self-control, while those more passive in character are to learn confidence and drive. All participate together in the same activities, but some events seem more slanted to disrupt passivity and others to teach discipline.

certain type of leader. A dynamic man who has learned to accept the nature of organization the hard way is the ideal person for top posts, while those who are harnessed and diligent but lacking in power make ideal subordinates.

Related to the issue of self-control is the value placed on hardship (*kurō*). One revealing example of this involves the rank of researcher (*chōsa yaku*). As noted, under close scrutiny this rank turns out to be a place where higher-ranking failures are shelved. The twenty-some chōsa yaku are given only minor tasks. Their basic assignment is to make work for themselves. The hardships of this existential situation occasionally produce reformations of character, and for this reason assignment to the chōsa yaku rank is regarded by the personnel section as a form of therapy. Creating hardships (delayed promotion is another example) as part of an education in character strength is not a constant policy, but it is a perspective that may be applied to a wide range of promotion issues.[8] This stoic outlook is also related to the opinion that because the length of a man's experience and his age are the best measures of his acquaintance with hardship, they are valid measures of his readiness for responsibility. The evaluation of people in terms of kurō definitely favors the older man.

SCHOOL BACKGROUND AND PROMOTION

Uedagin members pay most attention to personal character in cases of promotion to high office. The outstanding individuals are generally recognized and agreed upon, and competition between them focuses on the relative merits of one personality or another. The variable of educational background, however, is also of great and enduring interest. Like the concept of competition within the age set, this is a source of calculations about the average individual's chances for promotion.[9]

Ostensibly, management avoids all discrimination between high school and university graduates. *Nōryokushugi*, "ability-ism," implying judgment on the basis of ability alone, is the official policy, and to illustrate its success the bank can show that presently half of all

---

[8] Ironically, the welfare programs of the organization are at odds with the value placed on hardship, but this is a common paradox in Japan, where male values and dependency are both pronounced. The two inclinations conflict and reinforce each other.

[9] Glazer (1969) reports a survey of Japanese executive opinion that indicates educational background to be one of three major factors governing promotion, the other two being ability and seniority. In industrial situations, where educational differences are more pronounced, this factor would have greater weight than it does in Uedagin, although it is of considerable importance in the bank too.

branch and section chiefs are high school graduates. But, in fact, they are part of a generation that experienced considerable educational disruption during the war years, making their educational background rather unrepresentative. Today, young high school graduates feel they are at a great disadvantage in comparison to those of their age group with a university degree. They are not as bitter about this as they are discouraged. They give up easily, is a common remark. Precise figures comparing promotions of high school and university graduates are not available, but we can consider some observations. Of late, deputies promoted at age thirty-three (the top men in the age group) are almost entirely university graduates. Of the ninety published biographical sketches of newly appointed chiefs I collected, only forty-eight contain information about educational background. Of these, thirty-six (75 percent) are university graduates. The large number of cases of unstated educational background prohibits too much reliance on this figure, but we can also note that the ratio of university graduates to high school graduates among Uedagin men above forty years old is at least one to three, and by this we may interpret the bank's statistic showing half of all chiefs to be high school graduates as an indication that university graduates have actually enjoyed a much better chance to reach chief level. Finally, of the present fifteen members of the board of directors, only two are high school graduates. In summary, high school graduates are not excluded from high positions in Uedagin, but their chances are considerably less than others their age with a university education.

A related topic of interest is the apparent advantage graduates of particular universities have in the competition. This is a serious concern to the personnel department as well as to the average member. The basic question in the Uedagin case is not whether any one university clique (*gakkubatsu*) controls the organization, but whether there is a tendency to favor men from more notable universities. There is no resolution to this debate, for it is impossible to determine conclusively whether the school's name or the individual's ability explain any specific promotion. But it is an accepted fact that graduates of the region's leading national university, one of the most difficult universities to enter in the nation, have done very well in Uedagin, much better that the average of all men with a university degree, and in general this has begun with their first assignments after training. The personnel section is anxious to avoid my appearance of favoritism, and it considers the maintenance of a balance between men of various universities to be an important policy. It is feared that should the bank gain a reputation as a company favoring a given school, morale will suffer, and many good prospects from other universities will avoid Uedagin.[10] Yet, most people assume that graduates of top universities are virtually guaranteed chief rank.

CONNECTIONS

Another topic of general speculation is the influence of connections (*conne*) on the promotion process. It seems clear that a small number of sons of directors and of important bank customers do receive advantages in early assignments and promotions. More obscure connections, those involving outside sources of less influence or personal ties (e.g., senpai-kohai), are more difficult to spot and document. In some firms, personal connections and factions are believed to dominate company politics and related issues. The drama of factional struggles makes good reading, so journalistic attention often focuses on this sort of subject. Uedagin, to my knowledge, is not engrossed in this kind of intrigue. The preferences of the head of the personnel department and the president are the determining factors in the selection of chiefs and department heads, but up to that point more regular, less personalized, decisions are made. Had my research focused on the managerial level of the bank, it might have produced a rich portrait of factional intrigue, but well-informed people said that the president's power keeps such developments in check.

DEMOTION

Uedagin not only prefers not to fire members, it also avoids having to demote them in rank. This is best illustrated by the only demotions in rank that do occur, namely, the shifting of some men from chief and

[10] The competition to get ahead in Japanese society begins early in the educational career of some students, especially those fortunate enough to live in urban areas where particularly good schools exist. To come from families that are interested in advancement and wealthy enough to afford special schooling provides clear advantages in the highly competitive entrance examinations of the best preparatory elementary, middle, and high schools. While the odds favor these students in the university examinations, candidates less favored by special schooling also succeed in entering the top national universities. Of those graduates of the region's national university entering Uedagin, some were upper middle class and others clearly lower middle class (a carpenter's son, for example). These university graduates have the upper hand as far as promotions go, it is believed. Following them are graduates of prefectural public and private universities. The boys from private universities are generally upper middle class in economic background. Some are academically talented, but others are not. All, however, have an advantage over the high school graduates, who, primarily for economic reasons, did not go on to university. See Passin (1965).

assistant chief to researcher. This is the most extreme form of demotion, and even then an attempt is made to preserve the individual's dignity and status by giving him the title of researcher, one that outside the bank implies importance. Demotion otherwise does not involve rank, but rather assignment to smaller, less important offices. The size of a man's command is a secondary measure of his importance, and without losing the rank of chief a man may decline radically in terms of responsibility. He will immediately suffer a corresponding drop in prestige and authority in the process. Smaller branches are generally situated in more rural areas, and reassignment to such isolated and unimportant places is a kind of exile worse than a simple reduction of command. In a similar fashion, less competent men in the ranks below chief also tend to be given positions in the less important offices, some of them spending almost their entire careers moving from small branch to small branch and never experiencing the more glamorous and more challenging work of the main office. In these ways people judged incompetent or undesirable are shuffled about in the system without being dismissed or demoted. The problem of making room within each rank for the advancement of younger men of talent is affected only by the transfer of chiefs to the researcher rank, a rather insignificant factor. Otherwise, each age group must wait for places to open up as the result of company expansion, reorganization, and retirement. Early retirement at age fifty-five is often explained as "making room for younger men" or "giving the next group a chance to lead."

CORRELATIONS BETWEEN AGE AND PROMOTION

The essential character of the promotion system is now before us, but its rationale and significance remain unclear. Certainly, age is an important factor in the equation, yet why this is so is a question that remains unanswered. The criterion of age does not fit neatly into the dichotomy between "ascribed" and "achieved" status so popular in sociological analysis. Age is clearly not an exclusive indication of achievement in the usual meaning of the term, nor is it representative of or a label for ascription, if by that we mean inherited status. All persons are equally endowed with the capacity for aging, and the only factor which separates them and makes them unequal in this regard is time itself. Age may, however, represent achievement, in the sense of representing the accomplishments of experience. In instances in which skill and wisdom are equated with age (the criterion of length of experience), an age-based hierarchy reflects a form of achieved status. On the other hand, in situations where differences based on experience are less valued and achievement is measured according to other more variable criteria, the age factor may be viewed as similar to ascribed status.

The value of experience and the equation of seniority with ability are noteworthy elements of traditional Japanese thought. Experience and age have long been regarded as major indications of a person's reliability and skill. In traditional Japanese arts, for example, training and personal development have taken considerable time, and age has been regarded as a mark of accomplishment. Such examples are innumerable in the more traditional areas of Japanese life today,[11] and the close association of age and rank in Uedagin is intelligible and defensible in terms of this deep-rooted logic. Accordingly, it is inappropriate to separate seniority and ability as conflicting principles, even though, as is readily appreciated by all Japanese, the two are obviously opposed in some cases.

A second consideration is the "years of service to the organization" (*nenkō joretsu*) aspect. To the extent that promotion is a reward (rather than an attempt to match the abilities of men with work requirements), the "years of service" perspective may be relevant in a different sense. For example, a small number of older men are made chiefs of rather insignificant branches, more as rewards for loyal service than because they have outstanding talent. Extreme cases are, however, exceptional, and men do retire without being promoted to chief or even deputy.

The average age of the bank's directors is over fifty-five, of course, and the president is sixty-six. Before his death the former president remained active in Uedagin past his seventieth birthday, serving as chairman of the board. Where age is respected as a sign of experience, older men will be more able than younger men to influence and lead others. For this same reason older men will have comparatively greater confidence in themselves, and, as a result, their performances will be enhanced. Even some directorships, however, are said to be given as rewards for loyal service, rather than in anticipation of future contribution.

People are not blind to the possibility that younger men may be superior in energy and in knowledge of modern techniques, but overall leadership of the organization requires other qualities as well. A

---

[11] The occupations in Japan in which experience is recognized as of great significance include the arts, scholarship, medicine, politics, government, and even most traditional sports.

director should preferably have spent long years serving Uedagin in the ranks. His career at its conclusion should have a history of persistent contribution to the organization and be an example for others. He should be thoroughly respected by those around him. Furthermore, to get along well with the leaders of other organizations (older men themselves) being at least forty-five is a virtual necessity for a director.

Nor are older people denied the power to transform society. Led primarily by older men during this century of modernization, the country has shown a remarkable ability to adapt to the times and to technological innovation. The older man, if he is a wise and confident person, is well suited to encourage change, due to the fact that at the end of a long career, he stands alone at the top of a responsive hierarchy. While his knowledge of details may be antiquated, his ability to wield power in the organization is supreme, and this skill is often the most valuable in effecting change without causing paralyzing opposition or disorganization.

It is incorrect, however, to say the president holds his position by virtue of age alone. He is president because, over a long period symbolized by his age, he served the organization, developed his skills, and achieved the top position among his contemporaries. Time brings his personal qualities into focus, turns them into qualifications, and ultimately they become inspirations for his followers.

There are two more perspectives to be considered, and each potentially redefines the nature of Uedagin promotions. The first, the labor market approach, would see promotions as a factor in the competition for resources between companies. This is hardly significant for Uedagin because of the low rate of quitting by men, most of which comes before the time of promotions. The absence of market leverage is but a background factor. The second concept, of internal supply and demand, serves only to explain fluctuations in the lower age of promotion for each rank. Experience and service remain the more essential considerations in terms of the fundamentals of the system.

DISCUSSION

A thoroughgoing age-ordered organization is among the most regular and impersonal imaginable. In it, individual qualities must be subordinated to the mechanics of time. Uedagin's system is strongly flavored by such regularity, yet a strictly egalitarian operation of the seniority principle is neither expected nor possible. The bank has no intention of creating a chief position for every man over age thirty-

eight. This would be too costly. It would decrease the value of the
rank as a reward and thus strip the system of a key incentive. It
would also thoroughly confuse the ordering of responsibility and authority.

On the other hand, official disregard of the age-set concept and of
the years of experience and service perspective would certainly de-
moralize large numbers of Uedagin people. Yoshino has succinctly
described the reasons for this:

> Under the traditional pattern of career advancement, one is re-
> warded for his competence only after he proves his ability to
> the satisfaction of everyone concerned. There is an insistence
> on a general consensus that the person up for promotion is, in
> fact, competent and deserves to be given special recognition for
> it. Given the Japanese organizational climate, this insistence
> has its rationale. First of all, because of the high degree of col-
> lectivity orientation, opportunities to manifest one's individual
> competence are highly limited. Secondly, rewarding an indi-
> vidual for his competence prematurely in an intensely collec-
> tivity oriented organization (before subordinates, peers and
> superiors are convinced of his merits) is likely to breed resent-
> ment, disrupting the group harmony and adversely affecting
> the morale of the group and, therefore, its performance [1968:
> 237].

What he observes to be a general rule holds for the Uedagin case.
The exceptionally rapid promotion of one or a few individuals would
almost certainly undermine the motivation and commitment of the
rest. In their eyes, the seniority system safeguards the spirit of more
or less equal respect and opportunity, and it mitigates against the influence of cliques and other forms of favoritism in the organization.
Since all begin low and move up in a similar manner, older men are
as likely to resent too rapid promotion of young men as are their peers.

Although it is a clear statistical fact that students from rural areas
and poor families are at a disadvantage in gaining a public university
education, there are enough graduates of national universities from
such backgrounds to confuse the issue of special advantage. In any
event, the average Uedagin man, who enjoys an average promotion
pattern, prefers to see the customary limits on individual differences
retained. After all, everyone works equally hard for the bank, he
thinks.

The seniority factor is also consistent with the widely observed inclination of Japanese to accept authority most readily from older men.

The present promotion scheme prevents the development of what informants say would be a much more uncomfortable and seemingly more authoritarian situation, namely a hierarchy in which age was not recognized.

The ideal of membership, one that views relations among members as between equals in terms of commitment and interest in the organization, is also represented by the slow and "more-or-less" equal emphases. Women are, of course, a glaring exception. In sum, differences of rank and authority, although necessary, should be palatable, and the age criterion advances this purpose.

That promotion, like membership status, can be used as a means of making the organization more inclusive, especially when alienation increases, is exemplified in the 1970 promotion of the first three women to the rank of regular. Like other banks in the seventies, Uedagin finds itself not only increasingly dependent on female labor, but faced with the greater assertiveness of today's young women. The response has been to begin to allow women, particularly those who do not marry early, something like a career path leading to low-level supervisory positions over other women. That this may not be the end of the road is indicated by the 1973 promotion of a woman as high as section chief in another large bank.

The bank's promotion system is not, however, the only way talent, authority, and work are adjusted in the organization. We have seen that although promotion is a slow process, future differences of rank become highly predictable just a short time after any age group is assembled. This early informal recognition of differences achieves semiformal status beginning with the first (A group) promotions to regular at age twenty-eight. Before and after this event there are other sources of recognition for those judged more talented, including: a greater familiarity on the part of the personnel section, the bank's leaders, and their own office chief; assignments to important offices and branches; and special assignments and responsibilities. In all of these, one can read the message of who is highly regarded.

More importantly, the abilities of younger men are not lost to the organization during the period when they are low in rank. Creative planning, reorganization, special projects, and analyses are all kinds of work that are not directly ordered by considerations of rank. There are, for example, instances of young deputies making basic strategy for the entire branch system, assisted by a group of bright, hand-picked regulars. The ultimate authority over such projects lies far above the young men, but they are allowed to conceive the plans free of senior interference. At the branch and section level, the opportunities provided by group discussions and other informal contacts also open the bank to influence from low-ranking young men with ideas and energy. Opportunities of this kind are not, however, institutionalized. They depend on both the flexibility of older leaders in delegating special creative tasks and the initiative of younger men in accepting the challenges of doing work far above their formal authority. When both requirements are met and integrated, the system works exceptionally well, but when one or the other is missing, the liabilities of the age-ordered hierarchy cannot be erased. A characteristically Japanese question about organizations is how well the older leaders utilize young men of talent.

The Uedagin solution to the rather abstract issue of the relationship between equality, authority, ability, and the division of labor in a complex organization is somewhat different from that of the typical American business arrangement. While a semblance of equality is maintained by the seniority principle, and while authority ultimately rests with the senior men who lead the organization, and while men of rank have authority and influence over task-oriented groups, the creation of new policy and numerous special assignments can be delegated far down in the organization. This may be typical of large bureaucratic systems, but it has a special flavor in Japan.

The relationship between older leaders and younger men of talent is, of course, central here, for they must cooperate and trust each other, if the two separate but equally crucial parts of the arrangement are to fit together. Responsibility for the outcome of the tasks cannot be separated from the formal system, just as the latitude to do original work must be given to men of lower ranks. The success of the technique of using young talent, therefore, hinges on good working relationships between men of quite different age and rank, the senior often covering for his subordinate, more than supervising him. Obviously, a most satisfactory basis of cooperation in this case is the senpai-kohai pattern, and in fact this is the model for and image of successful teamwork along the vertical, informal lines within the bank.

This informal delegation of what we would view as leadership functions has repercussions for another issue facing Japanese companies today. University graduates are increasingly looking for job situations that will allow them to show their talents quickly. No matter how naive this ambition may be, it is clear that those working in Uedagin who view themselves as talented and who do not receive informal recognition are likely to be dissatisfied. Similarly, those who are recognized are likely to enjoy their work without too much regard for rank because they are fairly secure in the knowledge that they will be promoted as soon as it is feasible for their age group. It is the dynamic, growing company that most often gains a reputation for using its younger men well and thus attracts talent easily. Again, growth can be understood as highly beneficial to the organization, regardless of the profit picture that results.

7

WHO GETS WHAT, WHEN

There are a number of reasons why responsible tasks may be assigned to young men, low in rank, without their insistence on receiving either promotions or higher pay for performing such important work. It is highly improbable that they will leave Uedagin for higher rank or pay elsewhere. Such demands, furthermore, would be regarded with great disfavor by others, high and low. And, as just explained, the speed of promotions is governed by the notion that considerable experience is a requisite for each advance. Finally, salaries are related in only a small way either to rank or to actual work performed. This aspect of the individual-bank relationship is the focus of the following chapter, in which the relative weight of seniority, need, and ability in governing the allocation of rewards will be analyzed.

In no sense may we limit ourselves to a consideration of a single salary system in our description of what people receive in exchange for their work. Salaries and other direct payments are distributed through a set of overlapping systems so complicated that many of the younger men admit to understanding only its more important aspects. In addition, noncash benefits assume many forms, and considerable detailed explanation is required to untangle the factors governing their distribution. Only a patient attempt to understand the full range of considerations will permit us to grasp the underlying character of remuneration—a matter of considerable importance to the overall understanding of the bank-individual relationship.[1]

Salaries, granted to everyone on a monthly basis, are the most im-

[1] Three articles in Ballon (1969), one by the editor and the others by Tomita and Isomura, discuss specific aspects of the remuneration systems of both industry and government bureaucracy. Much of the material they present is valuable and is in accordance with what is described for Uedagin. Ballon's presentation of a statistical survey of the major components of salary, bonus, retirement, and other remuneration is particularly thorough. Dore (1973), chapter 3, should also be consulted.

portant form of payment. Supplementing salaries is a bonus paid in cash every July and December. These two are the regular, direct payments granted by the bank, and for most purposes an individual's income is calculated on this basis. The personnel section is responsible for salaries and bonuses. Other benefits including housing, insurance, medical care, and retirement payments come under the jurisdiction of the welfare section. We will take up each of these in turn, beginning with the monthly salary.

SALARY

The formula for calculating what each member earns each month is an imposing one: base pay (A) plus adjustment of base pay (B) plus temporary increase (C) plus family allowance (D) plus housing allowance (E) plus job pay (F) = monthly salary. Adding to the complication is the fact that some of these components are governed by even more involved formulas. All of the following statistical material on salary components is for the year 1967.

A. Base pay (kihonkyū)

The most significant element in determining how much people take home each month is their base pay. The exact proportions will differ, but base pay generally constitutes about 60 percent of total monthly pay. This most important component, interestingly, is not a reflection of job description, education, or estimated potential. Years of service alone is the determining factor. Each additional year with the bank brings an automatic increase in the base pay of members and quasi members, and though the increment of growth varies from time to time, the overall trend recently has been for an annual 5 percent increase.[2] Figure 8 and Table 1 illustrate this for 1967 in greater detail.

[2] Exceptions to the rule of 5 percent annual increase come at the beginning and at the end of each career. We have noted that Uedagin makes it a policy to avoid discrimination between university and high school graduates on the principle that four years of experience in the bank are equal to four years of education as preparation for working in the bank. High school graduates entering banks and other institutions today are offered starting salaries lower than those offered to university graduates, and Uedagin makes it a practice to offer no more than the going rate. This creates a problem, namely that the base pay of high school graduates, if increased by 5 percent annually for four years, would not be equal to the base pay of incoming university graduates of the same age. To resolve this, the bank boosts the rate of increase for new high school graduates so they have the same base pay as university graduates their age.

Starting salaries for high school and university graduates entering Uedagin in 1968 were:

Base Pay (thousands of yen)

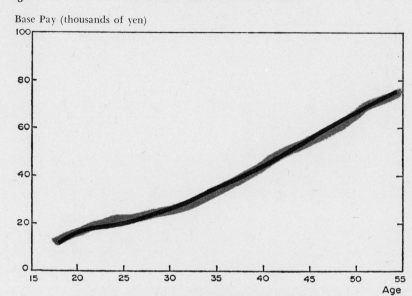

FIG. 8. The relationship of age and base pay (1967).

TABLE 1

1967 Rate of Annual Increase in Monthly Base Pay

Age	Annual amount of increase (in yen)	As a percentage of total base pay
19–23	1,900	13.9
23–24	950	5.0
24–25	1,500	7.5
25–27	1,200	5.6
27–28	1,250	5.3
28–30	1,300	5.2
30–33	1,700	6.2
33–35	1,750	5.4
35–44	1,900	5.3
44–50	2,300	4.3
50–55	2,250	2.9

	Base Pay	Temporary Supplement	Adjustment	Housing	Total
High School Graduate	¥13,600	¥4,100	¥800		¥18,500
University Graduate	¥18,300	¥5,000	¥1,700	¥1,000	¥26,000

As long as the person continues to be enrolled in the bank as a member or quasi member, he will enjoy a similar constant improvement in his income.

B. Adjustment pay (chōseikyū)

This element of the equation is granted according to rank. A man promoted to chief, for example, would enjoy an increase in adjustment pay that would be equivalent to between 7 percent and 9 percent of his base pay (depending on his age at promotion and the consequent amount of his base pay). For someone never promoted above regular, however, this element would amount to only 3 percent of his base pay at the time of retirement.

TABLE 2
Adjustment Pay Distribution

Type of work (rank)	Amount
Department, branch, section chiefs, and vice-chiefs	Y5,400–6,600
Deputy	Y4,200–5,000
Regular	Y2,300–2,600
Common	Y800–1,600
Quasi members	Y800–1,300

C. Temporary supplement (rinjikyū)

Like base pay this component is applied without regard for rank or ability, but unlike base pay it does not increase with years of service. It is virtually the same for all Uedagin people. Above age twenty-five it is Y5,000, and below that age it is Y4,100. In a minor way it favors the young, for the temporary supplement in an eighteen year old's salary represents 15 percent of the total while for a man in his fifties it is less than 5 percent.

Toward the end of a person's career the percentage increase dips until during the last five years the growth rate of base pay is down to 2.9 percent. One reason for the decision to slow down the growth of base pay during the last ten years could be that pensions and lump-sum retirement pay are calculated on the basis of base pay during that period. Of course, the distinction between percentage and real increases should be kept in mind, since even at a lower percentage the real increase of latter years is large.

D. Family allowance (kazokukyū)

The family allowance is given to heads of households for the support of dependents without regard for years of service or rank considerations. The standard rate of pay is: Y4,600 for the first dependent (usually the wife), Y1,700 for the second dependent, and Y600 for the third dependent.

Every Uedagin man, that is, receives a salary increase when he marries, and when he has his first and second child. Other relatives, such as brothers and sisters, count as one of the two allowable dependents if they are officially registered as dependents of the principal's household and are under twenty-one years old. Adult relatives and parents are, however, ruled out. Obviously, Uedagin women do not qualify for this payment because they leave the bank before beginning their own families.

The full amount awarded to a man with a wife and two children is small compared to the full cost of their support, but the increase it represents in the monthly salary of young men in their early thirties is considerable. For them, the family allowance accounts for 10 percent or more of their total monthly salary. Over a full year the family allowance is equal to approximately one and one-half times the average monthly salary. For older men, the steady growth of base pay, coupled with any increases resulting from promotions, makes the family allowance of less and less significance in total income.

E. Housing allowance (jutakukyū)

Regardless of what form of housing he actually occupies, every member receives a small housing allowance. In many cases it is not much, and never is it the full amount persons must pay for housing, but it does help. Variations in amount are governed by differences in seniority, but even the top amount would cover no more than a third of what a family would expect to pay for a modest apartment in public housing.

At one time or another, bank policy makers, it seems, determined that marriage was better made after age twenty-five. There is no other explanation for the arbitrary distinction that grants a larger allowance to married men twenty-six and over.

F. Job pay (shokumukyū)

My literal translation here can be misleading, for job pay is granted on the basis of rank, starting with regular and increasing rather steeply with each promotion thereafter. Job pay is the major salary component designed to reward ability and outstanding performance.

TABLE 3
Job Pay Distribution

Type of work (rank)	Amount
Department head	Y28,500
Department vice-chief	Y25,500
Branch chief	Y19,500–25,500
Section chief	Y19,500–23,500
Assistant chief	Y14,000–18,000
Investigator	Y14,000–16,000
Researcher	Y14,000–17,500
Acting branch or section chief	80% of regular chief's pay
Deputy	Y10,300–12,800
Director of extension office	Y11,300
Regular	Y 2,500–3,500

From the time of promotion to deputy, job pay accounts for from 15 percent to 25 percent of the individual's monthly salary. Young men promoted ahead of their age group to deputy and chief find their job pay to be proportionally a larger part of their total salary than older men of the same rank, since a young man's base pay is less.

Within each rank, there are several small step increases in job pay. As a rule these are made after a certain number of years in the rank.

In addition to these regular components of monthly salary, there are a few supplements that arise from special situations, namely, a living supplement, a special work supplement, and a commuting allowance.

All of the components mentioned are combined to arrive at an individual's monthly salary. In order to illustrate this and to present graphically some of the implications of the salary system, I have constructed Figure 9. It charts the increases in salary according to age, promotion, and other factors for a selected individual career. To define this individual career seven assumptions have been made:

(1) The individual is male.
(2) At age 27 he is promoted to regular and he marries.
(3) His first child is born when he is 30.
(4) His second child is born when he is 34.
(5) At age 34 he is promoted to deputy.

Yen (thousands)

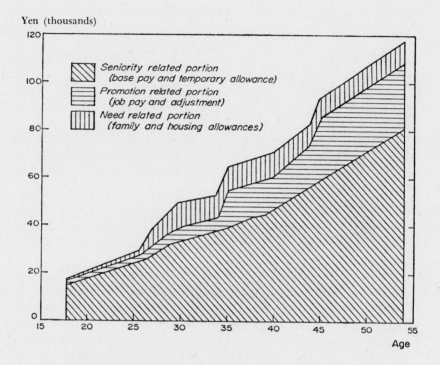

FIG. 9. The monthly salary pattern of a selected career.

(6) At age 45 he is promoted to chief.

(7) His first child becomes twenty-one when he is 51.

While this career is not an average one, since it includes promotion to chief (a rank which only about 25 percent of the men can expect to reach), it is characteristic in terms of the timing of marriage, the arrival of children, and the timing of earlier promotions. To permit us to visualize the shifting proportion of total salary governed by considerations of years of service, rank, and living needs, we have combined the components of salary into three basic subdivisions:

x: The portion related to years of service (base pay and temporary allowance).

y: The portion related to rank (job pay and adjustment).

z: The portion related to living needs (family allowance and housing allowance).

The overwhelming importance of the portion related to length of service is readily apparent from Figure 9. Even for a department head, who receives a larger amount of job pay than our selected individual at age fifty-four, years-of-service pay comprises almost two-thirds of his total monthly salary. Rank-related increases assume an important role in differentiating the salaries of men of the same age, particularly in mid and late career, yet, the maximum rank-related difference is never as large as the difference in base pay between men separated by ten or more years of service.

An upper limit based on rank has been placed on the base pay scale. This actually precludes such situations as a fifty-four-year-old ordinary receiving a monthly salary larger than a forty-year-old chief. The full schedule of upper limits on base pay reads:

Ordinary	Y53,000
Regular	Y58,000
Deputy	Y65,000
Chief	Y90,000

The maximum possible difference in salary related to differences in rank for persons of the same age appears in the comparison of two men at retirement: one a department head, the other an ordinary who has never been promoted. The former would be receiving a salary twice the amount of the latter. This represents the extreme. Characteristically, salary differences within an age group become significant around age thirty-eight, when a few in the group are promoted to chief. From that time differences between chiefs and regulars amount to approximately 25 percent of a chief's salary. Considering that more than 90 percent are promoted to regular by age thirty-three and more than 75 percent to deputy by age forty, we may conclude that the age-oriented promotion policy also serves to keep salaries rather uniform for age mates.

Obviously, the Uedagin system does not operate exclusively by the "equal pay for equal work" principle nor by the ideal of "work to one's ability and receive to one's need." Although based primarily on years of service, it contains considerations of need and of individual reward. Its strength may well lie in this ambiguity, since diverse goals such as family security and career motivation, may be realized in such a mixed approach. Nor is the criterion of years of service inimical to either individual or company goals, for to a large degree ability and personal need are or can be correlated to years of service.

BONUS

Until 1969, the bonus was calculated essentially as a multiple of an individual's monthly base pay. The formula was:

(3.30 × base pay) plus (.30 × temporary supplement) plus (2.75 ~ 3.00 × job pay) plus (Y2,500) = bonus.

The base pay multiple was negotiated each year between the union and management, but it generally remained close to three and one-half times monthly base pay. The centrality of base pay and its multiple in this equation emphasized seniority. In 1969, this emphasis was reduced when a new formula was established:

(base pay) plus (3.5 × job pay) plus (Y20,000) plus (sum based on evaluation of performance) = bonus.

This represents an obvious shift toward making the bonus more responsive to rank and performance, at some loss of influence for the seniority principle. In particular, the shift to a 3.5 multiplier for job pay works contrary to the interests of older men with low rank. The addition of a performance evaluation is another new twist. Until 1969, the bonus was commonly viewed as automatic and a regular part of the salary system, even though some leaders still wished to interpret it as a sharing of the bank's profits. The performance evaluation factor upset both of these interpretations, making the bonus, in part, a reward for individual good work. The value of this factor may range from zero to eighty thousand yen, and, in theory, differences of this extent may appear in the amounts of bonus granted to people of the same age and rank. In practice, little change was noticed. Only those chiefs whose branches performed very poorly were penalized by lower bonuses.[3]

Table 4 presents a compilation of the data on salary and bonus presented so far. Among the many interesting comparisons that are possible using this table, we find that an average department head earns 2.3 times what an average regular earns; that women of ordinary rank earn on the average only 60 percent of what men of their

[3] Taking the bank's figures for the average base pay and average total monthly salary for the different ranks, we can calculate what an average bonus would be under the 1967 and 1969 systems. The results are surprising. The 1969 formula (excluding the performance factor) produces a smaller average bonus for every rank, making the increment based on evaluation crucial to whether an individual's bonus improves or not under the new system.

TABLE 4
Average Annual Total Pay by Rank (1967)

Rank	Average base pay	Average salary	Average bonus	Base pay percentage of salary	Total payments
Department head	80,000 (estimate)	121,000 (estimate)	348,000 (estimate)	.65	2,148,000 (estimate)
Chief, assistant chief	59,000	98,000	251,700	.60	1,578,400
Deputy	43,000	73,000	174,900	.59	1,235,800
Regular	33,000	57,000	119,900	.59	923,800
Ordinary (male)	23,000	35,000	78,400	.61	576,800
Ordinary (female)	17,000	22,000	58,600	.75	381,200
Quasi member	22,000	38,000	75,000	.63	606,000

rank earn; that quasi members and ordinary men have, on the average, about the same annual total; and that, for men, promotion represents the following percentage increases in average annual pay:

Ordinary to regular	—60%
Regular to deputy	—33%
Deputy to chief	—27%
Chief to department head	—36%

The difference in average earnings between men and women of ordinary rank derives from two factors: the higher average age (and thus higher base pay, bonus, etc.) of men in the rank, and the welfare supplements paid to men but not to women.

WELFARE BENEFITS AND FACILITIES

Housing is undoubtedly the most important of the many contributions the welfare section makes to the lives of Uedagin members. As noted, Uedagin has a number of bachelors' dormitories. Presently 65 percent of the company's bachelors live in one of these, 27 percent live in rented quarters, and 8 percent live at home. The bank also owns 250 units for families, including both apartment buildings and single-family dwellings. Since this number is far from sufficient, it rents another 645 units on a contract basis. The annual outlay for this rental in 1967 is reported to have been Y47,407,000. This effort accounts for only 900 units out of approximately 1,350 required to house every Uedagin member's family. The remaining people, some by their own choice, find housing on their own and receive a housing supplement from the welfare section. The supplement is determined by the guidelines governing the bank's rental of housing:

Ordinary	Y5,000
Regular	Y6,000
Deputy	Y7,000
Assistant chief	Y8,000

This amount is increased by 1,000 for large cities, but is still insufficient to cover more than approximately half of the rental of an average apartment. Women, once more, do not share in these benefits. Men of higher rank receive substantially better housing than their subordinates. The president's house, a modest upper-middle-class one, is also owned by the bank. Reportedly, it will be given to him when he retires.

Special loans for the purchase of private housing are also available. It is common for Uedagin people to buy land in their late thirties and to build in their middle to late forties.[4] While loans are available to all members, the amount is limited for lower-ranking people, and interest rates are higher for younger members. There were 581 such loans in 1968.[5]

A variety of welfare and recreation facilities are also offered by the bank. For those families that wish to keep their children in school in Aoyama following transfer to another city, the bank maintains a student dormitory for them. This is actually an old house with a retired member to serve as caretaker and guardian. The gym, tennis court, and other facilities connected with the bachelors' dormitory and neighboring welfare building in Aoyama are also available to all.

Care for all these facilities, including the seven bachelors' dormitories and the mountain lodge, requires a considerable staff. Of the thirty-four people in the welfare section, nineteen are attached to one

---

[4] See chapter 11 for further discussion of the significance of this pattern in the lives of Uedagin families.

[5] According to several popular magazines many firms have begun offering larger and more attractive loans to their younger members as an alternative to the construction of more company housing. They have found that young people prefer to live apart from company housing and wish to own their own homes soon.

of these facilities. Most are quasi members, but there are also several commissionees (retired former members) and at least one man of researcher rank.

The mountain lodge is of particular interest since the bank has recently invested a considerable amount of money in its construction.[6] Located on a mountain side with a lovely view, it has room for seventy guests. Another one hundred sleep outside in tents during the two-day bank summer camp in July. Ironically, this costly facility is not utilized extensively, for Uedagin people seldom take more than a few days' vacation, and most go elsewhere. This reluctance to take time off is quite typical of Japanese white-collar workers.

Office group recreation, in comparison, is vigorously pursued. The welfare section supplies financial support for office group trips (about six thousand yen per person per trip), the monthly recreation day events, and the purchases of uniforms and sports equipment. The bank's thirteen hobby clubs and its seven sports teams are also supported with welfare funds.[7] Similarly, money for the three annual bank camping trips (about three hundred people participated in total in 1969) and for the annual arts and crafts show comes from the bank. A compilation of these various expenditures into total and per capita costs is unavailable, and among Uedagin people there is considerable difference of opinion as to the value of these things, depending primarily on whether company-sponsored recreation is personally enjoyed. Certainly, the potential benefit of these programs is considerable when compared to the cost of enjoying such facilities and activities on an independent, individual basis.

The health activities of the welfare section include the rental and reservation of some twenty-five hospital beds, including some at tuberculosis sanitariums. The welfare section sponsors periodic physical examinations, blood tests, and the inoculation of all workers and

6 As Abeggien (1958) mentions, resorts for company personnel are common for large Japanese companies. Uedagin, because it is comparatively new, has fewer such facilities than older banks of its size. It is much more expensive to purchase land and build such resorts today than it was before the war.

7 The hobby-study clubs (kyōyō kurābu) include those for the study of the tea ceremony, haiku, traditional instrumental music (shamisen and koto), needlework, flower arranging, photography, Japanese chess (shogi), traditional reciting (utai) and singing (shigin), calligraphy (shodō), chorus, and band. Between two hundred and three hundred people, all from the Aoyama area, are enrolled in these clubs. Those in branches outside the area have more difficulty organizing exclusively on a Uedagin basis, but in some offices clubs do exist. More typically, people will pursue serious interests in these subjects outside the auspices of the bank and without the support of the welfare section. The sports clubs are fencing (kendō), judō, baseball, tennis, ping pong, badminton, and fishing.

their families during periods of danger from epidemic. A nurse is kept on duty in the main office. Occasionally such things as ~~booklets on nutrition and first-aid are distributed to all families~~. Monthly, in the company magazine, a five-page section is devoted to child care, home economics, and health. The welfare section, because of its jurisdiction over the health of all persons connected with the bank, is given responsibility for sponsoring numerous physical fitness activities, such as the morning and afternoon daily exercises, the monthly recreation day activities, and the like.

The welfare section has also been given charge of certain public-oriented activities, including the distribution of Japanese flags to each household and the organization of the bank's contribution to public campaigns such as the "clean street campaign." It also conducts an annual campaign to collect blood from Uedagin donors. Contributions are to be used in the event anyone associated with the bank should need them.

Incidental benefits originating with the welfare section also include money and materials for business suits and shirts. Summer and winter uniforms and money for accessory clothing, such as blouses, are provided for the women and quasi members.

~~INSURANCE AND OTHER SPECIAL PAYMENTS~~

~~The bank participates in a group-plan life and disability insurance program and offers a second, voluntary group plan as a supplement.~~ In both cases, the ~~costs of the premiums are shared.~~ Almost all of the men and virtually none of the women participate in the voluntary program. The value of the insurance in the bank's program varies with rank. Coverage is extended for five years past the individual's retirement from the bank, but no coverage is extended for women who marry and leave Uedagin. The voluntary group plan allows each individual to elect the amount of coverage he wishes regardless of rank.

In addition to this ~~coverage the bank is prepared to offer further financial assistance for a wide assortment of needs and in certain emergencies.~~ These occasions are times when the union and the mutual aid fund (part company and part individual contributions) also offer financial help. A few examples of these payments are:[8]

(1) In case of death or disabling injury related to work, the following payments will be made by the bank:

8 The full list runs to some thirty items.

Department head	Y1,800,000
Assistant department head	Y1,700,000
Branch/section chief	Y1,600,000
Deputy	Y1,400,000
Regular	Y1,200,000
Ordinary	Y1,000,000
Quasi member	Y1,000,000
Commissionee	Y1,000,000

An additional 300,000 will be paid for wives and 200,000 for each child up to two children.

(2) When a person marries, the bank will pay:

After three years' or less service	Y10,000
Between three to five years' service	Y15,000
Over five years' service	Y20,000
Women on marriage receive	Y 3,000

(3) In cases where destruction is done by some sort of calamity such as fire, typhoon, or flood, the bank will give assistance based on its determination of need.

RETIREMENT PAYMENT AND PENSION

Considering the early age of retirement, the pension is a most significant matter for men facing the uncertainty of working once they have left the bank. At the time of retirement, a lump sum equal to a determined number of months of base pay (at retirement time) is offered. Seniority is the basis of the calculation as illustrated in Table 5. A man must work for Uedagin for at least five years to qualify. No one asked to leave by management may receive this payment, but people who go because of long illness are included.

A similar formula is used to calculate the monthly pension paid after retirement (Table 6).

The pension and lump sum payment along with the extension of life insurance are the final benefits the bank offers. People who have spent their entire careers in the bank are provided with funds sufficient to provide a living for an elderly couple without other income for an estimated two years. The pension of 30 percent of their last base pay is not likely to satisfy their needs after that, and most retirees take a subsequent job out of economic necessity.

Because base pay is used to calculate the payments made to retired personnel, years of service (not difference of rank) is the source of

TABLE 5
Calculation of Lump Sum Retirement Pay

Years of service	Number of months base pay	Years of service	Number of months base pay
1	0.35	15	5.25
2	0.70	16	5.60
3	1.05	17	5.95
4	1.40	18	6.30
5	1.75	19	6.65
6	2.10	20	7.00
7	2.45	21	7.47
8	2.80	22	7.95
9	3.15	23	8.45
10	3.50	24	8.98
11	3.85	25	9.53
12	4.20	26	10.10
13	4.55	27	10.72
14	4.90	28	11.35

TABLE 6
Calculation of Monthly Retirement Pension

Years of service	Percent of base pay at retirement	Years of service	Percent of base pay at retirement
1	0.77	15	13.05
2	1.53	16	14.25
3	2.30	17	15.45
4	3.06	18	16.65
5	3.83	19	17.85
6	4.59	20	19.20
7	5.36	21	20.55
8	6.12	22	21.90
9	6.89	23	23.25
10	7.55	24	24.60
11	8.55	25	25.95
12	9.54	26	27.30
13	10.65	27	28.65
14	11.85	28	30.00

differences in final income, although the limit on base pay for ordinaries and the fact that men of higher rank have had greater opportunities to save for their retirement must not be overlooked. Those men who are selected to continue past retirement as directors and auditors are the only ones who enjoy large incomes during later life; for five more years they continue to receive what have by then become quite substantial salaries and bonuses.[9]

Twice a year the bank holds an elaborate awards ceremony. Branches are praised for their performance and individuals are cited for outstanding contributions to the bank. Citations are accompanied by special diamond, gold, or silver Uedagin lapel pins which the recipients may wear during the following year. Diamond and gold awards are rare; only two or three are given each year. The person awarded must either have an outstanding record as a leader or have performed a noteworthy feat, such as in a recent case when a branch chief apprehended a robber. Silver awards are not so precious: about 150 are passed out yearly to younger, lower-ranking people. That is, each year 5 percent of the company receives special thanks and congratulations for service. Since repeats are infrequent, in a five-year period almost a quarter of the membership is likely to receive silver awards. Neither cash nor anything of material value is given, and the special lapel pins are returned at the end of the year. Just as the bank eschews any commission payments to its salesmen, it refrains from making cash rewards for outstanding performance. All of this is consistent with the understanding of the bank as representing the interests of its members. Uedagin people proudly display their framed citations in their homes and appear satisfied with their awards.

A campaign to sponsor suggestions for greater efficiency is also regularly conducted, and most issues of the Uedagin *News* contain a list of awards to members who have contributed ideas. There are three kinds of awards, and the two most important are worth one thousand and five hundred yen respectively. Their cash value, however, is usually not included in the announcement. Each month about forty persons are recognized in this manner, and perhaps half of these receive one of the small cash prizes.

9 To put retirement pay into the context of general Japanese practice, the reader is urged to consult Fisher (1973).

SUMMARY

This exhaustive and unfortunately rather exhausting enumeration of detail can be discussed at great length, but for our purposes a summary of the more important points will suffice.

It is impossible to determine exactly what any individual of a given rank receives for his work in the bank. We can calculate his monthly salary and bonus, if we know his years of service, rank, and family situation. These are the most important elements in the total picture, but no precise monetary value can be placed on the many benefits offered by the bank according to the variable conditions of need and housing, recreation, and health. Security and personal satisfaction are important issues, and the Uedagin approach is to solve these problems on a community basis. Rather than offering larger salaries and encouraging individual solutions, the bank has opted to finance company housing, recreation, health, and other programs. The total costs of community housing, insurance, recreation, and the like are probably considerably less for both the bank and the individual member. Obviously, all of this is only possible if continuity of membership is assumed, for company investments in such facilities would have little meaning to individuals expecting to depart the company at any time.[10]

The latitude the bank enjoys in its policies governing the distribution of salaries and benefits would not be possible if Uedagin had to find people in an open labor market. The emphasis on years of service, on welfare payments, and even the expenditure for recreation would all become irrational if salaries had to be directly competitive with those in other companies.[11]

[10] The recent shift from investment in new company housing to encouraging private home building is sponsored by the bank's interest in shifting this cost to individuals, who appear to be increasingly willing to pay for better accommodations. Perhaps this trend toward autonomy in housing will be followed in other areas of company welfare as prosperity and the efficiencies of Western-style management continue to influence company policy. But we must also note the continuing programs to build more bachelors' dormitories and the recent completion of two company apartment buildings in large cities. The present housing pattern and the community welfare programs in general are not likely to disappear or even decline radically in the near future.

[11] The history of Japanese wage systems (one subject that can receive a rather detailed historical treatment) and the role of labor market factors are matters of great scholarly interest among industrial relations specialists; see especially Taira (1970) and Cole (1972). This group, however, seems to me overly preoccupied with a distinction between "rationality" (market and profit-oriented calculations) and "traditionalism" (the feelings of involvement, loyalty, and empathy in employment

Of importance in an era of narrowing labor supply and rising labor costs is the fact that the company welfare system is an increasingly expensive one to administer. The overhead (in terms of labor and outlay, to build, maintain, and staff company welfare facilities, and to manage the details of so many programs) is a negative factor receiving more consideration today.

The many differences based on rank and age are deceptive. For men this is essentially an equalitarian system of material reward. Individual and family needs have a place in the calculations, but more significant is the years-of-service factor, which places all men on an equal footing. Given "lifelong employment," seniority distinctions make for a uniformity of income for age mates. Rank and ability distinctions do produce a degree of reward inequality over time, but all Uedagin men can expect to enjoy a high base pay in their forties and fifties. The participation of quasi members in the total reward picture is limited, but they also have a system of rising base pay. Nonmembers, on the other hand, are excluded from automatic years-of-service increases. According to the view of men in the bank, a woman after marriage enjoys the benefits of her husband's base pay increases, whether he works for Uedagin or another company (see chapter 11). Only the nonmember is excluded from the opportunity of an ample income during the middle and late years.

We must also consider the disparity of rewards between people at the very top and very bottom of the system. The president's income from the bank was estimated by one man near him to be about five million yen annually. Like the other directors, he receives some of

---

situations). Their effort is admittedly aimed at exorcising the influence of Abegglen's (1958) interpretation of industrial relations in large Japanese manufacturing firms as "paternalistic," based on lifelong commitment and traditional values. Obviously, this approach, one that is not taken very far by Abegglen, contains many implications distasteful to proponents of the viewpoint that industrial relations are everywhere essentially matters of power and of conflicting interests between employer and employee. I view the history of white-collar, managerial and clerical organization (for men, at least) as different from that of blue-collar workers, and secondly I would argue that the inclusiveness, security, and special wage arrangements found in the large late-Tokugawa commercial houses (not in their mines or factories, however) form a pattern that has not only persisted as the white-collar model but is also the pattern that seemed desirable to male factory workers and was gradually extended to them for business reasons. At any rate, when labor shortages arose, managers, making rational calculations, determined to extend this pattern to groups of factory workers they wished to retain, and over time the "paternalistic" arrangement came to characterize the industrial side of large firms as well as their offices. There is in this much less of a dichotomy between rationality and traditional values than the industrial relations specialists argue, but this is true only if tradition is regarded less an explanatory concept (as in Abegglen) and more as a part of a description of daily reality.

this in the form of large bonuses payed in years of good business. Because the figures are not available, the precise division between regular salary and bonus for directors is impossible to report, but it is asserted that larger bonuses make the major difference between what they and department heads receive (see Table 4). If five million yen is a good approximation, then the president makes about fifteen times as much as the average female member and about eight times as much as the average quasi member.

Some may see such disparity as excessive, yet others may not. In Japan during the time of this study, it was common among management specialists to claim that Japanese executives were underpaid by international standards, and some companies were making a point of raising the salaries of their top men. We should not ignore, however, the fact that the president receives many side benefits. He lives in a company house and has a chauffeur-driven company car and a sizeable expense account, including a golf club membership. These extras are normal for Japan, and, with the exception of the house, no doubt necessary for the conduct of the president's job. Other directors are in slightly more modest circumstances, but they too have considerable resources at their personal disposal. The average man naturally views all of this with great envy, and a common image of the powerful, successful business leader has him gaily enjoying a private party in an expensive nightclub, surrounded by lovely hostesses. In reality, many executives find such a life necessary but tiresome, yet the image and the sense of disparity remain. Whether American executives earn five times as much as the Uedagin president may not matter in the final analysis compared to whether this salary system appears to be equitable to the average Uedagin person. The heavy bonus component in the president's pay may be crucial here, for in times of business downturn his salary is likely to shrink dramatically, and only after heavy cuts in their own pay are executives likely to ask that everyone take a cut. Mutuality can thus be symbolized at what is likely to be a critical time.

In the preceding chapter we observed the close association of age and rank. Importantly, the age factor creates a close relationship between increases in base pay and the rising costs of caring for a family. Many young bachelors express the opinion that they would prefer a low wage before they marry, as long as they know they will have a proportionally larger income when they have a family to support. "If I had a lot now I would only spend it, but later I will really need it," was a common remark. As children grow, they require more space, and more money is required to care for them. They become more expensive to house, feed, and educate during their years in high school and college. The curve of increase in base pay follows rather closely the curve of increasing family expenses. Individual family planning, as we shall see in chapter 11, counts on this.

Finally, we must note that this entire list of payments and benefits ignores the reward that Uedagin men prize above all. More than material comfort or the power and independence that money can buy, they desire the status and distinction that only rank can provide. No matter how well off he may be due to the base pay system, a man who has not reached the rank he and his family desire is not likely to be happy. Conversely, popular opinion assumes that a man who has reached chief is a satisfied and proud person. Issues of motivation, so commonly figured in terms of money when Western business organization is considered, must be discussed primarily in terms of the Japanese white-collar worker's ambition for high rank: he pays most attention to the promotion, not the wage system.

8

THE BANK'S UNION

Considering the company welfare program and the ideological emphasis on unity and "lifelong employment," it is a bit surprising that there is a union in the bank. Indeed, the Uedagin union is hardly a major force at present, but to understand why we must consider it in some detail. What is the manner of articulation between the company and the union? This is the primary question before us, and to answer it we must consider (1) the definitions the union leaders offer of its nature and its role in the total enterprise, (2) the constitution and activities of the union, and (3) the actual manner in which it conducts relations with management.

Large federations of unions, aggressive small unions, strikes, and the political activities of labor have received considerable attention from scholars interested in the Japanese labor movement, but concerning the dormant union, probably the most typical, particularly among white-collar firms, we have much less information.[1] How such unions continue to exist without reliance on the usual functions of aggressive unionism is another question we will explore in this chapter.

THE UNION'S RELATIONSHIP TO THE BANK

Goyō kumiai, "at your service union," is the expression used to characterize the employees' union (jūgyoin kumiai) by persons in the bank inclined to sarcasm. The implication is that the union is subservient to the wishes of the bank's leaders, and often enough this is the case. The full story, however, is more complicated.

The Uedagin union, along with virtually all other Japanese unions,

---

[1] Cole (1971a) provides detailed glimpses of two unions in medium-size manufacturing companies; one is rather aggressive, and the other much less so. Levine (1958), Cook (1966), and Ōkochi (1958) are the best sources of information on the broad outlines of Japanese unionism. It is important to keep in mind that the Uedagin union is not an industrial union as are most of those studied by the above authors.

is company, rather than occupation, based. Only members and quasi members of Uedagin may join. Temporary and commissioned employees along with high-ranking members are excluded.[2]

Uedagin's union neither has nor seeks the greater power and leverage that unity of action with other bank unions might bring. Although it holds membership in the League of Cooperative Bank Unions, its ties with that organization have never been other than formal and tenuous. Because of lack of commitment from its large unions, the league itself has been unable to generate any significant combined action.

One stated reason for the bank union's satisfaction with its company basis is the fact that Uedagin personnel enjoy higher wages and a better standard of living than people working in other cooperative banks. This disparity is due to the greater size and economic success of Uedagin in comparison to its rival banks. With interbank labor mobility virtually zero and profit distributions determined by a government ruling, such differences in reward within a class of institutions, such as cooperative banks, arise essentially from differences in size and success. The unions of smaller, less prosperous banks have long indicated more interest in concerted union efforts across company lines, but what they wish to demand of management are goals that have already been realized with little effort by the unions of the larger banks. It is impossible, under these conditions, to establish a concrete set of demands that might become the basis for unified action. Furthermore, representatives from the more well-to-do companies are inclined to an attitude of superiority and self-satisfaction regarding other league members.

It is not surprising that Uedagin's union strongly subscribes to the belief that what is good for the bank is good for the union's members. The validity of this interpretation has been evidenced, they say, by the steady improvement of their income and welfare benefits over the last twenty years in the absence of strikes, work stoppages, or even propaganda campaigns against management. In fact, the absence of such disruptive tactics is one reason given by all sides for the bank's and consequently the union's success. With the exception of annual talks with management about increasing base pay and bonuses, the union's activities appear to be designed primarily to build morale and thus to support the efforts of the bank's regular leadership. The union works actively to prevent divisiveness between different levels within the Uedagin hierarchy, and, along with the personnel department, its

2 The exclusion of nonmembers is common throughout Japan.

leaders are charged with the responsibility of seeking reasonable remedies for the dissatisfactions that arise among the rank and file.

During the period of this research, the union played a minor role in the overall affairs of the bank. But, if the experience of a few other companies is indicative, there is always the possibility, however remote at a given time, that the pact of trust and reciprocal good will between the different levels in the company will collapse, and at this juncture a company union, even a dormant one, is likely to be thrust into the crucial role of representing the disaffection and animosity of the lower-ranking people.

The collapse of the internal order may have a variety of origins. The simple fact of economic failure has forced managers in other companies to dismiss personnel, an action that is obviously contrary to the spirit of the tacit understanding between company and workers. Friction from such noneconomic sources as the tactless use of authority by company leaders may also increase hostility to the point of rebellion. The patience and good will carefully built into the Japanese company system are by no means unlimited qualities. Thirdly, should the union fall into the hands of leaders who seek to realize the "employee versus management" ideology of the national and international labor movements, the pact of trust with management would soon be broken as certainly as in cases when management mishandles its side of the bargain.

The Uedagin situation is characterized by a well-developed awareness on all sides of the union troubles of other companies, their causes and consequences. Such difficulties in other banks, particularly cooperative banks, are watched with special interest and concern. They are reminders of the potential for divisiveness and organizational collapse that exist in the company system. Undoubtedly, people are on their guard, and leaders are cooperative, in part because of this awareness.

We might at this point remind ourselves of the ever present complaints Uedagin people have about their company. Wages and bonuses are not matters people naturally take satisfaction in, especially those who are paid less (and receive less expense allowances) than their fellow age mates. Inflation, which has been at serious, if not impossible, levels in postwar Japan, compounds the anxiety over pay for most men. Some women feel that they are taken advantage of, compared to men. This sense of injustice is in proportion to their years with the bank and their lack of prospects of marriage. Housing, a serious national problem in Japan, worries men with families. There are many complaints about company apartments. Promotions are another major problem, and while talented young men are impatient for faster ad-

vancement, men who are being left behind complain of unequal treatment. Transfers that unsettle family arrangements, create extra economic burdens, or take someone to a remote and undesirable location
may also be cause for complaint. The long hours and the requirement
that all members seek deposits from friends and acquaintances are
also among the most universally disliked aspects of bank work. There
are complaints that center in some offices about high-handed or incompetent leaders, and there is always a vague, but real, sense of resentment over both being manipulated and being forgotten.

Since cooperation is their aim, Uedagin union leaders work to keep
such complaints and problems channeled in the accepted manner.
Public outcries are avoided, and the "unity of interest" theme is reiterated at union meetings even while criticisms of bank policy are
voiced. Other union actions serve the same end. Various programs of
the "rest and recreation" type are sponsored, private counseling is offered, and regularized negotiations with management are conducted.
Complaints the union wishes to present to management are made in
private and in the spirit of compromise. This is fully in keeping with
management's policy of granting the union recognition, respect, and
assistance so long as complaints and demands are dealt with privately
and amicably. The bank's leaders realize the potential for ruinous
trouble.

All of the ambivalence and delicacy of the union situation are expressed in the following speech, given by a union leader to the incoming group of young men during their initial training:

> We have three major goals before us: to create a bright and
> pleasant work place, to create a work place that has a passion
> for work, and to create a work place that is satisfying. All of
> you are automatically members of the union, and we hope you
> will cooperate with us and with the bank to achieve these goals.
> The history of our union is part of the general story of postwar
> labor union expansion. As you probably know, the American
> occupation encouraged the establishment of unions, and
> throughout the land this was taken as a directive. The era of
> Japanese democratization and social modernization thus began,
> and labor consciousness developed rapidly. Unlike American
> unions however, most Japanese unions are company centered.
> Our own organization, which was formed in 1946, shares in this
> general history. But many unions have acted politically and
> have, in some instances, failed to give cooperation to their com-
> panies. There are enterprises where a very large gap has devel-
> oped between management and labor, to everyone's detriment
> in our opinion. As a rule, the more disruptive unions have

been the least successful in raising wages and improving working conditions.

We might say that a company's management is a mirror that
reflects the character of the company's union. That is, successful management and a well-run union are closely interrelated.
If the union is uncooperative, then so will management become uncooperative, and vice versa. The reality of modern economics clearly indicates that companies grow and succeed as
the workers grow and improve individually. Companies that
succeed are places where their members enjoy their work and
therefore work well. Wherever companies succeed, wages are
higher and the general condition of life and work is better.

A union's essential strength lies in its solidarity and organization. We have many differences within our membership according to sex, age, rank, work category, and region, and these may
lead to divisions that weaken us. For example, a good welfare
program for one individual seems unnecessary or prejudicial to
another. Our first principle is, therefore, that we all must work
together as union members considering the other person's position and ideas. Secondly, we must have confidence in ourselves
as union members and in the union as an organization for our
benefit. We must act, rather than simply speak about ideals, for
in no other way will improvements be achieved. You are newcomers to the bank, and soon you will see the contradictions
and realities of Uedagin life. Probably you will discover a generation gap and find that the pressure of work causes friction
between people. We all must work to solve these problems. The
union looks on the introduction of the computer and other rationalization programs as both necessary to meet competition
and useful for the improvement of our own working conditions. We hope you will be alert to other ways improvements
might be made. Our procedures for negotiating any increase in
base pay begin at the office level, where everyone is to discuss
what amount the increase for the year should be. The results of
these discussions pass from regional meetings to the central
committee, where they are combined with the information collected by the union about wages in other comparable banks,
increases in the cost of living, and the conditions of bank business. All of these serve to define our position for negotiations
with management about increases in base pay, bonus, retirement pay, and other problems. Management has been very cooperative to date, and our rate of wage increase has been better
than the other cooperative banks. Recently we have also been
working with management to reduce the number of overtime
hours so that we all may have more time to ourselves. In conclusion, let us say that this union is your union. If you have

problems of any kind please consult us. We exist for your benefit and for the benefit of all Uedagin people.

Turning to another source of definition for the union, the "Union
Handbook," which contains the rules of the union and its agreement
with the bank, we find its objectives and goals stated as follows:

1. Based on the self-awareness and unity of our membership,
we will maintain and improve the working conditions of the
bank and plan the improvement of our general social and economic position.

2. We will plan the improvement of our work effectiveness
based on our mutual affection and trust.

3. Improving our own social consciousness and drawing together our strength and ambitions, we will work to democratize
the managerial aspects of the bank and thus improve the bank's
public mission as a financial institution.

The first article of the "Cooperative Agreement with Labor" (*rōdō
kyōyaku*) between the union and the bank is also instructive. It reads,
"The bank and the union will mutually respect the rights of management and of labor and together pledge to cooperate according to the
spirit of the agreement which they sincerely promised to defend and
respect. While administering according to the rights of management,
the bank will consult and cooperate with the union on matters regarding the status, salary, and working conditions of union members wherever there are unusual circumstances." The vagueness of such statements serves best to characterize these attempts at a formal definition
for the relationship. This agreement has virtually nothing to do with
a strictly written contract containing rights and duties, legal sanctions,
and the like. Although respective rights are mentioned occasionally,
there is almost no enumeration of what they may be. Cooperation and
consultation before management reaches a final decision is the key
concept, repeated time and again, and at every turn we find some sort
of release clause permitting management, after consultation, full latitude to act according to its own inclinations. Powers and sanctions are
not specified with any precision.

This, however, does not prevent the union from operating satisfactorily. This ambiguity illustrates a point that we have noted throughout our description of the bank, namely, that relationships in Uedagin
are not contractual, nor predicated on the assumption of a conflict of
interest. Official statements defining relationships are therefore pur-
posely vague in terms of rights, duties, and sanctions. In the words

of a leader of the union, a spirit of mutual trust and cooperation is the basis of the relationship, and this implies the avoidance of legalism and overt suspicion. When affairs run smoothly and both sides respect the nature of the arrangement, its success is accompanied by a low level of strife and ill will, and the high costs of enforcing and renegotiating a legalistic solution are avoided.[3]

Reciprocal good will, however, is difficult to achieve. As long as both sides appear to be making efforts to this end (showing their "sincerity"), the ideal can be preserved as the basis of the relationship. However, the opacity of the understanding makes subtle incursions possible, particularly from the management side. Furthermore, the absence of legal definitions means that open and total hostility can abruptly appear once the spirit of trust is lost. The history of Japanese unionism includes, along with unparalleled union-management cooperation, some disastrous strikes.

Another key to our understanding of the union is its history. During the first years of the allied occupation, a wave of unionization swept over Japan, and unions were created everywhere, virtually overnight. In some instances (just how many is far from clear) this was not the product of a spontaneous action of workers but was rather, as in the Uedagin case, the result of an effort on all sides to conform to the wishes of the American authorities. In 1946 they believed that it was required of every company to have a union, and they dutifully set one up, modeling it on the new labor law and what was known of unions at the time.

The postwar period was one of impoverishment and disorganization for all companies, but for Uedagin it was a particularly difficult time because previous mergers and amalgamations had given it an appearance of some importance, but they also had created considerable dissension and disillusionment within the company. It is notable that the union never served as a vehicle for discord at that time of great stress. Apparently, from the beginning it has been operated in a spirit of cooperation with the top leadership of the bank. In fact, the union's first two officers were men who later became the bank's president and vice-president.

ORGANIZATION OF THE UNION

The original construction of a union must have posed some problems for its founders since the usual principles of unionism and those of

---

[3] Union contracts are not legal documents in Japan, but there is annually a small number of cases in which unions resort to legal action (see von Mehren, 1963).

Uedagin must have seemed contradictory. Instead of unity, unionism is founded on division. Instead of a system of categories of membership and a hierarchy of ranks, unionism is predicated upon a conception of owners, managers, and employees. Furthermore, the high internal mobility within Uedagin and the place of age in the promotion system are particularly unsuited to the union form of operation, since today's "employees" are likely to be tomorrow's "managers." In any event, the essential questions at the time were, first, what categories of people to include in the union, and, second, where to draw the line between the "union" and the "company." The exclusion of nonmembers seems to have been both a legal and practical necessity. Because temporary and commissioned workers are excluded from receiving bonuses and from the assurance of a permanent place in the bank, these persons could hardly be included under the umbrella of union representation without creating serious problems of conflicting interests within the union.

The second issue was solved by making the division between the union and management follow the line already drawn between the ranks of deputy and chief, a decision that seems rather arbitrary considering how much managerial responsibility deputies are often given. Other ranks with significance just less than chief, such as assistant chief and researcher, were later added to the management side. The one exception to the rule that union membership was to contain all those of deputy rank and below was, and continues to be, that deputies in the personnel department are part of management, although they may rejoin the union when transferred to other departments. These men administer the salary, assignment, and promotion systems, and their participation in the union would be awkward.

Other fundamental rules of the union are that all persons who qualify must join, pay monthly dues, and attend the scheduled meetings in their place of work. The dues are small, and the meetings are normally held as infrequently as possible. Each office unit elects a representative to one of the regional meetings (which coincide with the blocs of branches in the regular organization). Local meetings are held to meet with union officials, who tour the branches to stimulate interest in union affairs and to listen to local complaints. Meetings are also held to plan union-sponsored activities. Representatives to a central committee, which gathers monthly in Aoyama with the officers of the union, are elected from each of the regional meetings. The union's officers, five in all, are themselves elected annually by a general congress consisting of representatives from every office plus the entire central committee.

The day-to-day activities of the union are conducted by a regular staff consisting of the five officers and two women assistants. They occupy a room reserved for the union in the Uedagin main office. The women are assigned to work for the union by the personnel section just as they would be assigned to any other office within the bank. Appearances to the contrary, the union's officers come to occupy positions of leadership in somewhat the same manner.

Although formally elected at the union's general congress, the officers are actually appointed to their positions. They are nominated as the official slate of candidates and are elected and reelected each year unopposed. The exact procedure for determining who will be nominated is not clear, except that the union's officers make the nominations in conjunction with the personnel department. By this method leadership selection remains firmly in the control of the outgoing leaders and personnel. Each year, two or three of the top people move back to regular positions in the bank, and their places are taken by others who fit into the ongoing regime.[4] Usually new officers have had some experience as central committee members, and prior to their selection to positions of union leadership they have generally held positions within the main office. The top three men are invariably deputies in their late thirties and early forties who are regarded as being in line for promotion to chief. Their subordinate officers are younger regulars with moderately promising careers.

Although elections occur annually, a normal term of office runs for three to four years just as for regular bank assignments. There is a definite pattern of top officers being promoted to chief upon completion of their years of service to the union. The Uedagin perspective finds nothing ironical in this direct movement from union leadership into management. In fact, becoming an officer of the union is a recognized avenue to higher position. The union director, who spends much

4 Election contests, although unknown in Uedagin, are a clear possibility, and in such cases a central issue is usually the degree of cooperation each slate will give management. The democratic form of selection, therefore, preserves the possibility of a "take-over" by a more aggressive leadership, one not sharing in the general viewpoint or the career expectations of the management. Two banks larger than Uedagin have in the early seventies experienced such union take-overs. The story is that young women, especially those involved in left-wing youth activities and older "specialists" doing the routine work of the main office, were the firmest supporters of the change. Other large banks are anticipating similar troubles, and one relatively high-ranking officer of a very large bank recently observed in private that rather desperate measures may be needed to cope with the threat of such unionism. How threatening such a change seems can be appreciated from this account. It would raise a basic challenge to the ideological and organizational foundations of the company.

of his time with executives of the bank and is included in the annual conference of branch chiefs, actually has a foot in each camp during his term of office. Not only must he satisfy his superiors or sacrifice his opportunity for promotion, management tends to treat him as a partner in the enterprise of managing the bank.[5]

UNION ACTIVITIES

The leader of the union has the important function of acting as a go-between and coordinator within the organization. By expressing the needs and problems of the relatively inarticulate lower-ranking majority, he serves management's need to know as well as the union membership's desire to be heard. For this reason, an active and aggressive director is likely to gain the admiration of those above, as well as those below. Thus, although the allocation of ultimate power to management would lead us to expect lethargy and subservience on the part of the union's leadership, this is not necessarily true. Some leaders are criticized by management for lacking initiative and courage, one indication of a basic understanding that union leaders have the duty to speak out in the proper context. In the recent past, a leader who represented the complaints of his constituency most firmly earned for himself a good reputation and rapid advancement in his subsequent career. His forcefulness in discussions with the president and other leaders, as well as his tact, reportedly won their high regard.

The limits on positive action by union leaders are much the same as those that hold for others within the bank. Whatever is done must not cause a breach in the public presentation of unity and cooperation. The director's speeches to the union members, for example, must not interfere with his effectiveness in face-to-face dealings with the bank's executives, for it is in such personal relationships that he has the greatest opportunity to advance the union's point of view. Careless conduct of union affairs can cause the disaffection of management and can end their willingness to support a particular leader.

Yet union meetings are a special context where it is possible for the full flavor and rhetoric of unionism, Japanese style, to emerge, how-

5 In a personal communication, Taishirō Shirai, an authority on unions, indicated that the practice of promoting retiring union leadership into management is a common problem for Japanese unions. Even industrial company unions tend to be dominated by leadership stemming from the white-collar side of the union, and these men are often lost through promotion to management level. The situation of union leadership is thus ambivalent (by our terms, at least) from the beginning.

ever briefly. General meetings are accompanied by a succession of aggressive postures and rallying cries precisely in the stereotype of the union image presented in the Japanese national press. Brave slogans, colorful banners, everyone in shirt sleeves, and poses before the camera with locked arms, all stylistic borrowings from the public displays of Japan's largest unions, are strictly observed. Nor are these things regarded with much skepticism. The union leaders do take the identity of their union, as a union, seriously, and they try hard to act in public as union people should. For this reason, the overt form of activities is stereotyped and offers little indication of the actual effort being made on another, more private, level to effect improvements on behalf of union members. To fulfill the requirements of form and satisfy general expectations while maintaining the cooperative relationship with management is the balancing act union leaders must learn. As part of its side of the arrangement, management allows the union to assume formidable postures and provides other face-saving devices.

While the leaders' single most important activity is to negotiate with management, the majority of their time and effort is consumed by programs directed toward the internal life of the union itself. Dues must be collected and recorded and accounting made of the various union expenditures. Reports must be compiled on such matters as: (a) wages, benefits, bonuses, and working conditions in the bank and in similar institutions; (b) negotiations with management; and (c) the conduct of union affairs. The annual total of such reports exceeds one hundred. The union magazine must be compiled. This is a digest of union activities and individual literary and photographic work that runs to approximately sixty pages an issue, four times a year. Union-sponsored recreational events, including softball tournaments, outings, and a monthly office recreation day, must be organized and coordinated. An elaborate annual arts and handicrafts exhibit is also conducted as part of this general program. The apparatus of union government, including the convocation of regular meetings, the use of committees, and direct visits to office groups also requires large amounts of the leaders' time. In addition, there is visiting back and forth between the officials of unions of different banks, and there are meetings of the league to be attended. The result of all this is not concerted action, as we have noted already, but a useful exchange of information and techniques. The director spends from two to four days a month on such matters.

Some of the above activities, particularly the publication of the magazine and the conduct of recreational affairs, reflect the close alliance between the union and the personnel department. These activities are conducted as the union's contribution to the bank-wide official effort to build morale. The interests of union and management converge at this point, and they often cosponsor such events. Equally as often, the personnel department contributes the money and labor required while the union acts as official sponsor. Not only is the union allied with personnel in this respect, it is actually dependent upon it in many instances.

The annual arts and handicrafts exhibit is a good example. Even though it is a union event, entries are so numerous, the arrangements so time consuming, and the cost so high that the union is unable to to conduct the show by itself. Each year it must turn to the welfare section for aid, and, according to informants who have worked on the exhibit, it is actually the product of the welfare section staff. The work of labeling and displaying all of the entries, inviting some six outside judges to visit the show, recording their commentary on each work, and arranging the awards banquet requires several hundred hours of work. The women of the welfare section have developed over the years an expertise in setting up the event. When the exhibit is opened, ceremonial formalities maintain the fiction of union sponsorship and independence, and, as in other ceremonies conducted in the name of subdivisions of the bank, the president is treated as an invited guest.

The union's magazine, *Building*, published four times a year, is also produced with considerable assistance from the regular bank organization. The authorities on this kind of work are the people who put out the monthly Uedagin *News*, and the union's magazine-publishing committee is dependent on them for advice and aid. Both magazines, incidentally, are published by the same company, a *kogaisha* of the bank.

Building supplements the efforts of the Uedagin *News* to present an optimistic picture of life in the bank. One woman who worked on the union publication described it as a "happy sheet" in which pictures of people enjoying union outings and other events are stressed, while the criticisms and dissatisfactions of union members are played down. She indicated that editorial work to this end by management people is not unknown, and added that this seemed improper.

The union's dependency on the personnel department, reflected even in its assignment to an office down the hall, is something that the average member takes for granted in the absence of serious labor troubles.

We might ask what benefit individuals find in the union. Their response to the union's negotiations for wage, bonus, and benefit increases is at best lukewarm.[6] It is generally assumed that the bank will offer to pay what other banks its size offer, regardless of union efforts. To most people the union is unnecessary except in times of serious trouble. The regional and general meetings are held on Saturday afternoons and Sundays and are for this reason unpopular and often resented by those who must attend. Duty as a branch representative is also neither sought nor enjoyed. Consequently, the job is usually assigned on a rotation basis. In a number of offices women have been elected as local representatives. This is not discouraged, but women in such positions constitute only 10 percent.

Union recreational activities enjoy much wider popularity. The arts and crafts exhibit, which includes a full spectrum of creations by Uedagin people and their families, is definitely a source of pleasure for a wide number of people. The approximately four hundred entries each year are evidence of their enthusiasm. Union-sponsored softball tournaments and office recreation days, on the other hand, appeal more to the young men. The cash payments the union makes as part of its tiny welfare program are of interest primarily to married men, who appreciate receiving even such small grants in aid.

More significant to most older men is the cautious opposition union leaders offer to management's plans for reducing the seniority-based aspects of the wage scale. Because the union's membership includes many men who would suffer from reductions in the power of seniority, the union is obliged to defend the existing system, or at least to warn against the deprivations some would suffer if ability factors were strengthened too quickly or radically. This defense of the status quo does not sit well with the union's leaders, for they tend personally to favor what they believe to be the more efficient and modern style of management.[7]

The recent union campaign to reduce working hours through automation and efficiency (overtime pay is separate) is popular among all elements within the union and receives the full support of the personnel section as well. Perhaps this campaign characterizes the ideal union role in the bank, for the interests of all parties are united in the project.

[6] This is a point made in Shirai (forthcoming).
[7] This is one illustration of how the management point of view is represented by the personal attitudes of the union leadership, men who have had considerable managerial responsibility as deputies and who expect soon to advance to chief rank.

DISCUSSION

Drawing together the various qualities presented as characteristic of the union, we should note in conclusion its almost complete integration with the regular company organization. Its criteria for membership follow the bank's categories and ranks, and its offices are defined in terms of the system of ranks and promotions. Union leaders are selected with the approval of the personnel department, and their salaries continue to be paid by the bank according to the usual salary determinants. Serving as a union officer is little different from other assignments in the bank, for rank, wages, housing, and the general course of one's career remain unaffected. The union's office and all of its facilities are provided by the bank. In many instances, personnel supplements union funds and gives other assistance to permit programs sponsored by the union to continue. Because it suits the overall purposes of the bank, the union is encouraged to conduct activities that are popular with the membership and to represent their criticisms and complaints to the bank's leadership. The aim is to build morale, and energetic union leadership is encouraged and rewarded as long as this is the result. Cooperation in these matters earns for the union's leaders a degree of reciprocal cooperation from management.

In keeping with this pattern, the only time the union may be expected to act in a totally independent manner would be following a major breach of the bank-union relationship. If such a breach occurs, there are almost no mechanisms by which to settle the dispute. Recourse to the law, formal bargaining, and arbitration are not possibilities built into the basic relationship. A prolonged dispute could spell disaster for all concerned (given lifetime employment), and the union therefore has good reason to continue to avoid forceful actions, including those which alliance with other bank unions might bring.

It is indicative of the character of Japanese unions that strikes and union strife are interpreted by outsiders as evidence of management's failure to maintain a well-run house. Company unions only cause serious trouble in extreme cases, it is believed, and because management is charged with the responsibility of preventing problems from reaching such a level, a strike is generally viewed as the fault of management, even by managers in other companies. It is useful to recall the family analogy to understand why management should receive the blame for union troubles.

Authority and power become visible when they are challenged, but the Uedagin union does not challenge the bank's top men. This permits them to take a cooperative attitude toward the union and provide it with a limited sphere of activity. This is a situation fully consistent with many of the most valued precepts of proper social relations in Japan, and it follows a pattern, typical of Japanese political arrangements, in which power is veiled and indirect, but nevertheless ever present.

Nakane Chie remarks in her discussion of the character of Japanese society that "the majority of Japanese people have not been historically conditioned to life in a stratified community with effective lines of demarcation between groups. What they are accustomed to regard as an organizational principle is ranking rather than stratification [1970:142]." She also comments that, "in Japan it is not a matter of workers struggling against capitalists or managers, but of company A ranged against company B. The protagonists do not stand in vertical relationship to each other but rub elbows from parallel positions. The organization of unions in Japan, their ideals and the peculiarities to be seen in the union movement cannot be understood without this kind of analysis [1970:87]." In a related interpretation, Thomas C. Smith has observed, "Status consciousness is relatively strong in Japan in part because there was no revolutionary struggle against inequality, but for that reason class-consciousness is relatively weak. These attitudes are by no means contradictory. The nervous concern of Japanese for status is quite consonant with their relatively weak feelings about classes—higher-ups to some extent being looked on as superior extensions of the self [1964:382]." Though as comments about Japanese society as a whole they require numerous conditional remarks,[8] these generalizations are consistent with what has been observed about the internal order of Uedagin, particularly the place and character of the union. The only clear-cut divisions within the bank of the class or strata type are created by the system of categories, and this tends to discriminate against a small bottom minority. Women are excluded on the special grounds of their temporary involvement. Among the male membership, rank is the crucial factor, and it is a continuous

---

[8] In most manufacturing companies advancement to management is cut off for a much larger proportion of men, and separate rank systems for the different categories of white- and blue-collar workers exist. For these reasons an ideological viewpoint like this cannot be asserted with anywhere near the same degree of success. Blue-collar workers, one would assume, are more likely to support aggressive unionism than white-collar workers, yet even this oversimplifies the problem. Young white-collar workers, particularly women, are often the most aggressive, I have heard. I know of cases in which young white-collar activists in manufacturing firms quit after their union activities undermined their career prospects.

status ladder from bottom to top. Whether high-ranking men are always viewed as "superior extensions of the self" or not, it is true that they are part of a continuous vertical line. Company ideology presents them as models of goodness, as benefactors, as links in a chain of reciprocal assistance and cooperation, and as occupants of positions soon to be inherited by the next generation. This is not fertile ground for the unionism we visualize, but the rough outlines of unionism can be adapted to such conditions, and if organizational breakdown occurs such a dormant union can become an extraordinary power. We can only understand this species of union within its company framework. Once more, we find that the meaning of a particular element is largely a matter of its place in a total context.

9

CREATING THE UEDAGIN MAN

The Japanese hold education in high esteem. Not only is it regarded as a main avenue to advancement for both the individual and the nation, it is also valued for its civilizing qualities. According to widespread belief, study and training are important sources of improved character, and this, in turn, is the hope for a better, more peaceful society. The bank, in its own extensive education program, confirms these ideals and seeks to realize the great potential influence for improvement education is believed to have.[1]

There are also practical and obvious reasons for an emphasis on company education. An organization that hires only people fresh out of school and then keeps most of the men until retirement cannot depend on a policy of hiring the skills it needs on an open labor market. It must itself assume much of the responsibility for developing the talents of its members, and this is precisely what Uedagin, in its numerous training programs, attempts to do.

The technical training in business that Japanese universities and high schools offer is, as a rule, minimal, and there is today no more than a handful of graduate schools of business.[2] Recent graduates entering the bank, therefore, seldom have any training in banking procedures or general business skills. In fact, it has been public policy to leave much technical and business training to the nation's companies, and because they have their own particular educational requirements and perspectives, companies seldom cooperate in joint education ventures. Each characteristically invests heavily in its own program. The low male turnover rate makes this a sound investment. Large outlays

---

[1] The importance of internal training programs in medium and large Japanese business organizations is mentioned in Abegglen (1958 and 1970), Ballon (1969), Whitehall and Takezawa (1968), and Yoshino (1968).

[2] In the last few years some large companies have in combination begun a business school on the American model to fill this vacuum.

and maximum return are two characteristics of training in large Japanese companies.

In contrast to the low rate of company-to-company transfer, the rate of lateral and vertical mobility inside the bank is high. Men are called upon to perform many varied tasks and to assume increasing degrees of responsibility and leadership. Whether they eventually occupy high positions or not, their career leads them through many kinds of work. They are expected to show flexibility, and they must be ready to learn new skills. Contrary to the classical theory of bureaucracy, individual specialization is not pronounced. A transfer or promotion often means that new skills must be learned, and to meet this demand the bank conducts over thirty courses a year. Even with on-the-job training conducted by office senpai, and the expectation that each individual will make efforts to educate himself, the personnel department finds it desirable to have a special course for almost every kind of assignment. These range from courses for new chiefs to instruction for entering women in the proper use of polite language on the telephone. More characteristic technical programs operated by the training section are the courses for salesmen and the course in office calculating machines.

Whatever the skill taught, the effect of so much internal education is to make the bank nearly self-sufficient in terms of skilled labor. Almost all of its requirements can be met through training, and only needs for such specialized skills as computer programming make it necessary that members go outside to special schools.

Training programs are also expected to further harmonious relations, company loyalty, and high morale, and even in the most technical of courses these goals are not forgotten. The fact that training is conducted by and for the bank makes this emphasis on institutional qualities practical and reasonable.

There are a number of courses specifically designed to assist in the sponsorship of good human relations. Office recreation leaders, for example, learn how to conduct games, folk dances, and other group activities. There is a course for women who are office senpai, and a group of deputies undergoes a five-day sensitivity training ("T group") session each year. These efforts seem rather insignificant compared to the much longer and infinitely more involved introductory training new members receive. This program, constituting, in effect, an elaborate socialization attempt, is far and away the most important educational effort in Uedagin. New men spend three months at the training institute before their first assignments, while entering women attend only for two weeks.

The content of introductory training is an amalgamation of three concerns: technical training, character building, and integration into the Uedagin community. In Japanese, the latter two efforts are lumped together under the heading *seishin kyōiku,* "spiritual education," a major subject of this chapter.[3] The term refers to any and all processes by which individuals develop stronger character and a more complete respect for social requirements. It is considered at some length here to illustrate the interpretations of human nature, of the "good worker," and of the relationship of individuals to the organization expressed in the ideology and asserted by the company's leaders. There is a long history in Japan for this kind of training, and many of the methods utilized by the instructors in the training institute have been borrowed from the Zen, samurai, and other traditions.[4] While all bank courses are colored to some degree with this emphasis, only one is exclusively "spiritual" in content. This is the course annually given for the fifty or so men in their thirties and forties who have the poorest career records. These men, judged to be the most lethargic and least happy in their work, undergo a three-day personal reform session in the hope that some at least will reverse their unfortunate performance pattern. The effort, in essence, is to revitalize them "spiritually," and this is worth trying because the bank cannot fire them however unproductive or demoralizing their conduct might be. Here and in other matters "spiritual," I find much that appears to parallel efforts in China today to improve people, not just technology, as the surest road to a better society.

THE TRAINING INSTITUTE AND ITS STAFF

In all, about one thousand people, one-third of the personnel of the bank, receive some sort of training each year. The institute is housed

[3] The descriptive material on company seishin kyōiku in Japanese includes articles in Nakamura (1966), the special issue, *Seishin Kyōiku Tokushū* of Sangyo Kunren (1968), and Rohlen (1969 and 1970). In English, there is only Rohlen (1970) for descriptive information. However, a large number of books in English describe educational methods in Japan that come under the broad heading of seishin kyōiku. They include writing on sports training, Zen, and prewar education. Of special interest is Minami (1970:142–167) for his discussion of wartime spiritualism. Benedict (1946) also discussed training and discipline in her analysis of Japanese character. Finally, Suzuki (1959) is helpful.

[4] My estimate that one-third of Japan's medium and large companies practice some sort of seishin training is based on correspondence with the Industrial Training Association in Japan concerning the number of their members practicing seishin kyōiku, on reports reaching me or the bank about other similar company training programs, and on mention in magazines, newspapers and on TV of the increase of seishin kyōiku in companies. It is, however, looked upon as a bit archaic and right wingish, and the bank acknowledges a sensitivity to public criticism of their program.

in the five-story Uedagin welfare building in Aoyama. It is a modern, air-conditioned building with a full complement of facilities, including a gymnasium, a library, several lecture halls, and a home economics kitchen. During introductory training as many as one hundred and fifty people sleep and eat there at one time. Although these facilities are not exclusively for training purposes, in practice the training staff uses them far more than any other group in the bank.

The equipment available is similarly extensive. There is closed-circuit TV, movie projection equipment, a rich film library, and much else.

Six men and one woman make up the training staff, which enjoys a special position in the organization due to the president's enthusiasm for training, particularly spiritual education. The men of the group who conduct all of the courses held at the institute are young and have promising careers. As a rule they are gregarious, and enjoy close association with young people. Several are considered ideal senpai by the younger men who have trained with them. Except for a single lecture on female physiological problems in work, the woman on the staff does no teaching. She helps with record keeping and correspondence.

The level of staff proficiency is impressive. In the classroom they are professional and effective. On outings and special events they have the energy and fitness to take in stride physical challenges the younger trainees find difficult. Their greatest effectiveness lies with their attention to and success in personal relationships with the trainees, particularly the impressionable new members. At the end of formal classes on almost any day, one can find an instructor or two casually chatting with the students.

INSTITUTE ROUTINES

No matter what the content of instruction, the daily routine is the same. At the institute the appropriate dress for each event or time of day is always announced in advance. Business suits are common for classes, except in the case of the new men, who normally wear a set of gray work clothes supplied by the company. White athletic uniforms are mandatory for all exercise and sports events.

A PA system is used to announce the day's schedule beginning with a call to rise in the morning. Trainees are expected to stay the night during their training, and each is assigned to share a room with a number of fellow trainees. Leaders are designated within each group and given the responsibility for organizing cleanup, meals, roll checks, and other minor chores.

Most programs last from two days to a week. They begin character-istically with an introductory lecture given by the training chief, who invariably mentions:

(1) The necessity for increased skill and serious education due to the intensified competitive situation of the bank and the nation, and technological change, which demands adaptability of indi-viduals and organizations if they are to survive;

(2) The opportunity for personal development which will benefit not only the bank, but the individual himself;

(3) The chance to prove oneself and enrich one's life;

(4) The educational value of group living;

(5) The fact that respect for the rules is essentially respect for others.

Each morning the trainees are awakened at 6:30, and, dressed in athletic outfits, they soon assemble in front of the institute where the bank and Japanese flags are raised, the bank pledges are recited, and exercises are conducted. Sometimes the entire group, led by the in-structors, jogs around a nearby park for approximately a mile before breakfast. The fresh morning air and softly lit surroundings make this a pleasant experience, at least in the summer.

Rakes are occasionally taken along for the purpose of cleaning up a section of the park. The president and other top executives will some-times show up before seven to join in the effort. When raking is finished, it is common for the president, leaning on his rake, to offer a few observations on the symbolic importance of the project. Public service and a sense of sanctity are mentioned, and the trainees (stand-ing at attention with rakes held at their sides) are urged to carry the spirit of the moment back into their daily life and work. The jog back to the institute is followed by a hearty but hurried breakfast. Before beginning to eat, the entire group has a moment of thanksgiving and gratitude. Each meal ends with a corresponding expression of thanks. The food is institutional, and no time is devoted to savoring meals. Following breakfast everyone is expected to clean up their rooms, and every few days a general cleanup is conducted. At sunset, a flag-lower-ing ceremony is accompanied by exercises and announcements similar to the morning ceremony.

Sometimes evenings are assigned to study, but often, particularly at the beginning and end of training sessions, some sort of group recrea-tion is planned. Square dancing, various party games, and singing are the most popular. Because no training sessions are coeducational, the dancing and other partying are purely recreational. They serve to relax the group, to provide opportunities to become acquainted, and to establish a sense of togetherness. Exchanging neck rubs and other activities reminiscent of Esalen are not uncommon. In sum, these evenings succeed by a combination of group recreation techniques common to such places as summer camps and resorts.

During introductory training considerable time is devoted to teaching everyone a number of songs, and as a result training groups are able to sing together when traveling on a bus, during an evening's recreation, or around a campfire, another illustration of the staff expertise in the mechanics of successful group organization.

Discussion groups, often without an instructor present, are also common to most programs. Because training groups tend to consist of people of much the same age and rank, they have much in common to talk about. Hierarchy is absent as a rule, and the trainees are able to share experiences, complaints, and self-criticism readily.

The recreational activities, the living together, and the discussions all contribute to the popularity of training among younger members. Not only does a trip to the institute provide a few days off from regular work, it also provides a special opportunity to meet with peers in one of the least hierarchically ordered situations within the bank. Roommates often talk long into the night, and when there is free time there are always informal discussions to be found. There is criticism from some quarters to the effect that such a pleasant atmosphere makes training more like a holiday than a program consistent with the pressure and hierarchy of actual work.

Throughout the institute are hung slogans of encouragement and inspiration, some by famous men and others obviously written for the program in session. In the dining hall are photos of the president and of the bank's new main office, and the ever-present bank motto "harmony and strength." Works from the bank's art show are displayed, and on every landing, facing the stairs, is a full-length mirror. People passing up and down the stairs cannot help noting and hopefully improving their appearance.

Another practice is to have each trainee keep a diary. These are turned in regularly to the teachers, who review them, often quite routinely. The diaries are meant to provide an opportunity to make observations or criticisms about training or one's own behavior. Characteristically, trainees write that they have not taken training seriously enough and will attempt to have a more serious attitude. The fact that the diaries are read by the staff strongly colors their content no doubt, but as a method of sponsoring reflection and self-criticism diary writing appears effective. Self-reflection (hansei) is nothing unusual as part

of moral education in Japan, and the use of a diary for this purpose
is also common.

Strict attention to detail and propriety is constantly encouraged.
People who dress in a sloppy manner or fail to comb their hair can
expect to be sent back to their rooms. Sitting straight and standing
straight receive constant attention. Such things as using the right side
of hallways, proper and cordial greetings, and polite entrances and
departures from rooms are strictly enforced. Routinely every lecture
begins and ends with the lecturer being greeted and thanked by the
audience standing and bowing in unison. This attention to details of
orderliness is connected to the often reiterated belief that order and
neatness are fundamental necessities for successful group living. "They
are expressions of concern for one another," it is said. Instructors also
assert that outward appearance is a clear measure of a person's inner
qualities.

The staff has prepared a handbook of instructions explaining the
proper forms of daily behavior in the bank. This is an exceptional
document in which such fine points of etiquette as the manner of
passing bank visitors in hallways, the appropriate angles for bows on
different occasions, and the proper way to pass a cup of tea to one's
superior are all illustrated in pictures and explained in detail. This
handbook has been prepared exclusively for Uedagin use.

Whenever the trainees are women, flowers are placed on the dining
tables and elsewhere. To make them feel at home and create rapport,
women are assigned to spend an hour or two cooking in the special
kitchen on the third floor. Other feminine projects, such as house
cleaning and making paper cranes, are often introduced as relief from
the routine of lectures and classes. It was explained that these special
touches have been added because past experience has shown a home-
like atmosphere to be essential to the happy participation of young
women.

A special theme in the women's training is the interpretation of
work as preparation for becoming good wives and mothers. The bank
has found it appropriate to tie their work to the more central and
enduring concerns of marriage and childrearing. It is said, for example, that learning proper etiquette and polite language, as taught in
the institute, will make them more cultivated, charming, and graceful,
and therefore more attractive to their husbands and better examples
for their children. Learning how to keep records and handle money
will aid them in their responsibilities as keepers of the family purse
strings.

This is not taken lightly. I have overheard these points mentioned by women as major benefits of their time in Uedagin. Their salaries and the opportunity to be away from home are more important, but the explanation that work is a preparation for the greater responsibilities of marriage is a useful rationalization. Most Japanese women take their roles in the family with extreme gravity.

As is already apparent, the training section devotes a major portion of its attention to Uedagin youth. There are many reasons for this. Young people are the most in need of technical instruction, they are the most numerous age group in the bank, and they can be spared from their jobs more readily than their seniors. There are other reasons, too.

The bank, like most institutions in Japan, has a youth problem. The problem is, however, somewhat different from what we might imagine after reading of recent student battles with police. There is no insubordination, but in the opinion of older men, even those in their late twenties, too many of the newcomers lack a sense of responsibility and commitment to their work and their fellow workers. According to complaints, too many are ill mannered and unintentionally disrespectful, they have no apparent resolve, and they seem unable to sustain interest and motivation. The conclusion many draw is that they have not been brought up correctly. A common opinion inside and outside Uedagin is that the postwar parents and school system, in their combined enthusiasm to be as democratic as possible, have produced a generation of young people who lack many of the experiences, the values, and the discipline that previously made for thorough, Japanese-style socialization. The emphasis on youth at the training institute is one product of this perspective. Management has resolved that at least its own young people will become proper workers and members of society. The president has expressed himself on this matter in the following terms:

> It is very important to have a mental attitude which enables one to overcome any kind of circumstance. In the past the military and the public schools had a daily training period which served this purpose, but today's young people have no chance for this kind of education. When people enter a company these days it is common for them to spend their whole working lives serving that one company. Therefore they have a right to be

cared for by their company even late in life, and their company
has this duty to them. At the same time that the company must
care for its people, it must receive the utmost effort of its people. To achieve this training is a necessity.

While efforts are made throughout the bank to develop such things
as affection for the company, strength of character, and enthusiasm, at
the institute this is a central and always conscious concern. Only there
can the effort be elaborated free of the daily preoccupations of office
business. The perfect illustration of how concentrated the bank's socialization effort can become is introductory training.

The year of this study, 120 young men came to the institute at the
beginning of April, about one week after their graduation from school.

Each day but Sunday there is a full schedule of lectures, practice
sessions, and other activities. Most class time is devoted to learning
the expertise of branch teller operations and to absorbing large quan-
tities of information about company documents and procedures. Discussions of the national economy or the bank's business strategy are
rare, and it is apparent that introductory training is not a course in
executive management techniques. Manual skills, a mastery of the elemental office routines, and a familiarity with the rest of the work of
the bank are the primary goals. Such training is practical, tedious, and
very important to the bank. A detailed description here, however, is
unnecessary. Learning to operate a business machine, to greet customers, or to fill out receipts are not procedures that are difficult to
imagine. As we might expect, thoroughness and attention to detail are
qualities emphasized.

A totally different kind of instruction, designed to mold character
and socialize the newcomers, is conducted simultaneously with the
technical course. We have already had glimpses of this in the previous
description of institute routines. Running each morning, cleaning a
park, living together, and inspirational lectures are all part of "spiritual education." Because of its association with Japan's defeated mili-
tarism, this kind of training suffered public eclipse for several decades,
but since the mid and late sixties numerous Japanese companies have
been reviving spiritual education in an attempt to give their new members the kind of education in social responsibility that family, school,
and military service provided in prewar days.

On the first day it was explained to the new men:

Our aim is to build you up as people so you can grow on your
own once you leave here. That's the reason we have tough
(*kibishii*) training. All of you are entering society for the first

time. Cooperative living is different from the kind of living you knew in your school days.

Your study here will also be different. In public schools, all you had to do was study for examinations. Whether you got along with your fellow classmates or not was not very important. Here, we have cooperative living as our style of life. It is simply a matter of fact that living in society is being given work—that is, being told to do things by others. We want you to become more careful and to do things in a more complete and thorough manner. We expect you to grow as individuals, and that means developing confidence, as well as ability.

The point that experience, not just knowledge and thought, is an important aspect of training is also introduced.

There will be many things you will not understand at first. We would like you actually to experience our training before you spend a lot of time analyzing it intellectually. Many of the things in our style of education cannot be understood by the head alone. You will have many doubts about the things we do, but we ask that you give us your cooperation and make an effort to understand what we are doing.

Further explanations are offered regarding the rudimentary perspectives and goals of training. The following excerpts are taken from a lecture titled "The Correct Attitudes of a Bank Member." A careful reading of this rather long quotation will greatly aid the reader in understanding the philosophy behind spiritual training.

Our discussion today of the correct attitudes for a bank member begins naturally, with the principles and the "President's Teachings." Basically what we want is that our employees think and feel that they are working for the good of the bank. At first this will seem strange, and you may sense resistance to this concept, but we ask you to experience life here in the training institute, and in the bank, before you reach any conclusions. Gradually, I think you will come to accept this basic orientation of ours that all of us are working for the good of the bank.

When you get into a branch your biggest problem will not be using the abacus; it will be human relations. You will have to be able to deal with our customers in the proper spirit. You will have to be able to work well with others. The president feels the ideas in our bank code and in his teachings are absolutely necessary in order to assure correct behavior on our part. The essentials for successful customer relations are proper attitude and behavior, and this means that disciplined conduct is very important. If your way of thinking, that is, your attitudes, are correct, then it will follow that your behavior and your respect for customers will be proper.

You will find that because you are inexperienced, much of your work will be difficult and unpleasant at first, but if your attitude toward your work is a good one and you learn to do it well through practice, the unpleasantness will disappear.

One of our ideals is that all of you become bankers who are pleased to receive whatever work you are given. We want men who can enjoy their work and whose opinions don't interfere with their performance or their satisfaction in their jobs.

Sometimes people are going to criticize your work. Don't take this as being a personal criticism and get angry, but consider that you are being instructed and that your teachers are anxious for you to improve. A strict teacher is a man whose interests are really with his students.

You know, if you look at a mountain, invariably one side is in sunshine and the other side is in shade. Everything is like this. If you look at the sunny side, you can go forward and get stronger. But, if you look at the shady side, everything suddenly begins to go bad. Remember this during the next three months. We want you to develop self-confidence through learning to overcome problems, and we want you to set for yourself the goal of being of service to others, so that when problems arise you have good reason to want to overcome them.

The themes of "spiritual" strength and the psychology of accomplishment (reminiscent of Samuel Smiles and Norman Vincent Peale) reiterate the perspective found in the president's essay on "spirit" quoted in part in chapter 2. Every executive and most guest lecturers who address the trainees repeat these themes, choosing their own words.

To teach this, the staff does not rely on lectures alone. In fact, lectures are only a preliminary part of the program. That experience, not words, is the best teacher is a key educational concept, and much effort has gone into arranging the three-month program to teach the values of the bank through actual experience.

Group living (*shūdan seikatsu*) is one important example. The direction of daily activities is placed in the hands of the trainees, who take turns commanding the twelve-man squads (*han*) and assuming overall leadership. Cleanup, kitchen, and service details, the morning and evening assemblies, scheduling, and travel are directed by the trainees on a rotation basis. It is expected that a strong appreciation for the burdens of leadership and the need for cooperation will develop under such conditions. The most poignant illustration of the necessity for order in group living comes whenever the entire retinue of 125 travels together. The value of group discipline and coordination is evident at such times. Waiting at stations and elsewhere, trainees enjoy watching other less-orderly groups of people struggle with the problem of keeping together.

Closely related to the matter of group living is the often mentioned theme of teamwork (*chiimu wāku*). The form of organization for most activities is the team. Study related to bank business, the pursuit of hobbies, and other matters are arranged to require teamwork. Competition between individuals is seldom encouraged, but group competition is a major means of motivation throughout the training period. Physical fitness is also emphasized. Each morning and evening there are group exercises. On three separate occasions, lectures on health and fitness are delivered, and whenever feasible trainees hike or run to their destination. The value of good posture, both to health and to mental concentration, is also stressed. Spiritual power (*seishin-ryoku*) depends on these things, the instructors explain.

SPECIAL TRAINING ACTIVITIES: TWO EXAMPLES

The more dramatic means for teaching the company's values through experience are a series of special training events. The two reported here are among the most fascinating of a larger group of such activities.[5] They constitute an important part of the introductory training program and find occasional application in mid-career courses. I participated in these activities, and, because individual experience is regarded as a key element, I will occasionally offer my own reaction to the events.

Rotō

For two days the group stayed at a government youth center on a mountainside overlooking an agricultural valley and its market town. Early one morning the trainees were instructed to go down into the town and find work from the residents. Instructions were to go singly from house to house offering to work without pay. They were to do whatever their host asked of them. It was strongly emphasized that this was not to be a group operation. Each was to go alone and work alone for the entire day. In addition, the trainees were not to make

---

[5] Other examples may be found in an article of mine (Rohlen, 1973) that discusses this subject at greater length.

any explanation of themselves or their reasons for volunteering for work. They could offer no more than their name and their willingness to work.

Dressed in nondescript white athletic uniforms, the trainees were thus sent out to make a most unusual request of strangers, without benefit of a social identity or a reasonable explanation. Their reliability would not be vouched for by their relationship to a known institution like the bank. The situation created by their instructors made them dependent on the good will of the people they approached.

In Japan, strangers as a rule ignore one another, and social intercourse between them is unusual and suspicious. Approached by an unknown person with such a request, the common response is a hurried and not very polite refusal. It was with considerable consternation, therefore, that the trainees left for the town below.

At first they wandered about from street to street. Many were reluctant to leave their friends and go alone to the front gate of some house. Some groups walked four or five blocks together before anyone mustered the courage to make a first approach.

The common experience was to be refused two or three times before finally locating a house or shop where one would be allowed in and given work. All agreed to having been very anxious at the start, but found the second and third approach easier to make. An impolite refusal created considerable upset, but these were rare. People who accepted them were regarded as warm and understanding, and the trainees were happy to work hard for them. It was common to volunteer to do things that even the host would not have thought to ask. This was partly to avoid going out again seeking another house and partly from a felt desire to be of help.

When the group had all returned, a general discussion was held. Each squad was told to discuss the relevance of their rotō experience to the question, "What is the meaning of work?" As usual, a variety of opinions emerged. Some had had such an interesting and pleasant time that it had not occurred to them to think of their tasks as work. When this was noticed, it was generally observed that enjoyment of work has less to do with the kind of work performed than with the attitude the person has toward it. The bank's reasons for utilizing rotō centered on establishing precisely this lesson.[6]

---

[6] The actual intent of rotō, as it is used by some Buddhist temples, is somewhat different: it is used as a method of shocking people out of spiritual lethargy and complacency. The word rotō actually means something like "bewilderment" and refers to the state of insecurity established when the individual is divorced from his comfortable social place and identity. In the course of begging for work, that

It has been the experience of some people that the meaning of work and attitudes toward work have been changed by doing rotō. The anxiety of rejection and isolation mounts with each refusal until finally, when some kindly person takes the individual in and gives him work, a cathartic sense of gratitude for being accepted and allowed to help is created. No matter what the work, "even cleaning an outhouse," the sense of relief makes the work seem pleasant and satisfying. Work that is normally looked down upon is, in this circumstance, enthusiastically welcomed.

After such an experience, it is difficult to deny the assertion that any form of work is intrinsically neither good nor bad, satisfying nor unsatisfying, appropriate nor inappropriate. Pleasure in work, it must be concluded, varies according to the subject's attitude and circumstances. Because it must assign rather dull and methodical tasks to many, management finds this lesson of obvious value.

Endurance Walk
Ever since the first day, the trainees had heard about the twenty-five-mile endurance walk held near the end of training. The almost daily mile run and the other climbing and hiking activities had been explained as preparation for this event. On the morning of the event, there seemed to be a high level of anticipation and readiness even among the weaker and less athletic trainees.

The program was simple enough. The trainees were to walk the first nine miles together in a single body. The second nine miles were to be covered with each squad walking as a unit. The last seven miles were to be walked alone and in silence. All twenty-five miles were accomplished by going around and around a large public park in the middle of the city. Each lap was approximately one mile. It was forbidden to take any refreshment. During the second stage each squad was to stay together for the entire nine miles, and competition between squads was discouraged. Finally, it was strictly forbidden to talk with others when walking alone during the last stage.

The training staff walked the twenty-five miles too, going around in the opposite direction, and a dozen or so young men from the bank

---

is, begging for acceptance by others, the subject learns of the superficial nature of much in his daily life. It is expected that his reliance on affiliations, titles, ranks, and a circle of those close to him will be revealed, and, perhaps for the first time, he will begin to ask who he really is. Rotō also provides a unique opportunity for a trusting and compassionate interaction between strangers. After a rotō experience it is unlikely that the person will continue to disregard the humanity of others, no matter how strange they are to him in terms of social relationship. It is hoped that this will foster a greater warmth and spontaneity in the individual.

were stationed along the route to offer the trainees cold drinks which, of course, they had to refuse.

This was the program, and there was no emphasis at all placed on one person finishing ahead of another. Instructions were to take as much time as needed as long as the entire twenty-five miles were completed. The walk began around seven-thirty in the morning and finished around three in the afternoon. There was no time limit, and many had not gone the full twenty-five miles, but the collapse from heat prostration of a few led the instructors to call the event off at a point where most had a lap or two remaining.

On the surface this program was simple enough, but in retrospect it seems to have been skillfully designed to maximize spiritual lessons. When we began, the day was fresh and cool, and it seemed as though we were beginning a pleasant stroll. Walking together in one large group, everyone conversed, joked, and paid little attention to the walk itself. The first nine miles passed quickly and pleasantly, and the severe physical hardship that we had been expecting seemed remote.

Forming up into squad groups at the beginning of the next nine miles, we were reminded again not to compete with other squads. But with squads close before and behind, the pace began escalating and resulted in an uproarious competition. Each time a team would come up from the rear, the team about to be overtaken would quicken its pace, and before long trainees found themselves walking very fast, so fast that those with shorter legs had to run occasionally to keep up. There was much yelling back and forth within each squad—the slower and more tired people crying out for a reduction in speed, the others urging them to greater efforts. A common solution was to put the slowest person at the head, thus slowing down the faster ones and forcing the slow ones to greater effort. By the end of the second nine miles the toll was obvious. Many, besides suffering from stiff legs and blisters, were beginning to have headaches and show evidence of heat prostration. Some lay under a tree by the finish line sucking salt tablets. It was noon by that time, and the park baked under the full heat of a mid-June sun.

Any gratification the leading squad found in their victory was soon forgotten. At the finish line there were no congratulations and no rest. Squads were instructed to break up and continue walking, this time in single file and in silence. Soon a long line of trainees stretched over the entire circumference of the course. Having already covered eighteen miles, the last nine at a grueling pace, most were very tired.

At that point everything was transformed. The excitement and clamor of competition were gone. Each individual, alone in a quiet world, was confronted by the sweep of his own thoughts as he pushed forward.

My own experience was to become acutely aware of every sort of pain. Great blisters had obviously formed on the soles of my feet; my legs, back, and neck ached; and at times I had a sense of delirium. The thirst I had expected to be so severe seemed insignificant compared to these other afflictions. Upon accomplishing a lap, instead of feeling encouraged I plunged into despair over those remaining. My awareness of the world around me, including the spectators in the park and the bank employees tempting us with refreshments, dropped almost to zero. Each step was literally more painful than the one before, and the temptation to stop and lie down for a while in the lush grass was tremendous. Near the end I could do no more than walk for a minute or two and then rest for much longer. The others around me seemed to be doing the same thing. For some reason it was heartening to discover that six or so of the trainees had fainted. Other moments brought feverish dreams of somehow sneaking away: no one would notice if I slipped out of the park and returned just when the event was closing. Bushes became places to hide. I kept going, I suppose, because I feared discovery.

Though in a feverish state, I was in some sense capable of looking objectively at my response to this new test of endurance. The content of lectures about spiritual strength came back to me. I could see that I was easily tempted and inclined to quit. Under such stress some of my thoughts were obviously not serving my interest in completing the course. Whatever will power I had arose from pride and from an emerging, almost involuntary belief in the spiritual approach. If I was to finish I needed spiritual strength. It angered and amused me to realize how cleverly this exercise had been conceived. I vowed over and over never to get involved in such a situation again, and yet within days, when the memory of the physical pain had dimmed, I was taking great pride in my accomplishment and viewing my completion of the twenty-five miles as proof that I could do anything I set my mind to.

SPIRITUAL EDUCATION: A BRIEF DISCUSSION

There are many parallels between the activities described above and the practices of such quasi-educational organizations in the West as summer camps, Sunday schools, sports teams, boy scouts, and military training. These all claim special abilities in the socialization of both youth and adults that formal public education cannot or will not offer. We have no overreaching word for the special kind of education these institutions offer in common, but it is not too difficult to appreciate similarities underlying all of them. In Japan the term "spiritual education" covers this general kind of instruction.

Many tests are devised for training purposes, and the key element in each is the experience of emotional wavering, the "spiritual" struggle within the individual to carry on until the test is completed. Passing is not a matter of scoring high or coming in ahead of others. The individual competes with himself, and success is marked by completion of the task. Enduring one test to its conclusion will make completion of subsequent similar tests less difficult, it is assumed.[7]

According to *seishin*-oriented thought, incorrect attitudes are often the source of personal difficulty.[8] The basis of a proper attitude is acceptance of necessity and responsibility. Instead of fighting life's requirements, it is better to acknowledge and accept necessary difficulties. The dimension of accepting-resisting, important in so much of Japanese life, is a key to evaluating attitudes. Complaining, criticizing, and other forms of resistance are examples of actions that evidence improper attitudes.

During training character strength is closely associated with worldly achievement. Trainees are told that success reflects a man's character, and because a major quality of spiritual strength is persistence, it follows that achievements that take a long time are the more notable. The accomplished person is one who has overcome barriers that try one's spirit, and as a rule it takes a life of persistent effort to be recognized as fully accomplished. This opinion fits well with the nature of rank and promotions in the bank.

Although these are rudimentary lessons, Uedagin executives have decided that today's young people are not learning them in the public schools.[9] Rightfully, they say, spiritual development should not be of concern to a company. It is more appropriately carried on in the

---

7 Many commonly encountered personality values, such as *nintai* (fortitude), *gaman* (patience), *shinbō* (endurance), *gambaru* (tenacity), and the like, point to this form of behavior. Of course loyalty is hardly meaningful without the ingredient of persistence.

8 Here I have in mind the expressions *kokoro-gamae, taido, kokoro no mochikata,* and *mono no kangaekata*, all of which translate as "attitude."

9 See Singleton (1967) and Norbeck (1970) for discussions of moral education in contemporary schools and the parental and political pressure for its increase.

family, in the school, and in other educational organizations, but in
their view a vacuum has been created due to the postwar loss of confidence in Japanese traditional values, and so the bank attempts to
compensate.

A question worth asking is whether this kind of education is anything more than a futile attempt by an older, prewar generation to
transform the present one into their image. What influence can it
have on trainees of the present generation, raised as they have been
in a world governed by strong Western influence and an equally
powerful rejection of Japan's own traditions? While generational differences are pronounced in contemporary Japan, we must doubt the
underlying implication that each generation retains intact the philosophy, values, and life style it expresses when first entering the adult
world. At least in Uedagin it seems that as men pass deeper into adult
responsibility, their attitudes about the bank merge with those of
preceding generations. Training may be an insignificant cause, compared to social maturation, but it does seem to crystallize the issues
and to shock the individual into a consideration of the fundamental
differences in outlook between spiritualism and modern thought. Although some young men are quite skeptical, in time they too are likely
to wish that their successors in the bank learn to appreciate the
"spiritual" point of view.[10]

Even more to the point is the fact that, without quitting the company and the life of a salaried worker, Uedagin men must achieve
some sense of themselves that is reasonably consistent with the requirements of their jobs and their participation in the organization.
The alternative perspectives of personhood and individual fulfillment
found in the society at large, such as those that stress individual gratification or independence, are not easily adjusted to the requirements
of work and company membership. The seishin perspective, on the
other hand, offers the possibility of bringing work and personhood
into a coherent whole. Cognitive dissonance and the stress of incom-
patible ambitions can be reduced, that is, and it is not surprising that
with time (and experience), most that stay with Uedagin move in the
direction of accepting the implications of the seishin outlook. External perspectives are not forgotten, but neither are they allowed to
dominate conscious concern. Only the most unhappy and isolated

10 I should add that while resistance and resentment on the part of trainees were
surprisingly low at the outset and virtually gone by the end of training, most experts would say that spiritual training is only of great effectiveness when it is
entered into voluntarily.

among middle-aged men consistently reject the seishin view and this, of course, is a poignant, if indirect expression of their general alienation.

I might add that the movement of Americans from job to job also has a lot to do with our sense of personhood. That is, movement serves to retain the promise of independence and success. Learning to accept work and its organizational framework is that much harder for us, because we have no articulated psychological point of view supporting this process. Economic necessity is no substitute for a promise of personal fulfillment such as offered by spiritualism.

Americans are likely to consider Uedagin training as a case of improper interference with the privacy and the independence of the individual. This kind of education has a religious flavor, and, to us, only totalitarian regimes make religion involuntary. We also consider companies to be singularly devoid of responsibility for moral kinds of education. Some Uedagin people also have reservations about spiritual training, but on different grounds: it is too old-fashioned to be effective, and it is wasteful of time and money. Even its critics, in other words, find it legitimate for the company to teach morality and sponsor personal spiritual growth. Companies are properly more than money-making machines.

We observe in this and elsewhere in Uedagin life a centripetal tendency in which the company takes upon itself activities and functions that could be dispersed and independent within the larger society. Medical care, housing, leisure facilities, and social recreation are other examples of this same tendency. The capacity and inclination to fully elaborate company life in this way belong primarily to large firms in Japan. Size is correlated with economies of scale, with adequate resources, with lower quitting rates, and perhaps with a greater need to overcome the alienating effects of large organization.

Finally, we should consider the apparent contradiction between the general image of the company as one that succors and protects its members and the fact that it forces such a severe training experience on its new men. What we would label "paternalism" in Uedagin has two contrasting sides (the mother and father aspects, one is tempted to say), and the strictness of training is best understood as being part of a complex that involves a general inclination to parental role playing on the part of the company. "Uedagin for all its rigor and strictness is, at heart, understanding and sympathetic," says the spokesman for the incoming men at the initiation ceremony. Self-reliance and the offer of dependent security are contradicting emphasis, framing a reality that is dynamic and destined to seem incomplete. That company training is designed to foster self-reliant people harnessed to the work of the organization appears necessary because of the strong tendency to seek and offer dependence both within the contemporary Japanese middle-class family, where mothers indulge their young children greatly, and within the company system itself.

10

DORMITORIES AND COMPANY APARTMENTS

Many Uedagin people live together by virtue of company housing. The bank's five bachelors' dormitories and seven family apartment buildings house a majority of the bachelors and slightly less than 20 percent of the married men's families.[1] There is nothing uncommon in this for a large Japanese company, particularly one that must transfer men from place to place. Company housing is an important aspect of the Uedagin pattern, one that virtually every man experiences during at least part of his career with the bank.

In considering this, we will be interested in a number of questions about the contributions of coresidence to interpersonal relations within the bank. Does the fact of living together make for greater cohesion? Does it facilitate better working relations? What is the degree of influence the Uedagin administration exerts over the life of people in the company's dormitories and apartments? Does company housing mean living under the authority of Uedagin twenty-four hours a day?

We must also inquire into the nature of relationships among people in these units. The fact that coresidents are generally of the same age and rank makes their situation particularly interesting, given the usual emphasis on hierarchy in the work organization. Does the relatively egalitarian basis of these relationships distinguish them from other forms of relationship in the bank? To answer these and related questions, the bank's two largest residential units will be described and discussed in some detail.[2]

---

[1] Residence is also a factor in the lives of many of the bank's quasi members. In most branch office buildings there are small apartments for the families of quasi members who live where they work.

[2] There are no extensive studies of Japanese company dormitories in either English or Japanese, but Cole (1971a) discusses the place of dormitories in the life of blue-collar workers, and Shibusawa (1958) and Sumiya (1963) relate the history of the dormitory system in prewar industries, especially those employing women.

THE AOYAMA BACHELORS' DORMITORY

The company has recently built an impressive four-story dormitory (*dokushin-ryō*) for its bachelors, replacing a smaller, more run-down building that had been in use from the earliest days of the bank. The new dorm is located immediately behind the welfare building and training institute and shares with them a lawn, garden, and recreation facilities. This complex is located in perhaps the most exclusive residential area of the city, and the property alone represents a substantial investment. At present, the dormitory's capacity is described as one hundred persons, but because this figure is based on a calculation of one bachelor to a room, there is a strong possibility that it will soon increase, for there are plans to begin doubling up people in rooms as the need arises. The total number of unmarried young men working for the bank in Aoyama is above one hundred, and those bachelors whose parents live outside the city are given preference to stay in the dormitory.

The system of recruiting men from a wide geographical area and the system of transfers combine to create a large population of young men who are working in offices far from home. Probably more than three-quarters of all bachelors are in this category. The alternative to dormitory living for them would be to rent small rooms on an individual basis. These are generally expensive, of poor quality, and difficult to find, and the young men taking them would find themselves scattered over the city leading separate and rather lonely lives. To avoid this situation, the bank has built and continues to build dormitories wherever feasible. Presently there are dormitories in the five largest cities served by the bank. The newest one, built in 1968, is located on the top floor of a new branch office. In total, about two hundred bachelors reside in these five dormitories.

In cities and towns where branches are small, the young men generally have to live on their own. Although branch chiefs and senpai try to be of assistance, seldom can this extra attention make up the difference. Young men just out of school expect to find their friends among the other men of their new company, and few alternative sources of friends exist, particularly since companies typically strive to facilitate companionship among their own. The result is a low level of interaction among young people, particularly white-collar

---

The following brief description of the Uedagin dormitory is based on countless visits and interviews with residents and the dormitory director. I lived next door to the dormitory during most of my study.

people, of different companies. ~~Uedagin bachelors seldom make new outside friends once they enter the company.~~

Another possible consequence of solitary living is the development of mental unbalance, particularly depression.[3] While the dormitory system by no means totally eliminates personal problems, records clearly indicate a high correlation between their incidence and living outside a dormitory. Personnel's explanation is that the dormitory provides a stabilizing influence and that newcomers greatly benefit from the guidance of dorm senpai.

Contrary to what we might expect, Uedagin young men much prefer dormitory living to living at home or in rented quarters. Besides the company of friends, it provides an inexpensive and convenient way of life. The dormitory is located in a pleasant district close to transportation. For much less than it would cost elsewhere, the bachelor receives two meals a day and laundry services. All he must do to maintain himself is clean his own room. The recreation facilities, including a TV, ping-pong table, tennis court, gym, and grassy lawn, are far superior to what he could find elsewhere. Every new member interviewed expressed a desire to live in a company dormitory.[4]

From the bank's point of view, the expenses of building and maintaining a large dormitory system are justified because they (1) benefit many individuals, fulfilling a goal of the company's welfare program, (2) help to reduce the number of personal problems among bachelors, (3) are a promising factor in the development of a greater community among the young men, (4) serve to direct off-hours activities to the benefit of Uedagin, and (5) are good advertising for the bank at recruitment time. That large and luxurious facilities symbolize for the public-at-large a company's status and beneficence is another factor that cannot be ignored. All of these considerations are important, and there is no answer to the question which is more significant, the interests of the bachelors or those of the bank.

[3] A psychiatrist who consults for companies told me he often recommends improving dormitory life in order to solve psychological instability among young workers.

[4] Industrial relations specialists, viewing the question of company dormitories from the angle of the prewar development of the dormitory system for factory workers, strongly emphasize that they were created as instruments of managerial policy. The desire to restrict mobility (Cole, 1971a:178) and generally to control the lives of workers (Shibusawa, 1958 and Sumiya, 1963) are cited as explanations for the development of dormitories. The convenience, relative cost, and social relations side of early factory dormitories deserve more attention in the historical treatment of the subject.

AOYAMA DORMITORY: FACILITIES AND RULES

The building itself is an imposing gray concrete structure of modern, but not particularly graceful, design. Along the street in front of the dormitory stands a six-foot wall with a heavy iron gate. Compared to most other company dormitories in the same neighborhood, this seems larger and more luxurious (a distinction Japanese are liable to make). The few bachelors who own cars park them on the narrow street outside. If the automobile boom continues, the dormitory will face a tremendous parking problem some day soon.

Behind the dorm building, there is ample room on the lawn to play catch, lift weights, practice judo, or just lounge on the grass. On Sundays in good weather there is always activity outside. A tennis court is available, but because few play it sits idle most of the time, an empty symbol of the bank's largess. The most popular team sports in the bank, baseball and Japanese fencing, are both supported primarily by young men from the dormitory. Because the bank does not own a baseball field and the few public fields are hard to reserve, a game requires arrangements made far in advance. This inconvenience dampens enthusiasm, and it seems there is always a movement afoot to revive the flagging baseball team spirit. The fencing team, by contrast, has its own gym in the training institute next door. Practice begins at six-thirty in the morning, and the rest of the dormitory and neighborhood awake to the eerie sounds of clashing bamboo swords and combatants' screams.

The first floor includes a large common room used for both dining and recreation, several Japanese-style rooms, a kitchen, a room for the director of the dormitory, and a large communal bath. Eating, bathing, and watching TV are the main activities here. A small house for the director's family is attached to the main building, and next door to that are small apartments for the six women (ryō obasan or dorm "aunts") who work in the dormitory kitchen and do the cleaning. The bachelors live in singles on the three upper floors. Their rooms are uniformly and attractively provided with Western-style furniture. They resemble American college dormitory rooms, but they are smaller.

When a young man is sick or has any special need for assistance, the director and the six women gladly try to make him more comfortable. While the food is inferior to meals at home, the young men otherwise find the care satisfactory.

Residents have the opportunity to develop and express their own interests in the decoration and provisioning of their rooms. Many have their own televisions and record players. Pin-up girls, a few books, some souvenirs from trips, and an album of photographs of high school and company excursions constitute the typical decor. Drinking is allowed in the rooms, and most young men have several bottles of whiskey prominently displayed. Bachelors with many younger friends maintain large supplies of liquor since their rooms are often full of visitors. Alcoholic treats are clearly a part of good relations in the dorm.

At night, however, the place is almost never boisterous. People come back from work at different times, and while some wish to sleep, others remain downstairs watching TV or talking. It is almost unknown for the entire dormitory to be engrossed in a single activity or mood, and typically less than a dozen men are eating at the same time. Because each has his own room, those that choose to may develop an independent style of living in which contact with others is kept to a minimum.

The new dormitory is too luxurious, according to those who concern themselves with the flagging state of morale there. In the old dormitory, they say, people lived on top of one another tenement style, and the winter wind whistled through the cracks in the wooden walls. The spirit in the place was much better. As the director of the dormitory explained:

> There is no sense of sharing a rugged existence where even one's laundry is done by others. In the old dorm, we did our own and hung it up in the middle of the room. We probably complained, but we enjoyed living that way.

He went on to criticize the single-room arrangement of the new dormitory:

> No one should feel lonely living with one hundred other young men, yet there are some who are lonely here. They stay in their rooms watching TV or listening to their new stereos instead of joining activities downstairs. It is perfectly understandable that the top men of the bank should have desired to build this handsome dormitory to make life easier and more attractive, particularly with a growing labor shortage, but the luxury and the single-room arrangement have killed the old fellowship. Management couldn't foresee the consequences of their generosity.

There is a rule that activities on the first floor should end by eleven at night. People out on the town should make an attempt to be back by that time. If they are going to be late they are expected to phone. There is no fuss made if people stay out late or even overnight, as long as they report their plans. The duty of sitting at the telephone desk for an evening rotates to each resident about every three months.

Dormitory Self-Rule

Self-government within the dormitory involves a general meeting, at which discussions and decisions can be made by the entire dormitory on democratic principles, and a group of elected officers, who have the task of organizing dormitory affairs. General meetings are not held on a regular basis but are called by the officers when there is something to be discussed. The average seems to be a meeting every two months. Any subject may be discussed, but in practice the younger men simply listen and are not inclined to air their opinions publicly. The selection of topics and the responsibility to discuss them rests with the older residents, particularly those interested in the dormitory.

The election of domitory officers is a function of the general meeting, but never have candidates been raised in opposition to those nominated by the outgoing officers. The elected leaders are charged with making plans, balancing accounts, collecting dues for food, consulting with management on behalf of the dormitory, and bringing up new questions before the general meeting. The jobs are not popular because they take time and invite criticism.

From the bank's point of view, administration of the domitory is the responsibility of the welfare section. One man from this section (a former chief demoted to researcher) resides next to the domitory, and as its director he represents the administration. He also serves as liaison, representing the dormitory's interests to the welfare section. The man is terribly conscientious and devoted to making improvements for the bachelors' benefit. Because their duties overlap considerably the director and the officers are both in a position to run the daily affairs of the dormitory. In practice, the director, though he would prefer it otherwise, has almost complete charge of routine matters. The officers, busy in their work, prefer to depend on his initiative. Ironically, it is part of the director's job to encourage the young men to take more positive action on their own behalf. In the face of a seeming paradox, the director continues to make great efforts to stimulate dormitory life. He leads a singing group, teaches judo, and has organized a morning jogging group. Often he stays up to open the gate for revelers who come back after eleven. He pampers them like a devoted father, doing for the young men more than they are willing to do for themselves, yet his enthusiasm and devotion foster the very dependency he wishes would disappear.

A third locus of responsibility is the older residents. The single most active leader, Takeda, is twenty-nine years old and has lived in the dormitory for his entire ten-year career. He is the unquestioned leader among the bachelors. A member of the training section staff, he is in an ideal position to handle leadership responsibilities because as part of the personnel department, it is easy for him to consult with management. He comes to know and be liked by incoming new members during their introductory training, and in addition, he is the captain of the fencing team. Mr. Takeda has no official dormitory office. Jobs such as dormitory president and treasurer are held by younger men. Takeda's influence is based on the loyalty of numerous young men who turn to him for assistance, advice, and leadership. While the term is not quite appropriate (since today it has a pejorative connotation), Mr. Takeda is a kind of *oyabun* ("boss," literally "fictive father") for the dormitory.[5] His great influence depends on personal relations and the acceptance of his authority by others. He works hard for the benefit of the dormitory and yet has no particular expectation of personal gain from his efforts.

Sharing the responsibility of leading the domitory with him are a few other older bachelors, collectively referred to as *ryō senpai*, "dorm seniors." Among the older bachelors are many too busy, unpopular, or disinterested to do the job. Takeda's lieutenants, including the dorm's officers, consult informally about dormitory problems, particularly before and after general meetings. Since he is a high school graduate, Takeda has his greatest appeal among other high school graduates, to whom he is something of a hero. Most university people show less interest in Takeda and in the dormitory. In fact, only a minority of the bachelors over twenty-three concern themselves with dormitory life. Most have made their personal friends and are capable of finding entertainment outside this context.

The relationships between the welfare section, the dormitory director, and the leaders among the bachelors tend to be disjointed and ambiguous. The official policy is for the dormitory to be run by the residents on a home-rule basis, with the administration holding only a veto power over improper activities. The various parties interpret

5 While *oyabun* is a term used primarily in joking or in pejorative descriptions today, actual oyabun in some parts of Japanese society continue to perform valuable and appreciated service as leaders in low-level economic and political organizations.

this differently. The elected leaders show little inclination to direct the daily affairs of the dormitory, yet they complain about their lack of independence from bank supervision and opinion. They would like more recreational equipment and more parties. Their ambitions have the support of the director, but they feel they are opposed by the chief of the welfare section and some higher executives. The areas of disagreement are not discussed openly between the two sides; only hints and vague suggestions are exchanged. People in the dormitory only know for certain that their hints for improvement have gone unanswered. They explain that their wishes involve one of three sensitive problems: money, girls at dorm parties, or keeping the garden and lawn untrammeled—issues they assume the older men of management are reluctant to give way on. Takeda and the director, the two go-betweens, claim that the generation gap is perhaps more apparent in this situation than anywhere else in the organization. Management's attitude is a mixture of disappointment with the bachelors for failing to develop a satisfactory life for themselves, concern that life in the dormitory be improved, and fear that left totally on their own the young men would create incidents that would hurt Uedagin's reputation. They fear, for example, unsanctioned romance in dormitory-sponsored events, something that might offend parents. In summary, authority and responsibility for the dormitory, especially for its recreational activities, are vague and mercurial, with both sides pointing to the other as the source of the problem. Management has not relinquished its veto power, but it is ready to admit that it has little power over the bachelors' morale.

Girls, Dating, and the Dormitory

Though there is no rule forbidding it, no one would consider bringing a girlfriend to the dormitory. It is simply not done, and to do so would be to disregard the clear and virtually unchallenged barriers between the areas of life enjoyed exclusively by men and those where men and women may meet. Bachelors who do have regular girlfriends tend to secrecy and exclusiveness in the conduct of their romances, and it is unlikely that the dormitory would be turned into a social club for dates even if the administration encouraged such a change. In this sense, the dormitory is a different social entity from an American college fraternity.

Those who do date regularly are the subject of comment and some criticism from Takeda and other leaders. He notes that dating tends to isolate bachelors from dormitory life. This damages the chances that dormitory activities will receive sufficient support, and, as a consequence, it adversely affects the lives of the majority, who do not have girlfriends. Takeda, who has a fiancee himself, does not disapprove of romance. The problem, as he sees it, is the incompatibility of the traditional pattern of male camaraderie with the exclusiveness of the newer pattern of dating. He sympathizes with the younger bachelors who have no girlfriends and are, apparently, unable to organize entertainment for themselves. They want enthusiastic leadership in the dormitory, but dating has removed enough of the older bachelors from participation that activities are difficult to organize and maintain.[6]

At present, the absence of planned activities causes young men to go out on the town for entertainment, leaving the dormitory to the tired, the sleepy, and the less sociable bachelors. Many residents are less concerned with the decline of dormitory life than Takeda, yet it is usual for people to express nostalgia for the time past when the dormitory was a rousing place to live.

The Dormitory Festival: an Illustration

The 1969 dormitory spring festival (ryōsai or ryō matsuri) illustrates many of the above issues and indicates one possible compromise solution to the problem of girls and the dormitory. Traditionally, twice a year the dormitory has had some sort of outing, called a festival. These and the banquet at the end of the year are its main social events. For reasons that are not too clear, the spring party had not been held in 1968, and the younger residents were disgruntled with the dormitory president for this. Their complaints and the urgings of Takeda and other senpai resulted in the presentation of a plan for a spring party, one that would include any girls in the bank who wished to attend. The party particularly interested the younger men since this was a chance for excitement and an opportunity to meet girls outside their own offices. The older leaders were, in fact, arranging the party primarily for the younger men. The goal was to raise dormitory spirit.

Even though the request to include girls was unconventional, it was approved by the welfare section. Up to that time, all dormitory festivals had been all-male overnight drinking sessions at some seaside resort, and this was something new.

The night before, the young men worked hard preparing the food

---

[6] That eighteen to twenty-three-year-old men need help in organizing their own entertainment seems impossible by American standards, but in Japan this is not unusual and certainly not pathological. The "passivity" evidenced in this example is familiar to students of Japanese society, but a less ethnocentric label is necessary. Japanese do not experience anything approaching the education in peer-group activity that American teenagers do, and the informal "organizer" is neither an attractive nor familiar role for persons this age.

and collecting the equipment. The welfare section bought the soft drinks, and the residents paid for the rest of the food themselves.

Attendance the next day included about fifty men from the dormitory, thirty girls from various branches and the home office, and a handful of bank officials. Whether they were present to chaperone or to lend a hand is not certain; but whatever the reason, the chief of the welfare section, two deputies, several other married men, and the director of the dormitory were all in attendance. Management was obviously reluctant to allow the event to occur under bank auspices without supervision.

The day's activities began with a hike from a country bus stop up a mountain to the picnic area. A well organized two hours of folk dancing led by a professional instructor were followed by a leisurely meal and a walk back down the mountain late in the afternoon. All the precautions and supervision on the part of the older men might have implied that the young people were practiced and forward in relations between the sexes, but this was far from the case. They showed great hesitancy and embarrassment with each other. Young people from the same office tended to stick together, and choosing partners for dancing required the lead of the older married men.

Afterwards, everyone expressed great satisfaction with the event and with the fact that the dormitory president had finally begun to organize activities for the younger men. Senpai should do this kind of thing, they said. In fact, the restitution of this festival and the inclusion of women were Takeda's ideas. He reasoned that "mixed" activities, if held outside the dormitory and if limited to women in the bank, would improve dormitory morale without arousing a veto from management. Coeducational activities that avoid the dating pattern are a promising way out of the dilemma, he thinks.

Friendships within the Dormitory

Although its social life is unsatisfactory and there are few organized activities, the dormitory does produce and support many varied friendships.

Groups most often form among those working together in the same office. They usually commute together, end work at the same time, and often stop for a drink on their way home. Conversation and gossip about the office and their superior are easy and satisfying.

Membership in sports teams has much the same effect, particularly in the case of baseball and fencing. Often in the evenings, teammates sit around in each other's rooms drinking and talking.

Members of the same entering class (*dōkisei*), who went through training together, also tend to form into drinking and friendship groups.

A shared interest in mah-jongg is another social bond. Mah-jongg fanatics often play throughout a Saturday night, ending totally exhausted but happy the next morning. Sharing this kind of enthusiasm and experience creates a special familiarity that can be translated into deeper friendship quite easily.

Having graduated from the same high school or university is one more common basis for friendship, just as the same home region and the same dialect draw bachelors together. Others regard the men from one region or school as a group and thereby strengthen their common identity.

While members of the same office, sports team, or mah-jongg group will drink together on occasion, there is a separate type of group comprised of people who simply like to drink together (*nomi-nakama*), who go out often, and who seem to have similar styles of pleasure seeking. A bath group (*furo-nakama*), comprised of those who generally spend a long time in the bath together, is also recognized. It is common for them to sing, tell jokes, and generally carouse in the relaxed atmosphere of the large communal bath.

The internal structure of all of these informal groups follows one of two basic forms. If they are age homogeneous, they are comprised entirely of people who are within a few years of each other and regard themselves as the same age (*dōnenpai*). Otherwise, they are made up of one or more junior-senior relationships. Examples of the first category are the drinking, mah-jongg, and some of the entering class groups. In these, equality of status is the rule, and greater intimacy can reputedly be attained.

The drinking and mah-jongg groups tend to contain men of the same age for certain reasons. There is something obsessional to the enjoyment of these less than elevating pastimes, and the addiction, like a shared secret, creates a strong bond. The reason given why senpai-kohai relationships are separated from such activities is that mah-jongg involves gambling and this is best conducted when the participants are basically of the same maturity and economic status. Similarly, to enjoy fully the intimacy of drinking, they say, there should be no restraints created by inequalities of status and age. This underlines the general feeling that the ultimate in intimacy is obtained only when no hierarchy exists.

Hobby groups are not notably significant in the creation of friendship groups within the dormitory. While two or three bachelors may study singing or English together, unless they have other interests in common they do not make this the basis for general companionship. Nor is residence on the same floor of the dormitory the basis of close personal ties.

When the personnel section asserts that dormitory living brings stability and keeps young men from loneliness, it is the chance to make friends rather than the general social life of the dormitory that they are acknowledging to be important, and it is true that the dormitory facilitates friendship even though coresidence is seldom the cornerstone of the relationship.

How Bachelors Spend Their Free Time

In order to explore and document some of the less apparent aspects of the bachelors' social life, a simple form was prepared on which a person could quickly record on a daily basis the following information:

(1) The time of leaving work in the evening.
(2) The time of returning to the dormitory.
(3) What activities occurred between leaving the office and going to bed.
(4) With what people the time was spent.

Forty of these simplified diaries covering a month each were given to Takeda at the end of fieldwork. Several months later thirteen completed forms were returned. The following discussion is based primarily on the results of these thirteen diaries. They represent 16 percent of the dormitory population, and the age distribution of the sample closely approximates that of the dormitory as a whole, but a bias against bachelors with steady girlfriends probably exists since they would be the least likely to receive and fill out the forms. The observation that steady daters are more isolated from dormitory life is not confirmed because there are no such people in the sample itself.

The time of leaving the office varied considerably. During a single week it was common for most respondents to have quitting times ranging from six to nine o'clock. The average was roughly seven-thirty (excluding Saturdays when it was three-thirty). Relevant here is the fact that such long and irregular hours seriously limit social activities. It is difficult to know in advance whether work will end early or late, and, consequently, it is difficult to plan social get-togethers with people outside one's office. Saturday evenings are one certainty, and recently the bank has begun a policy of assuring an early quitting time one other night a week. Sunday and a few week nights, then, are the times it is most possible to join with friends for dinner, bowling, a movie, or an evening of drinking.

The late hours and fatigue of work explain why the thirteen respondents went straight back to the dormitory on most nights, ate dinner, and went to bed shortly afterwards. Watching TV, chatting, and reading were reported for these evenings. One nineteen year old indicated he spent over half of his evenings working alone in his room on a hobby, yet most listed no more than one such evening a month. There is almost an even split between instances of socializing and not socializing on the first floor these nights, and every respondent had a pattern of sometimes socializing and sometimes going to his room.

Only five reported having a date during the month. Of these, three had two dates, and one had three dates. Others, however, probably went out in groups with girls, particularly those from the same office.

The most interesting aspects of the diary data are not related to dating behavior or sociability in the dormitory. What is most striking is the prominence of other Uedagin people in their private social life. The separation of private life from work, a powerful theme for Americans, is not apparent in the data: such distinctions are obscured by the continuity of Uedagin people in the individual's private and company worlds. We have noted the frequency of recreation within the work group. When we examine the more voluntary aspects of the bachelors' social life, we find company-based relationships playing just as significant a role. In their off hours, with the opportunity to associate with whomever they choose, the young men of this sample spend their time with other Uedagin people no matter what the activity (see Table 7).

The fact that so much "private" time is spent with others in the bank reflects in part the absence of alternatives. It is not that old friends are

TABLE 7

Off-Hours Activities and Associates

	Movies	Bowling	Drinking	Dating	Hobby, etc.	Home	Total
With other(s) from Uedagin	6	29	34	1	9		79
With other(s) not from Uedagin	3		1	5		2	11
Alone	5	10	7		4		26
Total	14	39	42	6	13	2	116

forgotten or avoided, but it becomes difficult to see them once work begins. Old friends too work long and often unpredictable hours, and they too are liable to transfer. They are cherished but seldom seen.

Public meeting places for young people, such as sports clubs and youth organizations, are relatively undeveloped in Japan. The youth organizations that do exist (political, religious, and educational) are not natural places for aspiring white-collar workers. They are rather low status, take too much time, and are essentially for people lacking the benefits of connection with a large company.[7] Uedagin bachelors realize that membership in politically oriented groups is taboo; they generally find the religious groups objectionable; and they are a bit too sophisticated for the rest. Those that do find new friends outside the bank do so primarily by chance. Finally, the high degree of in-company friendship among white-collar workers gives rise to a shared expectation of disdain from "outsiders," and little possibility of more than a passing acquaintanceship when this proves not true.

THE COMPANY APARTMENT IN AOYAMA

In contrast to the many friendships found in the bachelors' dormitory, it is rare for married men living in the same company apartment complex (*shataku*) to socialize with one another as neighbors.[8] In those rare instances when men sharing the same housing do socialize, they do so on something other than a neighbor basis. Those who share the same office, who have worked together in the past, who have gone to school together, or who have previously been friends in a company dormitory might visit or combine to lead their families on a Sunday expedition, but as a rule Uedagin bankers prefer to keep office and personal relations separate from their families. This attitude encourages the view that the company apartment building is essentially the domain of wives and children.

Unlike their enthusiasm for the dormitory system, management sees no great advantages for the bank in its family housing program. It does

[7] Uedagin women are more interested in outside clubs and organizations. They are likely to be part of some circle studying an artistic skill, and a few join political groups.

[8] Company housing projects have not been described for Japan. See Dore (1958) for a description of relations in an older city neighborhood and Vogel (1963) for an account of neighborhood relations in a suburban area. Kiefer (1970a) has described life in a *danchi*, or modern apartment complex. Discussions of "neighborhood" ties in villages are numerous and include Embree (1939) and Beardsley, Hall, and Ward (1959).

permit the company to transfer families smoothly, and it has been a great benefit to individual families, given the postwar housing shortage, but considerations of individual stability and company socialization, so important in the case of the dormitory, are not considered relevant for married men.

Most of Uedagin's apartments were built in the early fifties when there was an acute shortage of housing throughout urban Japan. The fire bombings of 1945, overpopulation, and the astronomical cost of land combined to create a serious shortage. Periodic transfers compounded the problem for people (mostly white-collar) in larger companies. Like almost every company that could afford it, Uedagin built apartments to house at least some of its members' families. The housing shortage has eased considerably since the fifties, but still young family men and those transferred to big cities must rely heavily on company housing. Presently, 265 families (18 percent of all Uedagin families) live in company apartments. Lately new apartments have been built in association with new branches, but no new apartments have been constructed in Aoyama. This is a clear indication that company involvement with family housing is becoming less and less important as the housing situation improves. A new policy of encouraging Uedagin men to build their own homes with special bank loans is a further step in this direction. Ultimately, the housing pattern will probably include numerous apartments associated with big city branches, but no company housing in Aoyama itself.

Physical Arrangements

The apartment building we shall consider is the largest operated by the bank. The complex of forty-eight units is in Aoyama and serves families of men almost all in their thirties. The Aoyama apartments consist of two four-story buildings (here called A and B). Each building has three entryways, and groups of eight apartments share the same entryway and stairs. The six sets of entryway groupings are referred to by their residents as little neighborhoods (*tonari gumi*).

The apartments in building A are slightly larger than those in B, and because of this the occupants of the two buildings are clearly distinguished according to the husband's rank. The larger apartments belong to families of deputies or higher; the smaller apartments in B are occupied by families of regulars. Husbands in building A are older than their counterparts in building B, as are their wives and children. The average age difference in the case of children, for example, is five years. The families in A have also been in residence in the complex for a longer time. Often, they first resided in B and then, following the husband's promotion, moved over to an opening in A. The families in A have lived in the apartments on the average of four and a half years; the average is two years for the families in B.

The Aoyama apartments are in the central part of the city, making the main office and most branches easy to reach by bus or trolley, and daily shopping needs can be filled in the neighborhood. The surrounding area continues to be a pleasant part of the city.

If its good location is an indication of the bank's concern for the families, its physical appearance indicates a decline of enthusiasm since its construction. The buildings are of aging, light brown concrete devoid of detail and embellishment except for a tall narrow advertising pillar on the roof. On sunny days, laundry hung up to dry on the narrow balconies to the south of each apartment adds a touch of color to an otherwise drab scene. The only evidence of any communal interest or activity is a few flowers planted here and there in the sandy soil and some children's play apparatus in the opening between the two buildings. At the rear of the approximately half-acre piece of land stands a recently erected shed already overflowing with new Toyotas and Datsuns.

With the exception of the before school, lunch time, and after school migrations of school children in bright uniforms, the general atmosphere is quiet and sedate. Unlike some company housing, this complex has no gate or wall, and the postman, service people, occasional visitors, and housewives on shopping trips pass freely in and out of the area throughout the day. When the weather is nice, mothers of preschool children often spend time in the open space between the two buildings, watching their children and exchanging polite comments. It would be rare, however, for anyone passing by to notice more than two or three women gathered there. Only twice a year is a general meeting of all wives held in the automobile shed at the back of the lot.

The typical apartment in B building consists of a tiny kitchen, a bath, a toilet, a narrow entranceway, and two approximately twelve-foot square rooms: an incredibly small space for a family by our standards. The two main rooms are invariably crowded with dowry chests, a TV, often a stereo, bookcases, knickknack cabinets, and the like. The apartments cannot begin to accommodate the increased consumption of their occupants. Living being so cramped, it is little wonder that the men find it preferable to conduct their social life away from home. One apparent benefit of company housing, cramped and stereotyped as it is, is that children are allowed to roam freely because no differences of wealth or status create barriers between families in

the same building. A uniformity, much like that created by school
uniforms, is a by-product of this kind of living.

The narrowness and inconvenience bother the residents, but the
conformity of life style is not a problem they mention. The complaints they have are never openly expressed directly to bank authorities. Wives and husbands share their private irritations only with
friends. One wife, after telling me how her sons had virtually no
place to study in the evening, added, "Please excuse me, it's really not
right for me to complain about this since it is part of the bank; it is
what the bank has given us." It is a common sentiment that whatever
comes with life in the bank should be accepted or endured with gratitude. Private complaints are numerous, but, because of this attitude,
open criticism and concerted action are virtually nonexistent.

Organization of the Apartments

Meetings of wives are held by the automobile shed every six months
to elect a woman from each building to serve as a liaison between the
bank and the individual households on matters of administration and
upkeep.[9] While there is an election, there is never any contest for the
job, for no one seeks such work. The position can only be held by
those with children already in school, and, since the job changes every
six months, anyone who does not have young children can expect the
responsibility sooner or later. These leaders head a simple administrative organization. Each entry group of eight households is regarded
as a unit, with the job of entry leader rotating monthly among the
eight wives. In addition to informing the others of any messages from
the building leader, the entry leader is expected to select the day for
the combined entry cleanup, to relate complaints to the building
leader, and to organize assistance if a member wife has difficulties.
Occasionally such things as a going-away party or a gathering to welcome a new member will also be staged by the entry leader.

There is considerable shyness between strangers in Japan, and it
often takes the newcomers over a half year to become acquainted with
others in their little "neighborhood group." Entry leaders, although
expected to help, may fail to step forward and aid in the matter of
introductions. It is customary for newcomers to go around to the
other wives in the stairwell and also to the building leader, taking
some token gift (perhaps a small towel or a bowl of noodles), and

---

[9] The rest of this chapter is based on interviews of one to two hours with twenty-
seven wives living in the forty-eight-unit complex. Longer, more informal discussions were also held with four men living there, and I was an invited guest of a
few of the families.

thereby ask their favor and assistance. Some entryways try to hold a combined party for newcomers at least once a year, but the impression of the recently arrived wives is that the party and other welcoming procedures are more talked about than practiced.

Social Life in the Apartments

On the average of once a month the typical husband brings home someone from the bank as his guest. There is no set schedule or routine in this, but after beginning an evening with dinner downtown, husbands occasionally bring their younger office subordinates or an old office mate or university friend home. Since it is felt that the most successful and intimate times should not be preceded by elaborate arrangements, wives are not usually given any advance warning. Only the few men who host weekly mah-jongg bouts entertain at home on a regular basis.

Old friends and office subordinates may drop in unexpectedly, perhaps to talk over some problem, but whatever the reason, they will not be visiting because they are neighbors. Even the man next door is likely to define the reasons for a visit in office terms. In the Aoyama apartments, at least, it is fruitless to search for a society of neighbors among the men. They come home late and leave early. There is little for them to do at home and no neighborhood activities for them to join.

Their wives, whose existence centers on the children, do conduct neighbor relations in the apartments to a limited degree. Unlike men, wives often have no one but their neighbors to turn to for company and for assistance in times of trouble.

A tradition of neighborliness does exist in Japan's villages and older urban areas, and such things as mutual aid associations and neighborhood groups are still common. Men have come to ignore these forms, but among their wives the desire for a spirit of neighborliness persists.

While the entry-unit system seldom produces a circle of friends within a stairwell, having children of the same age does. Through school affairs, in particular, mothers of classmates have many opportunities to meet. Subsequently, they often consult each other and begin to reciprocate assistance. Pairs and sometimes tiny groups of mothers exchange such services as babysitting, escorting children to school, and even shopping. When a mother or child is sick, the fact is soon known by the other women in such circles, and they are usually the first to offer assistance. In this manner, relationships intensify, and longer chats over tea and expeditions together to downtown stores are eventually added to the activities as the wives become closer friends.

The agency of children and schools in the development of relationships among wives is influenced by the facts that the wives are usually of the same general age and that their husbands are likely to be the same rank. If not, they may have more difficulty becoming friends. If their children are the same sex, as well as the same age, the chances of the relationship between the mothers continuing to be important past kindergarten is greatly increased. Also, if several children in two families are paired in age, the chances are even greater that the two mothers will be drawn together. Uedagin children do not feel the hesitation and reserve toward others that their parents do, and they dash back and forth from one apartment to the next, serving, in effect, as go-betweens for their less outgoing mothers.

Another person likely to know immediately of a wife's troubles is the woman living directly across the landing, the closest neighbor. The usual pattern of friendship, in fact, includes this woman. She is the person most suitable for simple daily exchanges: watching the baby for a moment, lending a cup of sugar, or sharing a complaint about the administration of the building. Younger wives who have resided for the shortest period in the apartments usually consider her their closest acquaintance.

Two office groups are substantially represented in the apartments. Five men (two deputies and three regulars) from the personnel section and six men (two chiefs and four regulars) from the computer section have been assigned to live in the complex. The men from the computer section have been transferred within the last several years from one of the company's largest branches, where computer operations were originally located. Consequently, they share acquaintanceships from the time when they all lived together in that branch's apartments. Comments by wives in these two office groups reveal a pattern of social relationship rather different from most. For them neither the entry group nor the children are as important in forming friendships as their husbands' common office affiliation. When the need for help arises, they are likely to turn to others in the office group, particularly to the wives of the husbands' senpai. Mrs. Yamamoto, the wife of a regular, for example, has a special feeling of relationship and obligation to her husband's chief. He helped them carry things up to their apartment when they moved in. Later, when Mrs. Yamamoto needed a special kind of shallow bathtub for her child, this same man was able to produce one. Each New Year's she crosses from B to A building carrying a small gift for his daughters, presents to superiors being against regulations.

For these families, living in the Aoyama apartments is not radically

different from living in the smaller and more intimate company housing arrangements associated with branch offices. ~~It is said that when
husbands work together and live as neighbors a more relaxed, fluid,
and enjoyable neighborliness is possible.~~ Even some six or seven years
ago, Aoyama wives were in the practice of renting a bus and together
taking their children to the beach several times each summer. Cooking
classes for women and an occasional lecture on child care were also
part of the schedule of events shared by wives, but such activities have
disappeared. Elementary school outings are sufficient, some say, and
cooking classes are hard to organize. What social activities exist today
are small and rather cliquish.

Sixteen wives, one-third of those in the apartments, participate in
some sort of study circle. Two women in the same entryway study the
koto together, and the remainder study flower arranging in five separate small groups. Cultural pursuits of this kind are taken seriously
by the wives, but the chance to socialize is also greatly appreciated.
The flower-arranging circles are all based on relationships of the kinds
just discussed. The two instances in which women from A building
and B building study together also fit these patterns. Some of the
wives not included in any group have an interest in participating but
claim not to know anyone to ask to be included. Among the thirty
women not studying in any group, only one or two say that friendships or interests outside the apartments keep them from joining.

For some time there has been an underground discussion among
the younger wives about reviving apartment-wide activities, including
a single inclusive flower-arranging class. Some would like to reestab-
lish the excursions to the beach, and others have ambitious ideas
about mutual help on a large scale. Projects such as beautifying the
apartments and cooperative babysitting have also been mentioned.
Prior to the last general meeting some wives privately discussed bringing such proposals to the attention of the entire group, but at the
meeting the leaders of the younger group became reserved, and the
meeting adjourned without any issues being raised. Why this was so
is worth noting.

Discussing the general depressed state of wives' social activity, the
younger women point to the presence in the apartments of a few wives
of higher-ranking (chief and department head) men. They have lived
in the apartments for many years and are senior in age, often by as
much as ten years. Their presence, people say, makes it impossible to
organize apartment-wide activities. It is not a matter of active opposition from these older women. Their very presence apparently
inhibits the younger wives from acting. Leadership and direction

should come from the oldest in the group, they say, and stirrings of
discontent on the part of others would only cause resentment and
result in failure. The unfortunate thing, say the young wives, is that
the older women neither leave for private housing nor take an active
role in guiding apartment affairs. If they would do either of these,
the situation would improve. Among the group of senior women, the
lack of activities has not gone unnoticed, but their explanations are
rather different. "In the past we had a richer life here, but ever since
many of our age group moved away things have been on a decline."
Another commented, "These cooperative events are in some ways desirable, but there is also the danger that resentment and animosity will
arise over arrangements." Their own role in blocking the development
of a new era of activities led by younger wives is not perceived.

As a rule the wives interviewed indicated that, given the choice,
they would not live in the Aoyama apartments. They were assigned
to the apartments and feel they have no right to refuse. The financial
savings make the assignment a welcome one for some, but the narrow
quarters, the outdated arrangement for each individual apartment,
and the reserve among many residents combine to make this apartment
complex rather unpopular. They see the fact that their husbands are
all members of the same bank as primarily negative in its effects on
their own social life. It causes them to be especially careful in approaching each other, they say. Age, rank, and office group affiliation,
that ubiquitous trio of social distinctions within Uedagin, holds sway
for better or for worse over company housing as it does over the entire
spectrum of Uedagin life.

Enryo, "feelings of constraint and reserve," is a term commonly
used to describe the general tenor of relations among wives. Other
women are not accused of being cold or unpleasant, but instead differences in age and in husbands' rank are underlined. A few add
that the wives of bankers have too much dignity to preserve to allow
them to live easily with each other, and undoubtedly enryo is greatest
among women of higher social station. Whatever the explanations,
noncompany apartment buildings are viewed as warmer places to live.

Apparently, only in the housing for branch personnel may enryo
be forgotten. There, the smaller number of families, the office ties,
and sometimes the leadership of the branch chief's wife all apparently
contribute to better relations. One wife, recently arrived from a large
branch, reported that instead of going out to the usual bars and
cabarets her husband and his office friends preferred to spend an hour
or two together in their own apartments, drinking, discussing work,
and generally relaxing. Once a week on a rotation basis, a mah-jongg

party was also held. She and the other wives belonging to this group tended to be about the same age, and they too became close friends. There was little objection to the men socializing at home until late at night. The most surprising of her revelations was that in this situation couples, as such, occasionally visited one another after their children were asleep. Only one incident of this sort came to my attention during interviews in the Aoyama apartments.

SUMMARY

This discussion of residential groupings began with the question of their contribution as a cohesive factor in Uedagin life. For many young men in the dormitories and for husbands and wives in branch housing facilities, coresidence is a factor drawing them together and producing personal friendships within the organization. On the other hand, in the Aoyama apartments, few men interact with each other, and many wives find the social life reserved and unsatisfactory. Its larger size and the fact that the husbands work in different offices distinguish the Aoyama apartment complex from the more congenial branch housing arrangements. The size and luxury of the dormitory, combined with the emergence of regular dating on the part of some bachelors, are seen as key factors in the recent decline of camaraderie there.

We have also learned that although residential units are most homogeneous in terms of age, this does not appear to encourage active organization. With marriage and rank the major factors in the sorting process, people of approximately the same age are assigned to live together, and in these arrangements there is no one with strong official authority. Self-government and spontaneous association are the general intentions.

Neither voluntary organizations nor participatory government result, however, and there are a number of apparent reasons for this. Life in company housing is never totally out of the shadow of the company's authority, its rank hierarchy, and its moral expectations. The differences of age that do exist are also problematic: the younger defer to their seniors, yet seniors seldom provide energetic leadership. Official responsibility for organization in both situations is vague at best. Takeda's behind-the-scenes efforts illustrate that hierarchy, even in such relatively age-homogeneous groups, is crucial, and that successful organization hinges on the presence of a leader who qualifies and is willing to operate the ever present age framework.

Considering only the bachelors' dormitory for the moment, we can observe a number of ironical twists in the relationship between what is called "modern" and what is called "traditional." Relations among the bachelors are more egalitarian than those among men in the bank generally, but the opportunity to maximize this "modern" value is undermined by another "modern" value, Western-style romance.[10] The only person to act in this situation, Takeda, must use his status in the "traditional" senpai-kohai hierarchy to achieve a compromise between the goals of egalitarian fellowship and romance. The success of his approach will, unintentionally, encourage the preservation of a "traditional" age-based hierarchy. Similarly, the improvement of dormitory life will be a confirmation of a "traditional" bank policy, the use of dormitories to keep bachelors happy and closely tied to the company. If Takeda fails, social relations among the bachelors will decline, to be replaced perhaps by more individualistic, "modern" patterns. But, with the exception of dating and office recreation, there will be few alternatives to which the young men can turn for fellowship and a sense of belonging. Clubs, associations, political groups, and other similar noncompany possibilities are few and are usually seen as inappropriate as we have already noted. The basic choice for the Uedagin man is between a social existence within the bank, combining "modern" elements with much that is "traditional," or a more individual, but quite lonely, private existence.

Already there is evidence that the former possibility will receive increasing encouragement from the leaders of the bank. They are revising and updating their attitudes about "mixed" recreation, and they appear determined to make dormitory life more satisfactory and interesting.

Whether social life in the dormitory and the apartments revives or continues to decline, coresidence does contribute, if at times in only a small way, to the identification of the individual with his company and to the general sense of familiarity among Uedagin people.

[10] It is misleading to regard either egalitarian social forms or romance as "modern" in one sense, for there is overwhelming evidence of their existence in many villages and other preindustrial forms of social organization.

11

MARRIAGE AND THE FAMILY

Organizations like Uedagin do not exist in a social vacuum. Obviously changes in a variety of external factors (demographic, economic, political, and so on) can be of crucial importance to the survival of the company. One "external system" which students of organization seldom consider, but which anthropologists almost never ignore, is marriage and the family. In this final descriptive chapter we will examine the two-way set of influences between company and family life in order to further explore the meaning of some basic matters, including work and the company-individual relationship. Already it should be apparent that it is the total configuration of organization, explanation, and individual experience that is our primary focus, no matter how mercurial, complex, and imprecise some issues appear at times because of this approach. The major questions before us here will be: How does the bank influence the Uedagin family? And, how does the Japanese family pattern influence the relationship of husband-workers to the bank? To answer these questions we will need to know about such things as bank policies and covert opinions regarding marriage and the family, patterns of courtship at work, the typical middle-class Japanese views about marriage, romance, and parental roles, and the degree of conflict between work and a man's family responsibilities.

We cannot describe the entirety of marriage and family life but will limit our concern to how work in the bank affects these patterns. The reader who wishes to acquaint himself with the general picture of contemporary Japanese marriage and family life should consult Dore (1958), Vogel (1963 and 1967), Beardsley, Hall, and Ward (1959), Blood (1968), Pelzel (1970), and Befu (1971).

COURTSHIP AND MARRIAGE

The preliminaries for marriage in Japan hold a particular fascination for foreigners and Japanese alike. This is so because coexisting side by side for centuries have been the alternative patterns of arranged (*miai kekkon*) and love-match (*renai kekkon*) marriage-making. Many combinations of elements of the two are also possible and common, adding to the general interest of the matter, but popular discussion depends primarily on this simple distinction.[1] Today, arranged marriage is regarded as out of date, traditional, proper, secure, family oriented, and repressive of the romantic impulse. In contrast, a marriage based on romance and determined by the young couple themselves is regarded as modern, democratic, Western, and a bit risky.

Contemporary young people in the bank face a real dilemma on this issue, but it is not a dilemma we would expect. Rarely do their parents insist strongly on an arranged marriage, yet, and this is the crucial point, in many cases the young person is not able independently to find a romantic marriage choice. The great majority would prefer to find a compatible mate on their own, and some Uedagin women openly state that for them working is an opportunity to meet young men informally. There is a joke in the bank that the women's salaries are low and their working hours long, but at least they have the opportunity to find a banker for a husband. No one better symbolizes the steady, loyal, and increasingly prosperous, if unexciting, Japanese salaryman than the banker, and in Japan his attractions as a husband are considerable. The young men, too, harbor a strong interest in finding a good mate, if not in their own company then perhaps through company friends. Even so, as we shall see, more Uedagin men marry by arrangement than by personal selection.

Alongside the dichotomous categories of arranged and love-match marriage, a third type, the company marriage (*shanai kekkon* or *shokuba kekkon*), has entered common parlance. This term describes a marriage, assumed to be romantically based, between people working in the same firm. The considerable interest in and frequency of company marriage is unquestionably the result of the prominence of work relationships and the absence of other avenues for informal contact among young people such as those in Uedagin.

In my interview sample of thirty-nine marriages made within the last twelve years by Uedagin men, 56 percent are classed as arranged and 44 percent as love-match marriages.[2] Twenty percent of the total are company marriages. In the following discussion, we must keep in

[1] See Blood (1968) for a much more detailed discussion of the distinctions and variety within modern Japanese courtship.

[2] This sample is basically the same one as used in the discussion of the Uedagin apartments, but cases of marriages and family life of people not in the apartments have been added. All of those added are younger couples most of whom are in their late twenties.

mind that arranged marriages account for more than half of all marriages and that in the years before marriage only a minority of the young men and women are actively involved in a romance.

Dating

The bank assumes a neutral position on the question of marriage, yet it is ready to take a stand against romantic activity that interferes with the individual's primary responsibility to Uedagin. Young men are not only expected willingly to put in considerable overtime even on short notice, they are also expected to participate fully in the social activities connected with their office groups. Romantic attachments that create conflicts with these obligations are frowned upon, not only by supervisors, but also by many contemporaries. It is axiomatic that others suffer when an individual puts his own interests ahead of his responsibilities to the group, and a distracted Romeo is likely to be labeled selfish and foolish if his courtship interferes with his participation in bank activities. Only in exceptional cases does the bank deem it proper to interfere with a warning or a transfer, yet, the existence of this possibility makes everyone involved in romance rather cautious.

The opportunity for young Japanese to become acquainted on an independent basis no doubt expanded greatly in the postwar period, yet, as we have seen in our discussion of the dormitory, for Uedagin young people these opportunities lie mostly within the confines of their own company. Naturally those working together in the same office form the first circle of acquaintanceship, but there are other opportunities within Uedagin to meet the opposite sex. Company friends, especially senpai and dormitory mates, can also be avenues to meet young people of other companies. By no means are all courtships begun through the auspices of a company relationship, but it appears to be the single most common starting point.

The possibility of interference, whether from office superiors or parents, is real enough and the tradition foreign enough that dating (deitto), Western style, still has an element of the surreptitious about it, even though objections to dating as such are seldom heard. Young couples meet in coffee houses, go together to movies and concerts, and make outings to nearby parks, but isolation from friends, family, and office associates is desired. When in the presence of other Uedagin people, a young couple can be expected to avoid any display of mutual interest. Secrecy is necessary primarily because of the incompatibility of romance with the more serious matters of work, self-development, and group membership. The whole world does not love lovers.

Once marriage is set, however, the match may easily surface, for marriage itself has a definite place in the total scheme of social affairs, a place dating does not. This is most clearly seen in the case of office romances. Known pairings within office groups are viewed as disruptive, and warnings against such romance are heard from some chiefs and senpai. It is not a pleasant thing to transfer someone on these grounds, but it has happened and is talked about in the bachelors' dormitory.

But despite the risks office romances do occur and some result in company marriages. In one instance, the fact that romance was in the wind went undetected by the rest of the office until the day the couple hesitatingly approached their chief to ask his approval of their marriage. They had seen each other secretly for over a year, yet once the engagement was announced there was no difficulty in securing approval and congratulations. The chief became the official go-between, and everyone attended the ceremony. People commented on how well this office romance had been conducted. By great discretion the couple had been able to retain their separate identities and relationships in the office group and thus avoid disruptions and the possibility of censure.

The early marriage of young men is also officially frowned upon. In a lecture to the new trainees, the head of the personnel department expressly warned them on this subject. "Marriage," he said, "should come only after a man has spent at least three years adjusting to his new work. First develop the basic skills and establish yourself in the bank, then begin to look around for the right girl." It was clearly implied that his office, the source of assignments and promotions, would look with disfavor on those who married before they had had enough experience to perform satisfactorily for the bank. He continued, "Men who marry early tend to become soft. They lose their manliness and ambition. Furthermore, in the final analysis, the hardworking, ambitious young men will get the better wives, since girls and their parents are actually more interested in making marriages with that type of man." The best formula for finding a wife, according to his view, is to work loyally for the company and let one's reputation as a serious, dependable person with a bright future assure that a good marriage partner will be forthcoming. He did not specify what variety of marriage he was speaking about, but he left the impression that he favors arranged marriages.

Arranged Marriage

As a rule, the younger the person is the more enthusiastic he or she will be about romance and personal choice in marriage. The older they become the more ambivalent their stand will be. By about the age of twenty-two for the women, and twenty-six for the men, the possibility of making an arranged marriage seems reasonable. It appears less a matter of parental dominance and more a matter of simple convenience. The problem of making an acceptable marriage has to be solved, and totally failing to find a partner is certainly much worse than going through the brief trauma of an arrangement. As the proper time for marriage begins to pass, the convenience of an arrangement becomes appreciated, and parents and friends offer their services. The number of young people in Uedagin who are passive about this eventuality is large. Most may hope for a love marriage, but surprisingly few offer much resistance to an arrangement when the time comes.

A few more statistics might be considered at this point. As already mentioned, 56 percent of my sample are arranged marriages, and 44 percent are love marriages. Men making love marriages tend to marry earlier, their average age at marriage being twenty-five. This was two years younger than the average age at marriage of those marrying by arrangement. There is also a strong correlation between the type of marriage and the man's educational background. Thirty-three percent of the high school graduates in the sample have arranged marriages, compared to 62 percent for the university graduates. It follows that high school graduate men tend to marry earlier (in one case marriage took place as early as twenty-one), yet no high school graduates spent less than the officially recommended three years working in the bank before marriage. Company marriages also occur more frequently within the high school group, a fact consistent with their tendency to love marriages. Of further interest is the fact that the husband-wife age difference in love-match marriages is much smaller. A few women in such marriages are older than their husbands, in contrast with the uniform two or more years of seniority for the men in arranged marriages.

Uedagin high school graduates tend to be from rural areas, and their parents are of less help to them in locating a wife. They work in the bank with women their own age from graduation on, and it is not surprising that compared to university graduates they marry earlier and more often by their own choice.

Even though most young people express a personal preference for romance and freedom of choice, arranged marriages, rather surprisingly, are regarded as higher in prestige. Perhaps this is because marriage by arrangement, always more rigorously practiced by higher-ranking families, carries a flavor of upper-class propriety. Yet arranged marriages for our bankers are often made, as we have seen, because of the failure of the love match to materialize. It is interesting that in the bank this failure to find romance is generally attributed to the admirable qualities of the people in question. The modesty of the woman and the seriousness of the man are the usual explanations for the fact that they have arrived at the prime age for marriage without a candidate of their own choice. The fact that a much higher percentage of university graduates make arranged marriages also reiterates its status.

Company Marriages

Company marriages deserve our attention because they illustrate our point that working in Uedagin deeply affects the personal lives of its members, and because they illustrate how involved and variable marriage arrangements actually may become. In 20 percent of my sample, both partners had worked in the bank prior to marriage. In most cases, the couples agree to the label "love match," but two reported, "We were good friends, like brother and sister, so we decided to get married," and, contrary to popular interpretation, company marriages can also be arranged.

There is one instance in which the two young people worked in separate branches, and a chief, impressed by the fine qualities of each, suggested marriage. Although they did not know each other, the two consented to his proposal. "We both trusted his judgment," the wife says. In another case, a young man accompanying several inspectors visited the branch office of his future bride for approximately two weeks while it was under inspection. During that time he spoke with her on a friendly basis. When he returned to the main office, she thought nothing special of their relationship. He did write her a number of times, and she remembers being impressed by his handwriting (thinking it reflected good character). Suddenly, out of the blue, the young man's father paid a visit to her chief to seek his support for a marriage between them. The chief consulted the bewildered girl, and all of them went to her family's home to discuss the arrangement. After several weeks of checking into the man's background, her parents gave their approval. The first of these marriages occurred in 1961 and the second in 1958. If the contemporary activities of some senpai to find good marriage prospects for their kohai are any indication, "arranged" company marriages continue to be made today, although in a less precipitate manner.

To summarize the importance of company relations in bringing eventual marriage partners together, we should note that of the thirty-nine cases investigated in depth, over one-third either were company marriages or originated with introductions by superiors or senpai in the bank. In the bank itself, the topic is one of considerable interest, and many men say company marriages are preferable because they take less effort and because these wives understand better why their husbands come home late. On the other hand, there is much humor about company marriages, indicating a mild uneasiness on the subject.

The role of senior people as go-betweens in arranging marriages was for a number of years given publicity in the Uedagin *News*. During that time the bank built a marriage hall where Uedagin people could be married without incurring the usual heavy expense of renting a private hall. Today, it is clear that the facility has not been a success primarily because most parents choose to avoid the embarrassment of appearing sufficiently impoverished to require the company hall.

The Boss as Official Go-Between

It is a common practice to have an important man from the company serve as the official go-between (*nakōdo*) at the marriage ceremony. Most often this is the man's chief, but in some cases men of higher rank, occasionally even the president, agree to serve. The man's superior was nakōdo in just over half of the marriages in my sample. In the rest, a relative or important person unrelated to the bank filled the role. After the wedding itself, the nakōdo's theoretical role is to consult with the young people if they should have difficulties. In practice, because of his important social position, the young people are under some constraint not to disturb or embarrass the nakōdo by having difficulties in their marriage. In most instances, his is essentially a symbolic role, yet the fact that company leaders so often occupy this role has an underlying significance: with marriage, a man's wife becomes part of his relationship with the company, and she comes to share his responsibilities and dependent status within the general company framework. The bank also implicitly acknowledges a protective responsibility over the marriage through such participation.[3]

3 The president of the bank, when he was the official go-between for the first marriage in the new company marriage hall, offered his ideal conceptualization of the event in the following terms: "My wife and I have taken part today for two reasons. This is the inauguration of our new marriage hall, and it carries the further and special significance of being a marriage which brings together two people of our bank's second generation. This next generation which is being raised today will have the job of carrying the bank forward in the future. Each generation may expect to have the baton of responsibility passed on to them. Our dreams and our will to succeed are thus passed from parent to child time after time. I ask you, isn't this a most fruitful formula for understanding life? Other members of the second, then the members of the third generation, will continue to be married in this hall and the result will be the continuation and growth of the greater Uedagin family, the symbol of our unity and spirit of harmony." His reference to generations of Uedagin people as if the succession is between fathers and sons was actually true in this particular case, but it does not characterize the actual relationship of families to the bank, a matter we shall take up in the following section.

To recapitulate, the bank places some constraints on courtship. Dating and romance should not interfere with a full commitment to work, and men should not marry before a full adjustment to work has been made. This insistence on the priority of company responsibilities, coupled with many other factors including long and rather unpredictable overtime, serves to inhibit many young men from ever plunging into romantic attachment, and it creates a situation in which romance is kept separate from company life. More than half of the marriages are not built on romantic impulse. For the individual Uedagin worker, love does not compete with work on an equal footing, and we shall see how family life, thus begun, reiterates the first priority of work.

UEDAGIN FAMILY PATTERNS

What place does the family occupy in the bank's total scheme, and what kinship and family patterns are encouraged by the bank's policies?

The family recognized by the bank is a nuclear family with the wife and children dependent on the husband-father, who serves as its link with the bank and the outside world. The family is, thus, a dependency of Uedagin, and this view reinforces the principle of a strict division of labor between husband and wife. Properly the wife cares for the children and creates a stable and supportive home environment. The bank would strongly discourage any wife from working, for this would take her from her primary roles of mother and wife. The men in Uedagin, particularly the older ones, seem rather uncomfortable about the presence of unmarried women in their organization, and long before they actually marry, bank policy has given the women a definition that pushes them toward the more usual categories of wife and mother.

The concept of "one great bank family" envisions an organization of men and their dependent nuclear families. As we have noted, the bank has no inclination to extend its welfare support to the dependent parents of a member or his wife. Nor are adult children to be supported. On the question of the succession of fathers by their sons there is but slight ambivalence. The bank has a rule against nepotism, and the ties among scattered relatives within the organization have little influence. We do find the president and others speaking of the first, second, and third generations within the bank, and we may perceive within the hearts of those who have worked most steadfastly for the growth of Uedagin a desire for at least one of their sons to carry on the family tradition in the company. But for most, the family's association with the bank terminates when they retire. Even among the leaders, only a few imagine that the relationship between their family and Uedagin will be preserved over the years.

Father-son combinations are infrequent. Among the 120 young men entering in 1969, only one has a father in the bank. A few others have some less direct tie, such as uncles and father's friends, with people already in Uedagin. It is possible for a few young men to be related through marriage to senior men in the organization. The president eschews all such possibilities for his own family. His one son is a dentist, and his daughter is still unmarried.

Kinship ties are actually diminished by life in the bank. Young men leave home to begin work in the bank, and they may expect to spend much of their life on transfer assignment far from parents and relatives. This shifting around introduces instability into all kinship ties. However, when living near parents or siblings Uedagin people do take great satisfaction in exchanging visits and generally enjoying their company. The wives in the company apartment with the least interest in social contact with other wives are women with relatives in the city. It is also a general wish to be assigned near aging parents. Personnel takes such requests into account, but the fact that in their home towns Uedagin men attract more deposits is the basic reason for assignments near relatives and parents.

Usually assigned at a distance from parents, kin, and friends, the Uedagin family has little recourse but to depend on membership in the bank to provide the friendship and security it requires.

Corporateness and Succession in Uedagin Families

Unlike farmers, small shop and factory owners, and persons from families possessing an inheritable status, Uedagin families have little for their children to inherit. With the few exceptions of men who succeed to high office, Uedagin men consume in old age most of what they have succeeded in saving. In this circumstance, it is well to ask what happens to the traditionally important continuity and corporateness of the Japanese household (*ie*), as embodied in the succession from father to son or to son substitute.[4] When no son is available, adoption, particularly of a daughter's husband, has traditionally been practiced. In this way, the succession of a male household head able to serve the common interests of the household has been assured. In a few realms

---

4 Pelzel (1970) offers the best synopsis of the concept of ie, and his discussion of its implications are valuable as a point of comparison with the material presented here and in Vogel (1967), where the decline of the ie in urban situations is also discussed. See also Befu (1971).

of Japanese life, this continues in full strength today, but among white-collar workers the pattern seems radically weakened.

Until 1945 most Japanese families practiced primogeniture, and even now, under a new law of equal division of property, the practice continues among groups that must limit succession to preserve property or authority intact. Slightly over half of the men in my family interview sample, however, are first sons, and most of them chose to enter the bank over a career succeeding their fathers in such areas as farming, small business, and family professions. Often enough, however, they left a younger brother with the duties and the inheritance that go with household succession. None of the thirty-nine families interviewed indicated that they have any intention of practicing primogeniture in bequeathing property to their own children. The parents interviewed will not actually determine the distribution of their estate for many years, so there is reason for hesitation before concluding that perfect equality of inheritance will be practiced as they say, yet their unanimous intention to make equal distribution indicates that the Uedagin family is not conceived of as a corporate entity that exists over time.[5]

The most telling indications of the weakening of the principles of corporateness and continuity come in those cases in which a family has only daughters. Should they wish to continue their own household they must, according to traditional practice, find an adopted son to carry on the line. With the almost universal limitation of Uedagin families to only two children, approximately one-quarter will find themselves with only daughters. In fact, nine out of the thirty-nine families had two daughters and no sons. All said they intend to have no further children, and in the five cases discussed in depth the parents have no intention of adopting a son. Furthermore, all indicate having given the problem little if any consideration. These families are clear testimony to the general decline of the household ideal in the absence of any economic substance to the concepts of continuity and inherit-

5 Uedagin parents do not expect to be cared for in old age, but expect a son to care for their memorial tablets (*ihai*). Without significant property, the only corporate possessions of the household remaining to be inherited are the family name, its tradition and social status, the memorial tablets of deceased parents (and possibly other ancestors), and the responsibilities of commemorating the household's ancestors. Only men who are first sons and have inherited them possess the last two. There were three such families in my sample. All the rest had no ancestral tablets or memorial responsibilities. With few exceptions, first sons entering the bank have turned responsibility for these duties to the ancestors over to younger brothers, who also will inherit the household headship and property.

ance. This is a situation facing virtually all Japanese families connected to large organizations.[6]

Voluntary Associations

If kinship ties are tenuous, family involvement in other forms of social relationship beyond the Uedagin sphere is almost nonexistent. Many husbands and wives hold membership in hobby-study groups, but never together as a couple. Many of these groups are sponsored by the bank or are based on a common tie to the bank, as in the case of apartment wives' study groups. In some small branches, wives' groups have formed under the guidance of the branch chief's wife, and there is also a group of wives of high-ranking men that pursues a course of rather elegant entertainment together. PTA and school activities attract only a few mothers in the Aoyama apartments. When their children are grown some housewives gravitate to women's clubs, but the great majority do not become involved in such activities.

Husbands have little free time to spend outside the confines of the bank, and as a result there is almost no evidence of their active participation in religious groups, charities, civic or political organizations, or social clubs. In Japanese cities male voluntary associations, social, charitable, or otherwise, are usually formed along lines of economic interest.[7] The men of Uedagin below the rank of chief are not involved in any such associations, but many of their superiors, acting as representatives of the bank, do attend Chamber of Commerce, Rotary, and a limited number of other local business and civic meetings.

Although there are men deeply interested in the philosophical aspects of religion, and a few who practice *zazen* on an individual basis, no Uedagin men interviewed actively participate in a religious group. We have already noted in chapter 3 how men and women owing allegiance to any of the activist "new religions," such as Sōka Gakkai, are refused membership in Uedagin. Some families are affiliated with a temple of one of the older Buddhist sects. This is primarily because the husband's parents and other ancestors are buried there and memorialized by the priests of the temple. These families continue to pay for this service, but otherwise take no interest in the affairs of the temple. It is also common for Uedagin families to make the customary

6 See Moore (1963), Levy (1966), and Nash (1958) for general statements on economic development and the predominance of nuclear families. Vogel (1967) and Yamane and Nonoyama (1967) observe these trends for Japan.

7 Merchants' associations, farm cooperatives, intellectual circles, and the like are common, but outside the purview of Uedagin men.

annual visit to parental graves, but this again has nothing to do with organized religion.

The striking fact is that Uedagin people are hardly oriented to or active in any kind of voluntary organization. Clubs, civic groups, charities, religious groups, political parties, and the like, so common a part of the American social scene, are of virtually no consequence for people in the bank, and what personal hobbies they pursue are often followed within the company context. Because of this, neither the sense of personal latitude, nor the problem of contradictory involvements that accompany our pattern of voluntary affiliation is common to the Uedagin milieu. People in the bank are not encouraged to view work or company relations as a separate and narrow domain. The virtues, evils, and constraints of employment are not, that is, constantly being viewed in the context of a more attractive world of extracurricular activity and interest. The contrasts between work and pleasure, work and charity, work and public service, and work and personal preference (all so marked in our own contemporary thinking) are much less sharp for Uedagin people, and there is little choice in these matters, the company and work being so clearly predominant.

Family Planning

Bank influence extends also to family planning. It is not difficult for a man and his wife to calculate approximately how much income they will have at any given point during the remainder of the husband's Uedagin career, for base pay and promotion have a high degree of predictability. The sum cannot be precisely calculated, yet the general outlines of a man's career may be estimated with considerable accuracy. The projections that are invariably made allow young couples to pace their rate of expenditure and savings in order to achieve goals they set for themselves. Invariably, they wish children and almost invariably they have a project eventually to build a house of their own.

This house project usually involves the purchase of land long in advance of the actual construction of the house. Typically, the couple buys land during their mid or late thirties, and, depending on their financial circumstances and bank assignments, construction of the house is begun during the period before retirement. Some families may spend their last years with the bank living in their own home, but those who are assigned elsewhere have to wait until retirement to do so. This project constitutes a financial preoccupation second only to raising and educating children, and the effort to save and plan on a long-range basis, putting aside a little bit each month for many years,

is a virtual tradition among bank people and others like them. Japan,
incidentally, has the highest personal savings rate in the world.[8] Economy and self-control, however, are less necessary today to reach goals
such as the dream house, as indicated by the purchase of expensive
appliances and even cars along with the maintenance of family savings
programs.

To date, the object of limiting family size and spacing children has
been to have children born at such a time that they are completing
their education before their fathers are retired from the bank. Perhaps as incomes continue to improve families will be less subject to
the structure of the salary system and the deadline created by early
retirement, but today these factors, reinforced by recurrent transfer,
establish considerable uniformity in size, finance, and the goals of the
families interviewed.

Only four families in the sample varied from the norm of two
children. One of these had three and was regarded by others as extraordinary. The others had only one child and indicated that they expected to have another. Why do Uedagin people so consistently limit
their families? The reasons have nothing to do with a sense of social
responsibility to an overpopulated nation. Some have doubts about
being able to afford a third child, but many say they would have more
children except for company housing. Because of the savings involved
and the dislocation of recurrent transfer, all young families expect to
live in company apartments and company-rented housing at least
most of the time. The housing the bank offers is designed for a family
with two children, and even within this limit the living is cramped.
While only one-fifth of all families live in the company apartments
at any one time, most young couples of childbearing age live in them,
and this makes the effect of company apartments powerful.

A Brief Illustration

One spring evening I arrived at a deputy's house just as a young
man was leaving. He had come to consult with his senpai about his
marriage problems. The man faced his thirtieth birthday with no
good prospects before him. The girl he had hoped to marry had, at
her parents' request, agreed to an arranged marriage with someone
they selected, and the young visitor suddenly found himself without
a prospective bride. What was bothering him most, however, was not
the loss of the girl, but the fact that unless he found a suitable candidate and married her soon he faced a whole series of difficulties in

---

8 See Blumenthal (1970) and Sumiya (1969) for discussions of Japanese saving.

raising his family. Unless he married within a year or two and shortly thereafter had his children, he would be faced with the serious problem of supporting them during their school years on the reduced income he would have after his retirement from the bank. According to this man's calculations, in order to have his second child completing a university education before he reached age fifty-five, he would have to marry and have two children by the time he was thirty-three or thirty-four. With so little time left, no one was surprised at his consternation. The senpai and some other acquaintances agreed to scout around for an appropriate candidate. Like everyone else, this bachelor found that he had to adjust his life style and family pattern to fit the unalterable Uedagin career program. The predictability of the system may provide security and make sound planning possible, but its inevitability places heavy constraints on the course of family development and results in a marked uniformity among Uedagin families.

As Husbands and Fathers

The relationship between husband and wife, not necessarily intense to begin with, is subordinate in many ways to the man's involvement in the bank.[9] The single most significant fact in this triangle of man, wife, and bank is that husbands spend little free time at home. Six days a week they leave early in the morning for the office and return late at night. The average time to arrive home in the evening is eight. In some cases, husbands regularly return as late as ten and eleven due to the heavy work load in their offices or busy schedules of after-work entertainment. One or two nights a month, when the monthly accounts must be closed, all but a few men remain at the office until past midnight. Even with the effort to cut down on extra hours of work based on the introduction of computerized bookkeeping, a remarkable increase of time spent at home is unlikely.

Many men indicate that sitting around in their crowded apartments at night with only their wives and tired children holds little attraction compared to spending the evening out drinking or playing mah-jongg with friends from work. This apparent devotion to work and to the company of fellow workers is not due only to the requirements of the bank's pattern of organization; it is also the product of Japanese marriage and family patterns. Characteristically, the Uedagin family is not husband-wife oriented, and it has for men a centrifugal, rather

---

[9] Vogel (1963) offers the most detailed descriptive material on contemporary marriage in urban families similar to those in Uedagin. All of the subsequent discussion will benefit from comparison with his description, particularly because it is wider and more thorough.

than centripetal character when compared to American middle-class families.

It is perhaps an obvious point, but the man's relationships to wife, family and company are necessarily part of an integrated pattern of time allocation for him. There is always a potential conflict between the separate orientations of family and work, but actual conflict is not a foregone conclusion. The stricter the priorities set and observed, the less the amount of actual conflict. In practice, Uedagin clearly holds the highest priority, although sentiment about family living varies widely with different individuals. Growing interest in family-centered leisure activities may eventually be accompanied by more time spent with the wife and children and a demand that work not interfere with family life, a wish that Uedagin men hardly voice to-day.[10]

It is as mistaken to explain the salaryman's family pattern exclusively in terms of his involvement in his company as to explain the company pattern exclusively in terms of the family. The two have developed in tandem. Comparing the Uedagin family with farm and small-shop families does, however, underline how little time Uedagin men spend with their wives and children. In these other situations, work and family are more integrated, and the man is at home or with family members much of each working day. Blue-collar and small-company people appear to have closer ties to neighborhoods and old friends, in large measure because schooling and company transfers are not as likely to take them away.

The absent father and lonely housewife are problems mentioned by Uedagin wives as their greatest concerns. The centrality of mothers in child rearing and the restricted involvement between spouses, often viewed as typical of Japanese family patterns in general, are actually found primarily in households of the middle and upper-middle class, which are, ironically, the most Western in other respects.

Uedagin men are not likely to share their office experiences with their wives. Only about 10 percent of the wives interviewed know more about their husband's work than the name of his office and his relationship with some of the people there. Young bachelors occasionally visit the apartments of their office senpai, and this gives the wives

10 There has been much general discussion of something labeled *mai-homu-shugi* "my home-ism," and even the bank's leaders have criticized the new tendency for some to prefer car, family leisure, and home to work. Yet for all the discussion of this topic in 1968–69 the real question was not work versus family, but rather work versus time for individual leisure of all sorts, including much that was purposefully designed to avoid the tasks of father and husband. "My home-ism" has a humorous and deprecatory ring to it that must be acknowledged as part of the story.

some opportunity to become acquainted with their husbands' lives in
the bank, yet wives regard the bank and its affairs as their husband's
domain. Conversely, the daily affairs of the home and the children are
typically of little interest or significance to most men. They prefer not
to be bothered by troubles at home.

Love marriages are no exception to this rule of almost total separation between the husband's and wife's worlds. Many wives commented
that after marriage there are almost no perceptible differences in the
patterns of husband-wife relations between the two types. Wives of
both, for example, are equally vociferous about their husbands not
coming home earlier. One time a group in the apartments jokingly
discussed learning the arts of cabaret hostesses so that they could attract their men home. It is equally rare for men of either marriage type
to indicate a wish to spend more time with their wives.

Sunday is the man's day with his family. Excursions with his children, a drive in the country, or a picnic, usually including the wife,
are common recreation on this day. These activities are humorously
referred to as "family service." Occasionally there will be an outing
for families sponsored by the office or the union. One Sunday, for
example, over 350 people, union members and their families, traveled
by train and bus to an orchard where they picked plums, had a picnic,
and folk danced for the afternoon. Branches may also conduct some
sort of party for families, but a summer excursion to a nearby beach
for wives and children, excluding the husbands, is more common.
A family can expect to participate in two or three company events a
year.

Some fathers expect to be separated from their families by company
duties even on Sundays. Overtime work on that day, often voluntary
and without pay, is not remarkable. In addition, some men devote
some of their Sundays to leading and chaperoning hiking expeditions
and picnics for office young people. This they do if they are office
leaders, members of the personnel department, or union officers. The
men most active in such activities are typically the more dynamic and
responsible, and as leaders they are expected to participate unhesi-
tantly when needed. The greater the responsibility and the greater the
advancement potential a man has, the more his family life is pinched.
Spending Sunday with the family may be valued, but Uedagin work
does not have strict time boundaries, and the family's needs are seldom an acceptable justification for not participating.

In all of this the point is clear. In terms of time, attention, and
interest a man's company and his work should take priority over his

relationships at home. Only because of this emphasis can office life and company activities remain as elaborate and active as they are. The day the men of Uedagin decide to hurry home to their families when their minimum hours of work are completed will mark the end of the Uedagin system as described in these pages.

We might expect marital difficulties to be considerable given this situation, that is, if we assume that marital life depends on the frequent interaction of husband and wife. Uedagin wives do have many complaints, but their expectations for marriage do not apparently center on their husbands. Divorce among Uedagin couples is almost negligible. The personnel section has on record only two divorces among its present male membership. Husband-wife relations may be limited, and some are emotionally shallow, but marriages almost never break up. The low Uedagin divorce rate may also reflect the fact that divorce is highly undesirable from the bank's point of view. The resulting instability for the worker and the inconvenience and embarrassment to the bank should be avoided. With so few examples, however, it is difficult to gauge the effects of divorce on a man's career.

Even though they are away from home so much, the men still dearly need the services of their wives, for they have little time or ability to cook, clean, and care for themselves. Only two Uedagin men above the age of thirty-five have remained bachelors. The bank encourages marriage and is concerned about men who extend bachelorhood past age thirty. Informal assistance to help them marry is common. A wife to support the worker's efforts, but not to distract his attention, is a necessary part of the overall scheme. The bachelor's dormitory performs the same maintenance functions as a wife (or a mother) for the unmarried men, but older bachelors are not happy living there, and so marriage is necessary.

Socialization of Children

The children of Uedagin fathers grow up in a particular family environment, one that is shaped in part by circumstances related to

11 Vogel points to the same quality of middle-class Japanese life when he observes, "The effectiveness of each group in controlling its members rests partly on its success in keeping the exclusive loyalty of its members. In Mamachi, an individual rarely has divided loyalties which would make it difficult to control his behavior because generally he has only one group outside the family which is the object of his primary commitment: the work group for the man, the neighborhood group for the woman, and the school group for the child. Even for higher status salary men, who have more responsibility in the community wide organizations, no other outside group is permitted to interfere with his primary commitment [1963:140]."

the bank. The most significant aspect of this environment is the absence of fathers during the day and often the night. Sunday is the one day children can expect to spend any time with Uedagin fathers. During the week their mothers occupy the position of parent for them almost completely. There is little if any sharing of the task of child rearing, and the mother usually assumes the role of disciplinarian. Only when the children are grown to an age when they can stay up at night with their fathers and talk about adult affairs does the characterization "absent father" seem an overstatement.

On the average, Uedagin children are born when their father is between twenty-seven and thirty-two and their mother between twenty-four and twenty-nine. They almost invariably have only one sibling, and the difference in age between siblings is two to three years (with little variation).

Uedagin children grow up in company housing to a large degree. Because of this, they play with other Uedagin children much of the time. Company life, however, means transfers, and these bring drastic changes in schools, friends, and neighborhoods. Uedagin children do not know the life of growing up in a permanent neighborhood, traditionally a great source of security for Japanese children. Their family is not part of a local community, and the company apartment community is constantly shifting. Fathers may find community at work, but their children benefit very little from that connection.

A white-collar worker's children are raised with the expectation that they will have to fend for themselves in a job market where educational achievement reigns supreme.[12] From an early age, education is stressed as the child's most important activity. Even kindergarten children in the Aoyama apartments characteristically have special tutoring after school in reading and writing, and many are sent to music lessons. Pressure on mothers to provide every possible special opportunity for education develops not only because their children's future depends on their success in a series of entrance examinations, but also because mothers in the company apartments engage in a form of status competition to give their children the best, the most proper, and the most intense education. The results of this preoccupation on the child are not clearly understood, but the end product the parents have in mind is consistent with their view that life and work in an

---

12 See Vogel (1962) and Kiefer (1970a and b) for discussions of the place of education in middle-class urban families. They discuss the psychological costs of the examination "hell" and the obsessive drive for their children's educational success on the part of mothers. Passin (1965) is the best account of the relationship of educational achievement to jobs and career achievement.

institution much like Uedagin will be their children's general inheritance.

Sons never accompany their fathers to work, however, and father and son have no chores at home to do together. Primarily school, commuting around the city, and TV serve to expose the young boy to the male adult world.

One last consequence of the father's general absence is the overwhelming concentration of mothers on their children. Personal satisfaction and honor for the married woman stem primarily from her role as mother and from her close relations with her children.[13]

DISCUSSION

The conditions mentioned contribute to a situation in which the concepts of personal and family privacy are different from what Americans regard as normal. Courtship must often be kept secret because it is not fully protected by a conceptual separation of what is private from what is legitimately an affair of the organization. This is true also of married life. Company influence is extensive in the family realm, primarily because of the unintentional constraints created by transfer, housing, salary, and the weight of work involvement. While the distinction between individual matters and organizational ones is common to the thinking of Uedagin people, there is little insistence on the independence of personal affairs in the face of organizational demands and requirements. The rare demand for individual latitude falls on deaf ears.

It is most important that we take a retrospective look at how these patterns of marriage and the family fit with the overall character of the individual-bank relationship. It is not enough to list the effects of the organization on private life. We must also acknowledge the general consonance between interpretations of work and private existence. The bank did not create the view of marriage and the family that releases the worker from obligations to spend much time on such matters. Nor is the bank directly responsible for the almost total apathy of its members regarding all forms of voluntary association. These other realms of life have not, to my knowledge, been of great concern for white-collar workers throughout this century, and this is probably best explained as the inheritance of an earlier period. The life style of government officials in early Meiji, a group that was the country's elite, may have become the white-collar prototype, but this

---

13 Caudill and Weinstein (1969) offer a general discussion of the differences in child rearing between white-collar employee and small-business middle-class families in Japan.

is an historical question outside the capacity of this study to determine. The point is not so much about history as about the congruence between general patterns of social existence. Cross-cultural work on organizations must, it seems, cast a wide net in search of general underlying interpretations of basic categories of social life.[14] Management's worries about the emphasis in Japanese popular culture on such themes as romantic marriage, private leisure, and the joys of family life confirm this insight. These themes appear to them as vague threats to the coherence and acceptability of their company world, especially as it is represented in the company ideology and as it relies on the extensive and flexible allocation of individual time and attention.

[14] See also Crozier (1964) for a general consideration of this kind of cultural variation in modern organization.

CONCLUDING REMARKS

Writing an ethnographic account is an exercise in drawing a mass of highly varied observations, interviews, and other materials together to create a single, essentially coherent description. While this is necessary for reasons of both communication and aesthetics, it does cause the limitations and confusion actually experienced in fieldwork to be underplayed. There is no solution to this common dilemma short of writing a different kind of book, but as a corrective I would like to discuss the more apparent shortcomings in my data produced by the actual fieldwork situation I encountered.

My original contact with the bank was through the wife of a friend at the Japanese university where I was studying. This woman introduced me to a former managing director, her brother-in-law's father, and he in turn introduced me to the chief of the training section (at the beginning my purpose was to make a general study of spiritual training in Japan). At various times during the course of research, I was to wonder about the wisdom of my original course of entry, for neither man could give me a blanket O.K. to study whatever I wished. Starting with the training program also proved to limit other avenues of approach. At the time, there was no apparent alternative, and I was anxious to begin.

At our interview the chief inquired what specifically I wished to do, and I asked to participate directly in the men's introductory training program. Without apparent hesitation he accepted my request and laid down some ground rules that would cover my study. I was not to attend any lectures or discussions about bank financial plans or problems. I was always to ask permission to sit in on any activity. I could not stay over night at the institute with the trainees except on special occasions. Much later the chief confided that he had not really expected that I would ask to participate directly, but the top-level recommendation and the fact that I spoke Japanese combined to eliminate any objections he could think of at the time. It would have been easier to refuse, he acknowledged.

I attended the activities of the institute on an almost daily basis during the next month and a half, and I interviewed the staff there. I also began to learn about the bank in general from the daily lectures and mountains of printed material I found at the institute.

During the second month, I moved from the home of a Japanese family and took an apartment next door to the institute and the bachelors' dormitory. This was, in retrospect, a most important step toward deeper involvement with Uedagin life.

During the following months I gradually developed acquaintances with Uedagin people in other bank offices within Aoyama. Some I met through training, some through a shared interest in sports (I played tennis on the bank's court and joined the fencing team practices), several slated to visit the United States approached me, and others were introduced by the training staff at my request. Gradually, I found people in almost all areas of the bank (except top management) who were willing to talk with me at length, and some eventually became almost conspiratorial in their enthusiasm to help me obtain information. I hesitated, however, to approach the very busy executive-level people. Few understood why I was making the study, and most saw little of interest in the mundane activities I observed.

The single most important means to friendship was drinking, following the Japanese pattern of visiting bars and treating each other to drinks, cigarettes, and food. On a good day, fieldwork would not end until almost midnight because of such night-time activity. My weekly schedule of such outings must have been much greater than theirs, for otherwise I cannot understand how they continued to be able to get to the office at eight each morning. There was, in any event, a clear relationship between the helpfulness of people and the previous establishment of a personal relationship, usually through drinking. This procedure, however, was applicable only to men.

During the course of discussions, many activities of the bank calendar would be mentioned, and, whenever possible, I would seek permission in advance to attend. In this way, I learned to anticipate ceremonies and special activities. A large organization is not like a village, and there were many events I learned about only afterwards. I often found myself in the midst of something by accident, for the training institute is a center for many meetings, the site of a few marriages, and the place visitors to Aoyama often stay.

After three months, it became quite apparent that other bases of operation in addition to the training institute were necessary if I was to study the bank organization as a whole. It was relatively easy to initiate a study of the dormitory since I was already well acquainted there. I did, however, agree to teach a weekly English class as a means to greater involvement and in order to establish reciprocity. To study the Aoyama apartment complex, I first visited the apartment of one man I knew and then later asked him to ask his wife to introduce me to others in her entryway. Passed from acquaintance to acquaintance, I was eventually able to find introductions throughout the two buildings. About a week after some housewife had been particularly helpful, I would deliver a small gift for her or for her children as a sign of my appreciation. I also took small gifts with me when invited to someone's house for dinner, and when I left the country, I gave several key people expensive bottles of whiskey as signs of my gratitude. I made no other presentations except to buy a lot of drinks.

From April through June, I spent the majority of my time concentrating on the initial training program for new men. I participated in most of its activities, continuing to live in my apartment across the street. During this three-month period there was still sufficient time to continue meeting with others in the bank for interviews, particularly at night when the trainees were often studying on their own.

Throughout the year, I continued to make interviews on an almost daily basis with my acquaintances in the various sections of the main office. I visited some in their offices, but in most cases I felt this was a bad policy, for it would disturb others working there and give an impression of exclusiveness that could damage both my own and my informants' positions. I found that during office hours I could best meet people in the company library or in its coffee shop. The library also proved to be a fine source of written information.

During interviews I took written notes whenever possible. After a few sessions transcribing extended taped interviews, I gave up using my tape recorder except for lectures and speeches of special interest. When drinking with the men at night I often felt it was inappropriate to take notes directly, but I did learn to memorize key items of their accounts and then to recall the conversation in detail in the men's room or when I got home. Sometimes an excess of alcohol foiled my scheme.

The amount of printed material I was able to collect, including many years' worth of the company magazine, training pamphlets, personnel guidebooks, and union publications, was truly surprising and proved to be the single greatest source for company-wide statistics on the promotion, wage, and retirement systems. The over ten thousand pages amassed took a long time to cull through and analyze, but their contribution to my study has been immense.

While I had been participating more or less daily in the affairs of the training section, I had not made any formal observations of office routines and interpersonal relations. This was made possible through introductions by the training staff to other offices. After spending a week observing a particular office I was able to contact individuals in it for more detailed discussions of the situation among its members. It was valuable to have made the observations first, for my questioning was more to the point after I had seen the group in action. I never once actually worked in an office, however, and except for my long relationship with the training section, I never spent more than a week observing any other office group. In the dormitory, of course, I heard about office relations all the time.

There was a certain limit to what I could ask of the training staff and what they could do for me in the way of providing access to the information held by other offices. The complete backing of the top authority in the bank, the president, would have made my movement around the organization easier and guaranteed full cooperation. Proper introductions are always a problem in fieldwork, and in this case my haste to get started may have been costly. The point is that the participant study of modern organizations requires well-laid plans for entry, because office walls, busy work schedules, a sensitivity to publicity, and dispersed residence all contribute to a special degree of inaccessibility. The field worker will remain a stranger to most people in the organization, and, as such, he must expect to rely on introductions, official permission, and formal definitions of himself as basic means to each new contact and step in research.

The obvious limits of my study, as they were established by the methods adopted, include:

(1) Time and residential location. My apartment was across the street from the bachelors' dormitory and the training institute, and about four blocks from the bank's Aoyama apartments; consequently my coverage of these elements is proportionally greater than a balanced account would require. Private or rented single-family dwellings were scattered and therefore much less accessible.

(2) Age and sex. The information I collected directly from informants was in proportion to our closeness in age. I also collected much more material from men than from women due to the much greater ease of association with them.

(3) Lack of influential connections at the top. It was very hard to ask for interviews with the men occupying the highest offices in the bank. This lack of top-level acquaintanceship, in turn, resulted in a hesitation on the part of some officials to permit me access to sensitive information. My material on salaries and promotions, for example,

results from a careful study of the bank's published documents. The data were not given to me, and, no doubt, a more complete account of many things would have resulted from a closer relationship with top personnel officials. Nor did I have any opportunity to study high-level decision making, clique influence, and related matters.

(4) The starting point for my research. The training institute is one of the places in the bank where such things as ideology and personal character receive special attention, and I came to view many other aspects of the bank through these lenses, just as it is hoped the trainees will. If I had begun by observing the personnel section, personnel problems and the many exceptions to normative behavior that are known to that office might have become a major focus of my study.

(5) The knowledge that what I wrote of Uedagin would perhaps someday be published and even perhaps translated into Japanese caused most people and all officials (including union officials) to be cautious in their preliminary revelations regarding sensitive bank subjects. After personal rapport developed, many did show enthusiasm to help my study, but much remains to be learned.

(6) My research inclinations. In retrospect, four factors seem to have governed my selection of what to study and what to ignore: an interest in describing the basic social character of the organization; a sensitivity to those patterns that have existed in Japanese society before and beyond the existence of the bank; the assumption that the economic aspects of banking were not the subject of my study; and an ambition to see Uedagin in the conceptual terms of the people working in the bank.

(7) My own personality. It is wisely observed that an ethnography is a kind of projective test. Someone of different nature might well see very different qualities in the bank, much as Oscar Lewis and Robert Redfield saw the same Mexican village so differently. In this sense the reader should know that I am an optimist: gregarious and inclined to credit all people with good intentions.

THE ANTHROPOLOGICAL APPROACH TO ORGANIZATION

This study is obviously not the sort designed to answer a particular set of theoretical questions, and I have tried to avoid the pitfalls of a simple cause-and-effect framework of explanation. Rather, my aim has been to explicate selected fundamental matters of organization in terms of the general Uedagin context. I have included considerable detail because, for non-Japanese readers, it seems necessary in order to grasp the complex interplay of different spheres of activity, organizational form, and interpretations of them. Certain noneconomic sources of overall coherence, such as the meaning of membership, age, spiritual strength, "lifelong commitment," and the character of office group and family, have received emphasis. These are not, however, to be taken as mentalistic constructs, but rather their meaning, which we discover and they perceive primarily in the pattern of events and organizational order, is above all to be taken as part of the daily life of the company.

In emphasizing these matters, I do not for a minute wish to deny the coherence that comes from business calculations. These too are fundamental sources of interpretation, of course, and it is where many considerations, including business ones, intersect that the variation, paradox, and contradiction within the organization are most apparent. Here existence becomes most poignant and change most likely. The paradoxes of organizational life certainly have something to do with such ubiquitous distinctions as rational-irrational, practical-ideal, and modern-traditional; however, these perspectives are far too simple to provide anything like a thorough understanding of the complex levels and forms of meaningful action in organizations. Everything is related, yet actions may be understood in different ways. Several viewpoints dominate the organization—the company ideology of community and the logic of business, yet within each form of relationship, personnel policy and organizational context the nuance and consequences are different. While there are powerful reasons to argue that ultimately the logic of business dominates the whole, there are also powerful arguments pointing to the power of the company as community assumption. Finally, it is also clear that the nature of work groups, the family and the *senpai-kohai* relationship all greatly color the company system and its ideology. In other words, there does not seem to be one undeniably better starting point for an analysis of the paradoxical qualities of Uedagin organization. Certainly, the idealism vs. materialism question is too abstract for this level of consideration, and, in all probability, only a long-term historical account of the bank's response to various major changes in business and society-at-large could provide the necessary material for such a discussion.

For the anthropological observer, the organizational landscape is indeed difficult to describe in general and inclusive terms. The surface of routine appears so arid and flat, and yet as the perspective is rotated with the study of each additional element, the terrain becomes more and more uneven, shadows appear, and one comes to sense dynamic forces that, one assumes, lie below the surface. These forces, as I visualize them, are the pull of different great ambitions operating within the organization to perfect different versions of a more perfect order (goals, ideals, etc.). Each of these ambitions in its pure state appears to us dreamlike or visionary. Business dominion, a community of workers, a just salary and promotion system, and family security are typical of such visions, each of which is translated in practice into the language of the organization and expressed in the basic forms and daily routines that constitute bank life. Compromise among all of them must take place, of course; thus each visionary ambition earns the lables "impractical" and "unrealistic." They remain very *real* and crucial, however, to our understanding.

In the surface of daily events we may read the elaborate symbolic codes that speak of these underlying visions, their compromises and frustrations. Surface routine is thus richly expressive and meaningful due to the assortment of ambitions being worked out, mediated, and combined at what is seemingly a mundane level. It should be apparent that our common dichotomy between "reality" and "ideal" can be easily misleading, particularly when another culture is involved.

It is my impression that in contemporary organization the landscape (symbolic action) and the deeper dynamic (the ambitions) are both aspects of social consciousness and are, therefore, open to variation at what is termed the cultural level. It is not that differences must exist, but that they may exist, and, furthermore, that when they do, the differences are echoed and reverberated throughout the organization, coloring all else. The anthropological approach to organization is, I would say, destined to seek the differences and their echoes, but this is not to be equated with studying the obscure or the inconsequential, for, as I have tried to show in this book, the meaning of fundamental matters is involved. Instead of building on a foundation of our own cultural assumptions about organization, the anthropologist's task, to paraphrase Geertz (1966), is to seek first the architectural principles by which others build. To do this well requires a fieldwork approach, a readiness to assume that little is yet known, and a self-conscious scepticism about the adequacy of our own social science language for the task.

CONTEXT AND IDEOLOGY

Once we recognize the variety of meaningful perspectives within even a single organization like Uedagin, we must ask what underlies the order established among them. People in organizations do not all day long suffer a heavy sense of contradiction and paradox. This is not because they have come to take them for granted (although this too is part of the story). It seems that coherence for Uedagin people is served by two basic aspects of their organization: context and ideology. Just as the chapters of this book elucidate specific matters by isolating them from others, context in the bank separates many contradictory perspectives. The assumptions relevant at an executive session, a company ceremony, and a union meeting are very different, and in their purest state they cannot survive much exposure to one another. Most organizational contexts are, of course, intersections for a multitude of influences: in the office group, for example, the separating process is readily seen in such things as the shift from the work hierarchy to the social circle of an after-work party. People need not constantly be aware of the contradictory qualities of their own expression if there is a complex arrangement of time and place that corresponds to the multiplicity of perspectives. Successful leadership, obviously, involves the skillful management of context and appropriate meaning.[1]

Another obvious source of coherence within the organization is the general and inclusive interpretations that tie many aspects of organization together at a level transcending daily life. The company ideology, business calculations, and the union's potentially dichotomous view are the three most significant examples of such interpretations for Uedagin. Company ceremonies, for example, can be seen as attempts to draw the disparate elements of the organizational world together under a single radiant perspective, a canopy of symbols in which metaphor, analogy, and parable become means to the expression of a coherent whole. Ceremonies and other brief reiterations of transcendent meaning leave a glow, but they do not determine conduct in other contexts. They do, however, serve to confirm the meaningfulness of the most routine events.

Compared to, say, an American public school, Uedagin is not burdened with many contradictory ambitions or perspectives. Business reality and the company ideology are both of considerable power, but the union's voice, except for the narrow context of its own meetings, is presently weak and subservient. In an American school the differing perspectives of teachers, students, parents, administrators and so on converge, and as a public institution, the sway of the society's general values is much greater.

American companies, to make a different comparison, seem at first glance to be single-mindedly dedicated to a business logic, but on closer examination this is too simple an interpretation. The differ-

---

[1] The contradiction among general perspectives, it might be noted, is often experienced in daily routine as the incompatibility of fragments of several general perspectives.

ences between American and Japanese companies prove to be largely between fundamentally different understandings of work, satisfaction, participation, and the like, which in the American case leave the company to the utilitarian ethic largely by default. Unlike Uedagin, our white-collar world is greatly colored (or better, faded) by the importance of private worlds (family, leisure, charity, voluntary action, and the like) and by the confusion of multiple outside influences. Our great ambitions, private and social, tend to be contrary to what we understand the company to stand for, and the result is our view that work in large complex organizations is "meaningless." Nothing better illustrates this than the fact that the recent search for community, at least among intellectuals and youth, has been conducted without the slightest consideration of the company as a possibility.

CULTURAL STYLE IN ORGANIZATIONS

The word "style" is chosen carefully here to mean vague but commonly perceived differences between whole cultures of a gestalt kind. Lately, a number of authors have offered intriguing hypotheses about how a country's modern organizations are deeply flavored by the peculiarities of psychology and interpersonal relationship that hold for the society in general. Michel Crozier (1964), in perhaps the most culturally sensitive survey of organizational theory to date, has speculated that the French bureaucratic style, particularly its impersonal and hierarchical nature, reflects the fact that the office worker expects to find satisfaction and fulfillment in the private spheres of life rather than in his work or with his fellow office workers. This becomes a point of comparative interest considering the reverse situation in Uedagin, both in terms of the nature of outside expectations and the character of internal work relationships. We can say, I think, that the Japanese bureaucratic style is comparatively rich in direct proportion to the inattention given outside pursuits and satisfactions.

Turning to modern Japan, this study provides a rather firm basis for commentary on two recent theories developed specifically to explain the Japanese style in organization. The first emphasizes the special qualities of Japanese dependency. Originally introduced by Takeo Doi, this theme has become common in most psychologically oriented writing on contemporary Japan. The second perspective emphasizes the close personal ties between superior and subordinate in Japan. Nakane Chie (1970) provides the most recent statement of this interpretation. Both are essentially explanations of contemporary interpersonal and organizational patterns in terms of antecedent social pat-

terns: either the parent-child relationship or traditional social forms
(most often the family or the village). The antecedent pattern approach, of course, is emphasized by scholars who point to Japanese
cultural uniqueness and continuity.

Professor Doi has asserted that the Japanese have a special recognition of, acceptance of, and felt need for relationships involving the
rather explicit dependence of one party on the other. This he contrasts with the American emphasis on and training for adult independence coupled with the American anxiety about and rejection of
adult dependency. No one to my knowledge has ever challenged this
basic assertion of fundamental difference (one, incidentally, that helps
substantiate Nakane's presentation of vertical relations), and recent
psychological studies tend to confirm his approach as a fruitful one.[2]
The issue I wish to discuss here is how the insight Doi offers can be
coupled with organization research. How is dependency reflected in
the Uedagin material, if it is?

First, let us list the examples that would affirm the recognition and
acceptance of dependency. There is the senior-junior relationship and
the dependency aspect of the ideal boss-subordinate relationship. Second, there is the possibility of being dependent on the company.
Firing is virtually ruled out, and there are many "welfare" aspects to
the remuneration system, to the housing pattern, and to the style of
work relations. These are certainly powerful illustrations, and indeed
they are the ones most often cited when dependency in modern companies is discussed.[3] The bank's training program and much else,
however, point to a fundamental ambivalence about dependency. In
the bank's training, emphasis is placed on toughening up the newcomer, and this appears to be an effort to reduce dependency needs.
Furthermore, the bank's managers and the training staff constantly
assert the image of the independent but harnessed individual as the
goal they have in mind. In hiring, managers wish for less, not more,
reliance on connections and teachers. In their early recognition of
talent before formal promotion, and in their insertion of ability-ori-
ented factors in the wage system, management also seeks to underline
the same point—that dependency on the organization is undesirable
(understandable perhaps, but not to be encouraged). Can we interpret the *seishin* tradition as a counterweight to the dependency of
interpersonal relations which permeates Japanese organization? We
may conclude that while at the personal level dependence can be and

---

2 See Caudill and Weinstein (1969) in particular. Kimura (1972) argues that Doi
is still too "Western" in his thinking on this.

3 See, for example, Vogel and Vogel (1961).

is encouraged between persons of differing power and age, it is most certainly discouraged at the level of company-individual relations. There considerable ambivalence is created by the persistence of personal-level values at the organizational level (supporting the paternal role of management), and by the fact that in so many cases the personal and organizational are thoroughly intertwined. Independence is not being encouraged when dependency is discouraged; rather, the ideal organization man is one who allows others to be dependent on him, but who is not himself dependent on the organization.

The crucial factor, if organization is inevitably hierarchical, is that the more close-knit the organization, the more possible dependency becomes (this is perhaps a tautology in Japan), and the more likely that efforts to avoid excessive dependency will be established. I suggest that white-collar organizations (especially large ones) in Japan are more close-knit than blue-collar organizations, that they are characterized by a greater potential for forms of dependency, and also by greater efforts on the part of management to head off such behavior.[4] The inclination to dependency in personal relations does, indeed, flavor organizational life in a variety of ways. It does not determine it, however, but rather provides one of its significant dimensions.

Nakane's emphasis on close vertical relations also finds considerable support in this study, particularly in the importance of senior-junior ties and in the expectation that leader-follower relations in the office group will be emotionally close. We also find the ideology making much of lineal ties in the company history. These examples certainly stand in sharp contrast to the centralized, organizational processes of hiring, transfer, promotion, and retirement. On the one hand, we have highly personal ties that are crucial to individual motivation and commitment, and on the other hand, we have well-developed impersonal processes that serve to maintain a high degree of consistent order throughout the organization. Of particular significance is the fact that successful vertical relations greatly facilitate the acceptance of impersonal hierarchy and manipulation. That Americans think of personal relations as horizontal, whereas Japanese more often visualize them as vertical, is a crucial distinction, for in a large organization the vertical reinforces hierarchy and authority, whereas the horizontal challenges them.

Yet there are clear limits placed on close personal relations in any large organization. In Uedagin transfer inevitably separates senpai

4 Based in part on my 1972 study of a medium-size manufacturing firm reported in Rohlen (forthcoming).

from kohai, superior from subordinate, and members of office groups from one another, diluting close personal relationships over time. A large organization is different from a small group, and even while the ideology emphasizes the opposite, introductory training makes no bones about the necessity of organizational discipline. This is indeed a basic paradox, one that intertwines with the dependency versus self-reliance paradox, and, while both are probably issues of social life anywhere, they appear particularly acute in Japanese organizations. Probably the most long-lived and recurrent characterization of Japan's modern institutions is that of remarkable cohesion. Not all types of groupings in Japan earn such a comment; many forms of involvement are transitory or are incapable of drawing more than a limited degree of time, energy, and commitment. Villages,[5] companies, the newer religions, the older commercial neighborhoods, and government agencies have, however, been repeatedly seen as evidencing a high degree of community solidarity when compared to similar institutions in other complex societies. This quality is what theories like the two by Doi and Nakane we have just considered tend to explain.

It does seem true that wherever employment or fundamental interests of work and ownership are involved, Japanese are inclined to elaborate the social ties involved. The clear tendency of the new religions to draw membership from those groups in society that are not wrapped up in a work institution (for example the self-employed, day laborers, housewives of the lower-middle and lower class) is, in fact, further evidence of this general pattern.

Turning to Uedagin, we must conclude that the bank evidences a degree of social integration and individual involvement that we Americans would deem unusual and, in our terms, unhealthy for the individual. Although a bank, Uedagin reminds us of a village, so involved are its people in a multiplicity of mutual activities and concerns. This is one reason why an ethnographic approach to the bank occurred to me in the first place.

Yet, cross-cultural comparisons often end in a language of stereotypes and polarities that greatly misconstrue the actual situation within any particular organization. In Japanese studies, we also find a residual implication that some psychological propensity to solidarity explains the national organizational stereotype, but interesting as this possibility may be to some, the question is best left to studies of national character. Here, I have tried to examine a more limited problem: how a particular company arrives at the degree of integration it

5 See, for example, Barrington Moore (1966) chapter 5 and Dore (1971) especially pages 201–209.

does. Virtually this entire account can be seen as devoted to a discussion of this question. I have emphasized the various contributions and perspectives associated with particular elements of the full picture, and I have argued that these must be understood and evaluated as part of one large organizational configuration. Everything from the meaning of membership to the role of the husband in the Uedagin family is to be properly understood as both an element of and a contribution to a larger whole.

In adopting an ethnographic approach, I hope to have also put the reader in a position to understand the failures, limitations, and fluctuations of cohesion within the bank. I have tried to point out the internal contradictions, the forces of potential disruption that have arisen beyond the company boundary, and the exceptions to my every generalization about coherence. Hopefully, the reader has gained a sense of the likely nature of change and dynamic flux. Problems and change, it should be remembered, dominate the conscious concerns of Uedagin people. Good relations, personal commitment, and the sense of common interest and endeavor are goals never fully realized, and only the magnetism of such goals and the corresponding disappointment with "reality" are givens. A relatively high degree of cohesion does not mean that contradiction, confusion, and dissatisfaction are absent; it means that they take rather different forms than we might initially expect.

I do not wish to recapitulate further on the subject of Japanese organizational style except to comment briefly on a rather omnipresent concern of social science: the issue of how man is connected to "modern" society. The change from peasant to wage-worker undoubtedly represents a transformation of the essential character of social life in all nations. The question is: to what degree have the personal ties and intimate arrangements typical of village life been superseded by labor markets, impersonal procedures, and the rule of organizational rationality? During the last hundred years Japan has experienced utilitarian philosophical arguments, laissez-faire labor policies, and periods of fluid industrial labor markets. But the images of man and society, the fundamental assumptions about motives, and the capacity for certain types of cooperation have not so changed as to correspond with the organizational theories of the modern West. In fact, the formation of our own modern organizations has been greatly affected by our peculiar understanding of them as essentially mechanisms and by our assumption that the power of the labor market was natural and healthy. In Japan, the potential power of an impersonal labor market has been greatly modified (in practice more than in theory) by

the continuing high regard for the power and possibility of social cohesion. In Uedagin, at least, the ideals of harmony and strength are
more mutual than antagonistic, and, furthermore, they receive more
day in and day out reinforcement in practice than could be imagined
by people used to American thinking about organizations. A labor
market, that is, for all its power remains but part of a larger and more
complete picture of society, and in Japan that picture contains strong
cultural countertrends. Differences of degree will show up in statistics,
but a statistical approach will never serve to illustrate the market's
place in the larger picture.

The notion of cultural style in organization seems destined to remain as elusive as the idea of national character. For one thing, description and explanation cannot possibly be separated to anyone's
satisfaction when a collection of anecdotes (that appear to be of a
revealing nature) are strung together with a "theory" about their re-
latedness. Yet contrived experiments and other controlled approaches
that might verify theories often undermine the context that here is so
crucial. This is a dilemma that I am willing to accept, for cultural
differences in organization seem very real to me personally. Fieldwork
and like experiences must be appreciated as an alternative to "scientific" forms of verification. A more complete description of cultural
style emerges with a multifaceted approach, one that ties together
such general perspectives as psychology, social structure, and inherent
patterns of meaning. Even such a division continues to cut the pie
according to a social science view of the world, but the sense of cultural style that it conveys will be considerably richer than that of a
single "theoretical" approach. The goal, I would say, is to develop
pictures of organizations so complete that many abstract theories fit
the data; and that each theory in turn is so thoroughly conditioned
by the richness of the data that the variation, unpredictability, contradiction, and change in organizational life are fully accommodated.
Obviously, much more remains to be said about Uedagin before this
goal is satisfactorily approached.

THE MODERN-TRADITIONAL DISTINCTION
AND THE CONVERGENCE HYPOTHESIS

The contrast I have made between universal constraints and particular meaning, however, should not be viewed as coincidental with the
contrast between modern and traditional. Although we almost invariably make this connection (in defining the culture of a non-Western
society as traditional, in associating the personal with the traditional

and the impersonal with the modern, and so on), it is one that lies at the heart of many of our problems in attempting to study modern organization on a cross-cultural basis. When we assume the convergence of social character among industrializing nations,[6] as has been the tendency of Western social thought for the last two centuries,[7] we obscure some crucial characteristics of organizations. It is easy to assume that the difference between universal factors and particular meaning is a matter of opposition,[8] when, in fact, the issue is of profound differences of kind. An analysis of universal factors, its logic, vocabulary, and research procedures, are necessarily different from those applied when the meaning of a particular cultural context is studied and analyzed. In the latter case *their* vocabulary, not *ours,* is of central importance. In the typical functional analysis of organizational differences, for example, questions of type, size, kind of work, goals, and general operating environment are central, and whenever this kind of explanation is not sufficient, such factors may be treated as historically generated differences that are functionally equivalent.[9] None of this need conflict with the exploration of differences of particular meaning, unless, as in a court of law, only one explanation must prevail. Most scholars today appreciate this, of course, but rarely do we find studies of organizations giving as much time to *their* understandings as to our own.

When we introduce a time frame to the situation, we (both social scientists and people in societies with a progressive view of history) have been trained to assume that a conflict exists, and that with time the modern will supersede the traditional. With our focus on change, our Western experience and our own concerns usually determine the fundamental vocabulary. What does not fit is quickly labeled "traditional" and seen as destined for change. However, no social situation can be devoid of culturally specific meaning, and even the most "modern" attitudes and interpretations are only part of general frameworks of understanding that are relative to time and place. The rise of a particular organizational or economic type does not erode the im-

---

[6] See Kerr, et al. (1960), Feldman and Moore (1962), Moore (1963), Levy (1966), Karsh and Cole (1968), Weinberg (1969), and Cole (1971a) for discussion of this perspective. Croizer (1964), Dore (1973), Gusfield (1967), Bendix (1967a), Bennett (1967), and Befu (1970) should be consulted for formulation of the theory that attempts to accommodate cultural variation, normally in terms of "levels" of society.

[7] Bendix (1967a).

[8] For a recent example from the field of Japanese labor relations see Marsh and Mannari (1971).

[9] Cole (1972) utilizes the concept of functional equivalence in his recent discussion of Japanese and American interfirm mobility rates.

portance of culture, nor does time bring universal constraints into a special ascendancy. We only need to note the varieties of religious and social life associated with any given type of agricultural subsistence to appreciate that companies, too, can vary greatly in terms of culture.

To summarize, for the study of modern organizations to accommodate the real and vitally significant matter of cultural context, what must be avoided is the false assumption that a functional analysis is a complete analysis. The underlying definitional structure of any theory of progressive history must be kept distinct from the descriptive study of specific cases.

If we are to advance our understanding of organizations beyond the present boundaries created by the functional and historical perspectives, we must also learn to consider them in cultural terms, and this requires a solid empirical foundation developed through sensitive fieldwork, especially as it illuminates the character of immediate reality in each case.[10] For anthropologists, the fascination and the challenge in studying modern organizations derive from their obvious transcultural similarities. These uniformities have been so apparent, it seems, that anthropologists have shied from the subject on the assumption that it is infertile ground for their inherent concern with cultural difference. I feel that no better territory exists for such exploration, particularly since other social sciences have made so much of late about the eclipse of cultural differences that modernization brings.

I would like to underline the ultimate promise for anthropology that such work offers. By attempting to study the complexities of organization, anthropologists will not only be adapting their methodology and insight to a realm of vast importance and possibility, they will also be opening their discipline to the exciting prospect of dealing with modern societies at a crucial and dynamic level, one where the nature and meaning of modern life is being forged. Nothing better characterizes modern societies than their work organizations and these are still very much in the early stages of a process aimed at discovering internal explanations and social forms that will be of lasting significance.

---

[10] This seems to be taking place in the sociology and anthropology of schools, with the many studies of peer group subculture, classroom reality, and the differences of perspective between teachers, students, administrators, and parents. The multiplicity of meaning in schools for Americans is especially evident, but it is true for all organizations upon closer scrutiny.

REFERENCES CITED

ENGLISH

Abegglen, James C.
1958. *The Japanese factory: aspects of its social organization.* Glencoe, Ill.: The Free Press.
1969. Organizational change. In Robert J. Ballon, ed., *The Japanese employee.* Tokyo: Sophia University Press.
1970. The economic growth of Japan. *Scientific American* 222:3:30–37.
Adams, T. F. M. and N. Kobayashi.
1969. *The world of Japanese business.* Tokyo: Kodansha International.
Argyris, Chris.
1954. *The organization of a bank.* New Haven: Yale University Labor and Management Center Series. Yale University Press.
Arnold, Thurman.
1937. *The folklore of capitalism.* New Haven: Yale University Press.
Ballon, R. J., ed.
1967. *Business in Japan.* Tokyo: Sophia University.
1969. The Japanese dimensions of industrial enterprise. In Robert J. Ballon, ed., *The Japanese employee.* Tokyo: Sophia University Press.
Bank of Japan.
1969. *Outline of Japanese economy and finance.* Tokyo: The Bank of Japan.
Beardsley, R. K., John Hall, and Robert Ward.
1959. *Village Japan.* Chicago: University of Chicago Press.
Befu, Harumi.
1964. Ritual kinship in Japan: its variability and resiliency. *Sociologus* 14:150–169.
1970. Review of R. P. Dore, ed., *Aspects of social change in modern Japan. American Anthropologist* 72:1:160–162.
1971. *Japan: an anthropological introduction.* San Francisco: Chandler.
Bellah, Robert N.
1957. *Tokugawa religion: the values of pre-industrial Japan.* Boston: Beacon Press.
Bendix, Reinhard.
1956. *Work and authority in industry.* New York: John Wiley and Sons.
1967a. Tradition and modernity reconsidered. *Comparative Studies in Society and History* 9:3:292–346.

1967b. Preconditions of development: A comparison of Japan and Germany. In R. P. Dore, ed., *Aspects of social change in modern Japan.* Princeton: Princeton University Press.

Benedict, Ruth.

1946. *The chrysanthemum and the sword.* New York: Houghton Mifflin.

Bennett, John W.

1967. Japanese economic growth: background for social change. In R. P. Dore, ed., *Aspects of social change in modern Japan.* Princeton: Princeton University Press.

Bennett, John W. and Iwao Ishino.

1963. *Paternalism in the Japanese economy.* Minneapolis: University of Minnesota Press.

1968. Tradition, modernity and communalism in Japan's modernization. *The Journal of Social Issues* 24:4:25–45.

Berger, Peter and Thomas Luckman.

1967. *The social construction of reality.* New York: Anchor Books.

Bernard, Chester.

1938. *The functions of the executive.* Cambridge, Mass.: Harvard University Press.

Blood, Robert.

1968. *Love-match and arranged marriage.* New York: The Free Press.

Blumenthal, Tuvia.

1970. *Saving in postwar Japan.* Cambridge, Mass.: Harvard University Press.

Bodde, Derk.

1953. Harmony and conflict in Chinese philosophy. In Arthur F. Wright, ed., *Studies in Chinese thought.* Chicago: University of Chicago Press.

Broadbridge, S. A.

1966. *Industrial dualism in Japan.* London: F. Cass.

Brown, William.

1969. Japanese management: the cultural background. In Ross A. Webber, ed., *Culture and management.* Homewood, Ill.: Richard D. Irwin.

Cartwright, D. and A. Zander, eds.

1960. *Group dynamics: research and theory.* 2nd ed. Evanston, Ill.: Row Peterson.

Caudill, William and David W. Plath.

1966. Who sleeps by whom? Parent-child involvement in urban Japanese families. *Psychiatry* 29:4:344–366.

Caudill, William and Helen Weinstein.

1969. Maternal care and infant behavior in Japan and America. *Psychiatry* 32:1:12–43.

Cole, Robert E.

1971a. *Japanese blue collar.* Berkeley and Los Angeles: University of California Press.

1971b. The theory of institutionalization: permanent employment and tradition in Japan. *Economic Development and Cultural Change* 20:1:47–70.

1972. Permanent employment in Japan: facts and fantasies. *International Labor Relations Review* 26:615–630.

Cook, Alice H.
1966. *An introduction to Japanese trade unionism.* Ithaca, N.Y.: Cornell University Press.

Crozier, Michel.
1964. *The bureaucratic phenomenon.* Chicago: University of Chicago Press.

DeVos, George and Hiroshi Wagatsuma.
1970. Status and role behavior in changing Japan: psychocultural continuities. In Georgene Seward and Robert Williamson, eds., *Sex roles in changing society.* New York: Random House.

Doi, Takeo.
1962. *Amae:* a key concept for understanding Japanese personality. In Robert J. Smith and Richard K. Beardsley, eds., *Japanese culture.* Chicago: Aldine.

1963. Some thoughts on helplessness and the desire to be loved. *Psychiatry* 26:266–272.

1967. Giri-ninjoo: an interpretation. In R. P. Dore, ed., *Aspects of social change in modern Japan.* Princeton: Princeton University Press.

Dore, R. P.
1958. *City life in Japan.* Berkeley and Los Angeles: University of California Press.

1969. The modernizer as a special case: Japanese factory legislation, 1882–1911. *Comparative Studies in Society and History* 5:11:433–450.

1973. *British factory-Japanese factory: the origins of national diversity in industrial relations.* Berkeley and Los Angeles: University of California Press.

Dore, R. P. and Tsutomu Ōuchi.
1971. Rural origins of Japanese fascism. In James Morley, ed., *Dilemmas of growth in prewar Japan.* Princeton: Princeton University Press.

Drucker, Peter F.
1971. What we can learn from Japanese management. *Harvard Business Review*, March-April, pp. 110–122.

Embree, John.
1939. *Suye mura.* Chicago: University of Chicago Press.

Feldman, Arnold S. and Wilbert E. Moore.
1962. Industrialization and industrialism: convergence and differentiation. *Transactions of the Fifth World Congress of Sociology* 2:151–169.

Fisher, Paul.
1973. Major social security issues: Japan 1972. *Social Security Bulletin*, March 1973. U. S. Department of Health, Education, and Welfare.

Folsom, Kenneth E.

1968. *Friends, guests and colleagues: the mu-fu system in the late Ch'ing period.* Berkeley and Los Angeles: University of California Press.

Fuji Bank, Ltd.

1967. *Banking in modern Japan.* 2nd ed. Tokyo: Research Division, Fuji Bank, Ltd.

Gamble, Sidney D.

1954. *Ting Hsien: a North China rural community.* Stanford: Stanford University Press.

Geertz, Clifford.

1964. Ideology as a cultural system. In David Apter, ed., *Ideology and discontent.* New York: The Free Press of Glencoe.

1966. Religion as a cultural system. In M. Banton, ed., *Anthropological approaches to the study of religion.* London: Travistock.

1972. Deep play: notes on the Balinese cockfight. *Daedalus* 101:1:1–38.

Glazer, Herbert.

1969. The Japanese executive. In Robert J. Ballon, ed., *The Japanese employee.* Tokyo: Sophia University Press.

Gusfield, Joseph.

1967. Tradition and modernity: misplaced polarities in the study of social change. *American Journal of Sociology* 72:351–362.

Hall, Robert K.

1949. *Shushin: the ethics of a defeated nation.* New York: Bureau of Publications, Teachers College, Columbia University.

Hirschmeier, Johannes.

1964. *The origins of entrepreneurship in Meiji Japan.* Cambridge, Mass.: Harvard University Press.

Hsu, Francis L. K.

1970. *Americans and Chinese: purpose and fulfillment in great civilizations.* Garden City: Natural History Press.

Ishino, Iwao.

1953. The oyabun-kobun: a Japanese ritual kinship institution. *American Anthropologist* 55:5:695–707.

Isomura, Motoshi.

1969. Private pension plans. In Robert J. Ballon, ed., *The Japanese employee.* Tokyo: Sophia University Press.

Johnson, Harrison.

1968. The office caste system. In Robert Dubin, ed., *Human relations in administration.* 3rd ed. Englewood Cliffs, N.J.: Prentice-Hall.

Karsh, Bernard and Robert E. Cole.

1968. Industrialization and the convergence hypothesis: some aspects of contemporary Japan. *Journal of Social Issues* 24:45–64.

Kawashima Takeyoshi.

1963. Dispute resolution in contemporary Japan. In Arthur Taylor von Mehren, ed., *Law in Japan: the legal order in a changing society.* Cambridge, Mass.: Harvard University Press.

1967. The status of the individual in the notion of law, right and social order in Japan. In Charles E. Moore, ed., *The Japanese mind: essentials of Japanese philosophy and culture.* Honolulu: East-West Center Press.

Kerr, Clark, et al.

1960. *Industrialism and industrial man.* Cambridge, Mass.: Harvard University Press.

Kiefer, Christie W.

1970a. Personality and social change in a Japanese danchi. Ph.D. dissertation. University of California, Berkeley.

1970b. The psychological interdependence of family, school and bureaucracy in Japan. *American Anthropologist* 72:1:66–72.

Lebra, Takie Sugiyama.

1969. Reciprocity and the asymmetric principle: an analytical reappraisal of the Japanese concept of *on. Psychologia* 12:129–138.

Levine, Solomon B.

1958. *Industrial relations in postwar Japan.* Urbana, Ill.: University of Illinois Press.

1967. Postwar trade unionism, collective bargaining, and Japanese social structure. In R. P. Dore, ed., *Aspects of social change in modern Japan.* Princeton: Princeton University Press.

Levy, Marion J., Jr.

1966. *Modernization and the structure of societies.* Princeton: Princeton University Press.

Marsh, Robert M. and Hiroshi Mannari.

1971. Lifetime commitment in Japan: roles, norms and values. *American Journal of Sociology* 76:795–812.

Marshall, Byron K.

1967. *Capitalism and nationalism in prewar Japan: the ideology of the business elite, 1868–1941.* Stanford: Stanford University Press.

McFarland, H. Neill.

1967. *The rush hour of the gods: a study of new religious movements in Japan.* New York: Macmillan.

Michida, Shinichiro.

1966. The legal structure of economic enterprise: some aspects of Japanese commercial law. In Arthur Taylor von Mehren, ed., *Law in Japan: the legal order in a changing society.* Cambridge, Mass.: Harvard University Press.

Minami, Shinichiro.

1970. The psychology of the Japanese people. Translated by Albert R. Ikoma. Honolulu: East-West Center Press, Occasional Papers of Research Publications and Translations.

Misumi, Jyuji and Toshiaki Tasaki.

1965. A study of the effectiveness of supervisory patterns in a Japanese hierarchical organization. *Japanese Psychological Research* 7:4:151–162.

Moore, Barrington.
1966. *Social origins of dictatorship and democracy: lord and peasant in the making of the modern world.* Boston: Beacon Press.

Moore, Wilbert E.
1963. Industrialization and social change. In Bert F. Hoselitz and Wilbert E. Moore, eds., *Industrialization and society.* Paris and the Hague: UNESCO and Mouton.

Murphy, Robert F.
1971. *The dialectics of social life: alarms and excursions in anthropological theory.* New York: Basic Books.

Murry, Robert N.
1958. Recruitment, dependency, and morale in the banking industry. *Administrative Science Quarterly* 3:87–106.

Nakamura, Hajime.
1969. *A history of the development of Japanese thought.* 2 vols. Tokyo: Kukusai Bunka Shinkokai.

Nakane, Chie.
1970. *Japanese society.* Berkeley and Los Angeles: University of California Press.

Nash, Manning.
1958. *Machine age Maya: the industrialization of a Guatemalan community.* Glencoe, Ill.: The Free Press.

Niyekawa, Agnes M.
1968. A study of second language learning. Project report of the Bureau of Research, Office of Education, U. S. Department of Health, Education, and Welfare.

Norbeck, Edward.
1970. Religion and society in modern Japan: continuity and change. *Rice University Studies* 56:1.

Norbeck, Edward and Harumi Befu.
1958. Japanese usages of terms of relationship. *Southwestern Journal of Anthropology* 14:1:66–86.

Ōkochi, Kazuo.
1958. *Labor in modern Japan.* Tokyo: Science Council of Japan.

Passin, Herbert.
1965. *Society and education in Japan.* New York: Teachers College Press, Teachers College, Columbia University.

Pelzel, John C.
1970. Japanese kinship: a comparison. In Maurice Freedman, ed., *Family and kinship in Chinese society.* Stanford: Stanford University Press.

Perry, Linda.
1973. *Being socially anomalous: wives and mothers without husbands.* Unpublished paper.

Plath, David W.
  1964. *The after hours: modern Japan and the search for enjoyment.*
    Berkeley and Los Angeles: University of California Press.
Riesman, David.
  1967. *Conversations in Japan.* New York: The Free Press.
Rohlen, Thomas P.
  1970. Sponsorship of cultural continuity in Japan: a company training
    program. *Journal of Asian and African Studies* 5:3:184–192.
  1973. Spiritual training in a Japanese bank. *American Anthropologist,*
    75:5.
Forth- The work group in Japanese organization. In Ezra Vogel, ed., *Japa-*
com-   *nese modern organization.* Berkeley and Los Angeles: University of
ing.   California Press.
Shibusawa, Keizo.
  1958. *Japanese life and culture in the Meiji era,* vol. 5, *Life and culture.*
    Tokyo: The Tokyo Bunko.
Shirai, Taishirō.
Forth- Decision-making in Japanese unions. In Ezra Vogel, ed., *Japanese*
com-   *modern organization.* Berkeley and Los Angeles: University of Cali-
ing.   fornia Press.
Singleton, John.
  1967. *Nichū: a Japanese school.* New York: Holt, Rinehart, and Winston.
Smith, Thomas C.
  1955. Old values and new techniques in the modernization of Japan. *Far*
    Eastern Quarterly 45:3:355–363.
  1964. Japan's aristocratic revolution. *Yale Review* 50:370–383.
Sumiya, Mikio.
  1963. *Social impact of industrialization in Japan.* Tokyo: Japanese Com-
    mission for UNESCO.
Suzuki, Daisetz.
  1959. *Zen and Japanese culture.* New York: Bollingen Foundation.
Taira, Koji.
  1962. The characteristics of Japanese labor markets. *Economic Develop-*
    ment and Cultural Change 10:2:150–168.
  1970. *Economic development and the labor market in Japan.* New York:
    Columbia University Press.
Teraoka, T. W. M.
  1967. Accounting in Japan. In Robert J. Ballon, ed., *Doing business in*
    Japan. Tokyo: Sophia University Press.
Tominaga Ken'ichi.
  1962. Occupational mobility in Japanese society: analysis of labor market
    in Japan. *The Journal of Economic Behavior* 2:2:1–37.
  1968. Occupational mobility in Tokyo. In Joseph A. Kahl, ed., *Compara-*
    tive perspectives on stratification: Mexico, Great Britain, Japan.
    Boston: Little, Brown.

Tomita, Iwao.
    1969. Labor cost accounting. In Robert J. Ballon, ed., *The Japanese employee*. Tokyo: Sophia University Press.
Tsuda, Masumi.
    1965. *The basic structure of Japanese labor relations*. Tokyo: Society for Social Sciences, Musashi University.
Vogel, Ezra F.
    1962. Entrance examinations and emotional disturbances in Japan's middle class. In R. J. Smith and R. K. Beardsley, eds., *Japanese culture: its development and characteristics*. Chicago: Aldine.
    1963. *Japan's new middle class*. Berkeley and Los Angeles: University of California Press.
    1967. Kinship structure, migration to the city and modernization. In R. P. Dore, ed., *Aspects of social change in modern Japan*. Princeton: Princeton University Press.
Vogel, Ezra F. and Suzanne H. Vogel.
    1961. Family security, personal immaturity, and emotional health in a Japanese family. *Marriage and Family Living* 23:161–166.
von Mehren, Arthur Taylor, ed.
    1963. *Law in Japan: the legal order in a changing society*. Cambridge, Mass.: Harvard University Press.
Waldo, Dwight.
    1963. Theory of organization status and problems. In Amita Etzioni, ed., *Readings on modern organization*. Englewood Cliffs, N.J.: Prentice-Hall.
Weinberg, Ian.
    1969. The problem of convergence of industrial societies: a critical look at the state of a theory. *Comparative Studies in Society and History* 11:1:1–15.
White, James W.
    1970. *The Sōkagakkai and mass society*. Stanford: Stanford University Press.
Whitehall, Arthur M. and Takezawa Shin-ichi.
    1968. *The other worker*. Honolulu: East-West Center Press.
Wolf, Erik.
    1966. Kinship, friendship and patron-client relations in complex societies. In *The social anthropology of complex societies*. A.S.A. Monographs 4. London: Travistock; New York: Praeger.
Yamane, Tsureo and Hisaya Nonoyama.
    1967. Isolation of the nuclear family and kinship organization in Japan: a hypothetical approach to the relationships between the family and society. *Journal of Marriage and the Family* 29:783–796.
Yoshino, M. Y.
    1968. *Japan's managerial system*. Cambridge, Mass.: M.I.T. Press.

JAPANESE

Doi Takeo.
1960. Jibun to amae no seishinbyori (Psychopathology of *jibun* and *amae*).
Psychiatria et Neurologia Japonica 60:733–744.
1971. *Amae no kōzō* (The structure of *amae*). Tokyo: Kobundoo.

Hazama Hiroshi.
1963. *Nihonteki keiei no keifu* (The geneology of Japanese-style management). Tokyo: Nōritsu Kyokai.

Itō Chosei.
1969. *Shudan shugi no saihakken* (A reexamination of groupism). Tokyo: Daiyamondosha.

Kawashima Takeyoshi.
1948. *Nihon shakai no kazokuteki kōzō* (The familial structure of Japanese society). Tokyo: Gakusei Shobo.
1950. *Nihon shakai no kazokuteki kōsei* (The familial composition of Japanese society). Tokyo: Nihon Hyooron Shinsha.
1956. *Ideorogi to shite no kazoku seido* (The family system as ideology). Tokyo: Iwanami Shoten.

Kimura Bin.
1972. *Hito to hito no aida* (Between person and person). Tokyo: Kobundo.

Miyamoto Mataji and Okamoto Yukio.
1968. *Nihonteki keiei to wa nani ka* (What is Japanese-style management). Kyoto: Yūkonsha.

Nakamura Sentaro, ed.
1966. *Nōryoku kaihatsu keikaku* (plans for the development of personnel ability). Tokyo: Nikan Kōgyō Shimbunsha.

Nakane Chie.
1967. *Tate shakai no ningen kankei* (Human relations in a hierarchical society). Tokyo: Kodansha.

Office of the Prime Minister.
1970. *Nihon no shūyō kōzō: showa 43* (Japan's employment structure: 1968). Tokyo: Bureau of Statistics.

Ono Tsutomu and Wakita Mamoru.
1966. *Nihon no kachō* (Japan's section chiefs). Tokyo: Diamondosha.

Rohlen, Thomas.
1969. Shinnyūshain kyōiku no nihonteki tokuchō (The special Japanese qualities of new employee training). *Kyoiku to Iigaku* 17:11:33–40.
1970. Nōryokushugi jidai no seishin kyōiku (Spiritual education in an age of "ability-ism"). *Sangyo kunren* 16:173:41–48.

Sakamoto Fujiyoshi.
1967. *Keiei shiryōshū taisei* (Encyclopedia of materials on management). Tokyo: Nihon Sōgō Shūpan kikō.

Sangyo Kunren (Industrial Training).

1968. *Seishin kyōiku tokushū* (Special issue on spiritual education). 14:9.

Seisansei, Chubuchihō Honbu.

1964. *Shatei-shakunshū* (collection of company mottoes and statements of company principles). Nagoya: Seisansei Chubuchihō Honbu.

Sugaya Junbei.

1963. *Midoru manejimento* (Middle management). Tokyo: Jitsugyo no Nihonsha.

Sumiya Mikio, ed.

1969. *Nihonjin no keizai kōdō* (The economic behavior of Japanese). 2 vols. Tokyo: Tōyō Keizai Shinbunsha.

INDEX

Page numbers in italics indicate main entry for that topic.